New Risks, New Welfare

New Risks, New Welfare
The Transformation of the European Welfare State

Edited by

Peter Taylor-Gooby

OXFORD
UNIVERSITY PRESS

OXFORD
UNIVERSITY PRESS

Great Clarendon Street, Oxford OX2 6DP

Oxford University Press is a department of the University of Oxford.
It furthers the University's objective of excellence in research, scholarship,
and education by publishing worldwide in

Oxford New York

Auckland Bangkok Buenos Aires Cape Town Chennai
Dar es Salaam Delhi Hong Kong Istanbul Karachi Kolkata
Kuala Lumpur Madrid Melbourne Mexico City Mumbai Nairobi
São Paulo Shanghai Taipei Tokyo Toronto

Oxford is a registered trade mark of Oxford University Press
in the UK and in certain other countries

Published in the United States
by Oxford University Press Inc., New York

British Library Cataloguing in Publication Data
Data available

Library of Congress Cataloging in Publication Data
Data available
ISBN 0-19-926726-x (hbk.)
ISBN 0-19-926727-8 (pbk.)

1 3 5 7 9 10 8 6 4 2

Typeset by Newgen Imaging Systems (P) Ltd., Chennai, India
Printed in Great Britain
on acid-free paper by
Biddles Ltd., King's Lynn

Preface

Welfare states developed through political struggles in industrial society to meet the needs experienced by mass publics. Recent analysis has focused on the challenges to the industrial society welfare settlement resulting from population shifts, changes in the labour market and economic globalisation. This work shows that traditional patterns of welfare provision are remarkably resilient, but that current policy-making takes place in a climate of austerity and constraint. This book develops understanding of current welfare state transformations by directing attention to the new social risks that result from the transition to post-industrial society. Patterns of family life and employment are changing, with implications for the risks that different groups of citizens experience in everyday life, for opportunities to develop alliances to promote new forms of welfare, for the interests and roles of the traditional political actors (principally business, unions, and left- and right-wing political parties), and for the extent to which government can use welfare policy to promote national interests by mobilising the workforce and enhancing competitiveness.

Our work draws on the data gathered by a major EU Framework Five research project: *Welfare Reform and the Management of Societal Change*. We are grateful for the support which made collaboration possible. The arguments presented here were developed through discussion at a series of conferences in Canterbury, Paris, Madrid, Berlin, and Oxford, and via email. We also benefited from the unstinting advice of Professor Karl Hinrichs, our academic adviser, and from the comments of Professor Vivien Schmidt, and many others. Members of the group who are not named as chapter authors, but who nonetheless made major contributions to background work, debate and discussion are Professor Hellmut Wollmann, Mr Benoît Guy-des-Combes, Dr Anne Daguerre, Dr Ana Arriba, Mr Johannes Kapanen and Professor Ollie Kangas, and we are grateful for their support.

The Approach of this Book

This book discusses the emergence of new social risks and of policies to address them in the four European welfare state regimes: Nordic, corporatist, liberal, and Mediterranean, and also at the EU level. Analysis of policy-making requires the detailed study of processes in particular cases by an experienced scholar, preferably with extended experience of the issues and of how they have developed over time in the national setting. For this reason we proceed by case study.

The states chosen for detailed study include examples of the Nordic citizenship regime (Finland and Sweden) with their inclusive support for women as citizen–workers and their established activation policies; corporatist states with more (France) or less (Germany and Switzerland) overt commitment to women's labour market participation and traditions of job subsidy and early retirement, with recent expansion of activation policies; a liberal system, where government pursues care needs mainly by promoting private provision and workforce mobilisation through incentives and negative activation (the United Kingdom); and a Mediterranean state with strong family engagement, lower state support for women's employment and a de-regulatory approach to employment issues (Spain). In addition we consider the influence of the European Union, a highly consensual suprastate body with particular concerns about legitimacy and discourse, and a mixture of liberal economic and more generous social policies. The sample includes the three largest economies in Europe (France, Germany, UK), the largest Nordic member (Sweden), and a major Mediterranean state (Spain). Switzerland is also included because it illustrates the issues surrounding the evolution of consensus in new social risk policy-making in the most highly consociational institutional context in Europe.

The national and EU-level policy-making processes in the main new risk areas are examined in Chapters 2–8. Each chapter discusses the context in which debates about new risks and policies to manage them have emerged, the extent to which new policy implements are being introduced, the political processes involved in policy-making, the issues which remain unresolved, and possible future policy directions. Chapter 1 considers the relevance of the concept of new social risk, and the final chapter draws conclusions about the implications of the emergence and responses to new social risks for future welfare state developments in Europe.

P. T-G.

Acknowledgements

We would like to express our thanks to the European Union for FPV Project Grant no. 20000-00054 (2001–5), which made the work possible, and to OECD for permission to produce material calculated from published work: Tables 1.1, 1.2, 1.3, 9.1, 9.2, and 9.4.

Contents

List of Figures and Tables   x
List of Abbreviations   xi
Notes on the Contributors   xii

1. New Risks and Social Change   1
   Peter Taylor-Gooby

2. New Social Risks in a Conservative Welfare State:
   The Case of Germany   29
   Andreas Aust and Frank Bönker

3. The UK—A Test Case for the Liberal Welfare State?   55
   Peter Taylor-Gooby and Trine P. Larsen

4. New Risks—Are They Still New for the Nordic Welfare States?   83
   Virpi Timonen

5. France: A New World of Welfare for New Social Risks?   111
   Bruno Palier and Christelle Mandin

6. Spain's Transition to New Risks: A Farewell to 'Superwomen'   133
   Luis Moreno

7. Switzerland: Negotiating a New Welfare State in a
   Fragmented Political System   157
   Giuliano Bonoli

8. New Risks at the EU Level; A Spillover from
   Open Market Policies?   181
   Trine P. Larsen and Peter Taylor-Gooby

9. New Social Risks and Welfare States: New Paradigm and
   New Politics?   209
   Peter Taylor-Gooby

Index   239

List of Figures and Tables

3.1 Employment rates for different groups (%, 1994–2002)   74

1.1 Trends in state spending on new social risks (% GDP, 1980–99)   16
1.2 Women's employment and child care   18
1.3 Labour market participation and active labour market support spending   20
2.1 The supply of child care facilities in Germany (1965–98)   31
6.1 Female activity rates in Spain (1976–2003)   139
6.2 Territorial distribution of public expenditure in Spain (%)   147
7.1 Swiss social expenditure as a proportion of GDP, 1998   158
8.1 Selected equal opportunity measures adopted by the EU   194
9.1 Employment 2001   212
9.2 Spending on active and passive labour market measures (% GDP, 1997–2001)   213
9.3 Poverty and inequality (ECHP, 1999)   214
9.4 Social security contributions   217

List of Abbreviations

APA	*allocation personnalisée d' autonomie*
BMFSFJ	*Bundesministerium für Familie, Senioren, Frauen und Jugend*
CIS	*Centro de Investigaciones Sociológicas*
DGESA	Directorate General for Employment and Social Affairs
DIW	*Deutsches Institut für Wirtschaftsforschung*
GDP	Gross Domestic Product
EES	European Employment Strategy
IMSERSO	Institute of Social Services and Migrations
INE	*Instituto Nacional de Estadística*
NAPs	National Action Plans
NSR	New Social Risks
OMC	open method of co-ordination
PAYG	pay as you go
QMV	qualified majority voting
RMI	*revenu minimum d'insertion*
SHP	Stake-Holder Pension

Notes on the Contributors

Andreas Aust is research assistant in the research project 'Welfare Reform and the Management of Societal Change' at Humboldt University, Berlin. Publications include 'Konjunktur und Krise des Europäischen Sozialmodells: ein Beitrag zur politischen Präexplantationsdignostik', with S. Leitner and S. Lessenich, *Politische Vierteljahresschrift* (2002) and 'From 'Eurokeynesianism' to the 'Third Way': the Party of European Socialists and European Employment Policies', in G. Bonoli and M. Powell (eds.), *Social Democratic Party Politics in Contemporary Europe* (Routledge, 2003).

Giuliano Bonoli is a Lecturer at the Department of Social Work and Social Policy, University of Fribourg. Publications include: 'Switzerland: Adjustment Politics within Institutional Constraints', in F.Scharpf and V.Schmidt (eds.) *From Vulnerability to Competitiveness. Welfare and Work in the Global Economy* (Oxford University Press, 2000) (with André Mach); *European Welfare Futures. Towards a Theory of Retrenchment* (Polity Press, 2000) (with Vic George and Peter Taylor-Gooby); and *The Politics of Pension Reform. Institutions and Policy Change in Western Europe* (Cambridge University Press, 2000).

Frank Bönker is Assistant Professor at the Department of Economics, European University Viadrina, Frankfurt (Oder) and Research Fellow at the Frankfurt Institute for Transformation Studies. Recent book publications include *The Political Economy of Fiscal Reform in Central-Eastern Europe: A Comparative Analysis of Hungary, Poland and the Czech Republic* (Elgar, 2004) and *Post-communist Transformation and the Social Sciences*, co-edited with K. Müller and A. Pickel (Rowman Littlefield, 2002).

Trine P. Larsen is a Research Assistant on the project; 'Welfare Reform and the Management of Societal Change' at the University of Kent. Publications include a report to the European Commission: *Multi-career Families, Work and Care in Finland, France, Portugal, Italy and the UK* and 'European Families—Are They So Different After All?', *Social Policy and Administration*, vol 38, 2004.

Christelle Mandin is a young researcher at CEVIPOF and is working for her Ph.D. at Sciences Po, Paris, in the comparative analysis of policies on active ageing in Europe.

Luis Moreno is Senior Research Fellow at the Spanish National Research Council, CSIC, in Madrid. Recent publications include: *The Territorial Politics of Welfare*, Routledge (forthcoming); 'Mending Nets in the South. Anti-poverty Policies in Greece, Italy, Portugal, and Spain'(with

M. Matsaganis, M. Ferrera L. Capucha), *Social Policy Administration*, 2003; 'Europeanisation, Meso-a record year governments and Safety Nets', *European Journal of Political Research*, 2003; 'Spain, a *Via Media* of Welfare Development', in Taylor-Gooby, P. (ed.), *Welfare States under Pressure* (Sage, 2001;) and *The Federalisation of Spain* (Frank Cass, 2001).

Bruno Palier is CNRS researcher in Centre d'Études de la Vie Politique Française (CEVIPOF), Paris. His research interest is in welfare state reform from a French and a comparative perspective. He is a member of the Management Committee of Cost A15, 'Reforming Welfare Systems in Europe' and was responsible for the MIRE programme 'Comparing Social Welfare Systems in Europe'. Recent publications include: co-editor with Nick Manning of *Global Social Policy*, vol. 3, no. 2, 2003, 'Globalization, Europeanization, and the Welfare State'; 'Facing Pension Crisis in France', in Noel Whiteside and Gordon Clarke, *Pension Security in the 21st Century: Redrawing the Public-Private Divide* (Oxford University Press, 2003); *Gouverner la Sécurité Sociale*, (PUF, 2002); *Globalization and European Welfare States: Challenges and Changes*, edited with R.Sykes and P.Prior (Palgrave, 2001); and 'Defrosting the French Welfare State', *West European Politics*, vol. 23, no. 2, 2001.

Peter Taylor-Gooby is Professor of Social Policy at the University of Kent. Recent publications include: *Making a European Welfare State?* (edited) (Blackwell, 2003); *European Welfare States under Pressure* (edited) (Sage, 2001); *European Welfare Futures* (with Vic George and Giuliano Bonoli) (Polity, 2000); *The End of the Welfare State?* (with Stephan Svallfors) (Routledge, 1999); *Risk, Trust and Welfare*, (edited) (Macmillan, 2000) and *Choice and Public Policy*, (edited) (Macmillan, 1998).

Virpi Timonen is Lecturer in Social Policy and Ageing at the Department of Social Studies, Trinity College, Dublin. She has previously worked in the Department of Social Policy, University of Turku, and is the author of *Restructuring the Welfare State* (2003). She has also written a range of journal articles, reports, and chapters on welfare state restructuring in the Nordic welfare states and on social policy in Ireland.

New Risks and Social Change

Peter Taylor-Gooby

Introduction: The Post-Industrial Welfare State

This book presents a new perspective on the question of what to do about the welfare state. Changes in population, family structure, labour markets, and in the coming to maturity of expensive welfare systems present formidable challenges to the current welfare settlement. For the most part, discussion of these developments focuses on the pressures they impose on existing benefits and services (see, for example, Pierson, 2001*a*, *b*; Scharpf and Schmidt, 2000; Ferrera and Rhodes, 2000*a*, *b*; Kuhnle, 2000). Key questions in the literature concern the maintenance of standards and the politics of retrenchment, realignment, and recalibration. In this book, we consider different and parallel changes that require new policies and offer the possibility of more positive directions in welfare reform—the emerging policy agenda of new social risks.

The development of European welfare states in the 1950s, 1960s, and 1970s took place under highly favourable circumstances, aided by four key factors: a 'golden age' of relatively continuous growth in economies characterised by large stable manufacturing sectors which provided high levels of family-wage employment for the mass of the population; stable nuclear family structures which supplied care for young children, frail older people, and other dependent groups; governments able to manage their national economies through broadly neo-Keynesian policies which achieved continuing low unemployment and secure wages; and political systems in which coalitions of working and middle class groups were able to press effectively for the provision of benefits and services to meet their needs and in which the tax consequences of such provision could be

This chapter has benefited from debates in the WRAMSOC group, and particularly from extended discussions with Giuliano Bonoli and from his work on new social risks (Bonoli, 2002), which has been very helpful.

legitimated. These circumstances favoured the development of a family of European welfare states characterised by a specific division between the appropriate spheres of public and private action.

As an ideal type, the main business of the welfare state in industrial society was to provide for needs which were not adequately met through the market—interruption of income (retirement, unemployment, sickness, or disability) and mismatch between income and need during the life cycle (e.g. child endowment)—or for needs where state provision was widely recognised as desirable (e.g. highly-valued services in areas where the costs of privately checking professional expertise are high, such as health care or education). Social care, however, was mostly provided through the family system. Interventions in the family were limited and the corresponding services weakly developed in most countries. The outcome was the Keynes–Beveridge or Keynes–Bismarck welfare state: governments managed economies to promote full employment and organised social provision for needs which market and family did not meet.

Things have changed. In an ideal typical post-industrial society, economic growth rates are lower and more uncertain. Technological changes mean that stable employment in the manufacturing sector is no longer available on a mass scale, with implications for the job security of semi- and unskilled workers and for class structure and the political interests associated with it. Stricter competition promoted by economic globalisation has advanced labour market flexibility. The fact that women have succeeded in gaining greater advancement in education and in employment and are continuing to press for more equal opportunities means that traditional unwaged social care based on a gender division of labour imposes strains on the family (EU 2000*a*, *b*; Daly, 2000: 490).

These changes create new social risks and a new reform agenda for the welfare state. This book analyses the emergence of these risks in a range of European societies and examines political responses to them by governments and at the European Union level. In this chapter, we define new social risks, consider how they relate to old social risks, identify the implications for citizens and government, discuss how new risks are to be analysed, review the emergence of new risks and policy response to them at the national and EU level and consider the contribution of reforms in this area to innovation in welfare state policy-making.

New Social Risks: A Definition

New social risks are the risks that people now face in the course of their lives as a result of the economic and social changes associated with the transition to a post-industrial society. Four processes are of importance:

First, women have moved into paid work in large numbers, while the proportion of men who are economically active is falling. Men's labour force participation in EU countries fell from 89 per cent in 1970 to 78 per cent by 2001, while women's participation rose from 45 to 61 per cent (OECD 2001*b*, 2002*a*). One powerful driver is the importance of two earners to maintain a satisfactory family income. Another is the increasing demand from women for greater equality in access to education and to independent employment. Analysis of Luxembourg Income Study data shows that new social risks emerge most acutely for lower skilled women who find most difficulty in balancing work and family, especially in conservative and Mediterranean countries (Cantillon et al., 2001: p.447).

Second, the increase in the absolute and relative numbers of elderly people has implications for social care as well as for the cost of traditional welfare state pensions and health services. The ratio of those over sixty-five to the population of working age in Europe is projected to rise by 73 per cent between 2000 and 2030 (OECD, 2001*b*: 27). Most domestic care is still provided by women. Just over twice as many women as men spend time on care tasks for children and older dependants; women of family age (20–49 years old) who have care responsibilities for children spend about 46 hours a week on them compared to 22 hours for comparable men. Corresponding figures for those aged 50–64 who care for older dependants are 22 and 16 hours, respectively (Eurostat, 2002*a*: tables A.17 and A.19). Traditional patterns of care impose stresses on women seeking paid work and generate a demand for provision from alternative sources—men, the private sector, and the state.

Care responsibilities also impact on employment and on incomes. Data from the 1998 ECHP show that, for couple households with dependent children, 90 per cent of men of prime working age (20–49) are in employment compared with only 57 per cent of women. When we turn to older couple households with care responsibilities for dependent older people, employment rates fall to 47 per cent for men and 29 per cent for women—the same two-thirds ratio of women to men (Eurostat 2002*a*: table A.21). The impact of care responsibilities on women's employment in turn affects the risk of family poverty. The Luxembourg Income Study data show that poverty rates for couple households in the European Union where only one partner is in paid work are between three and six times higher than those where both work and here the effect is most marked in liberal countries with their weaker benefit systems (Esping-Andersen, 2002: table 2.5).

Third, labour market changes (to do primarily with technical developments in production, which have reduced the proportion of unskilled manual jobs in industry, and secondarily with the growth in scale and intensity of cross-national competition, which allows countries with lower pay levels to use their comparative advantage to attract mobile work) have tightened the link between education and employment. This in turn affects the risk of social exclusion among those with poor education. Those with a minimum level of education are about two and a half times more likely to be unemployed and nearly five times more likely to be in long-term poverty compared with those who have attended university (Eurostat 2000, tables 2 and 3; OECD, 2002d: table D). Education and skill levels are also linked to progress in work and in quality of working life. The Employment in Europe survey in 1996 showed that 47 per cent of employees had experienced a significant increase in the skill level of their job in the last five years, and virtually none a decrease. Skill increases are much more likely higher up the occupational ladder and the lower skilled more likely to anticipate insecurity and unemployment (Gallie, 2002: 113–18).

The fourth change lies in the expansion of private services resulting primarily from attempts to constrain state spending to meet the pressures on the old risk welfare state listed in the first paragraph. While privatisation is not in itself a risk, it can generate new risks when citizen–consumers commit themselves to unsatisfactory choices, and when regulation of standards in private provision is ineffective. The shift towards the private sector has been most marked in responses to the pressures on state pensions. A number of countries are also providing benefits which widen access to private provision as part of their care strategy for children and frail older people.

The United Kingdom, which already has the most extensive private pensions system, has gone furthest, by radically weakening the state second-pillar pension and developing private alternatives. Non-state pensions, which currently provide 60 per cent of income for the top 30 per cent of retired people are intended to provide 60 per cent for all by 2050 (OECD, 2000: figure 4.1; DSS, 1998). The Netherlands also has extensive second-pillar private provision. Other European countries are pursuing private pensions as supplements to state pensions. Germany provides subsidies and strong encouragement, Sweden requires workers to invest in complementary private pensions and Switzerland has well-established compulsory occupational pensions. In France, long-term tax-subsidised savings schemes are in process of implementation. The OECD concludes that the strengthening of private pensions is the most important trend in the current reform of pension systems (OECD, 2000: 46). Promoting the growth of occupational and private pensions is a major element in the EU's strategy for modernising social protection (EU, 2002*a*: 38). The UK private pension scandals are well known (chapter 3). While problems on a similar scale have not emerged elsewhere, successful regulation of new private services is essential to avoid escalating risks for more vulnerable groups (Esping-Andersen, 2002: 16–17).

This brief review of the way in which changes associated with the post-industrial transition affect people's lives indicates that more vulnerable groups are likely to experience new needs in three areas:

In relation to changes in the family and gender roles:

- balancing paid work and family responsibilities, especially child care
- being called on for care for a frail elderly relative, or becoming frail and lacking family support.

In relation to labour market changes:

- lacking the skills necessary to gain access to an adequately paid and secure job
- having skills and training that become obsolete and being unable to upgrade them through life long learning.

In relation to welfare state change:

- using private provision that supplies an insecure or inadequate pension or unsatisfactory services.

We go on to consider the context in which new social risks have emerged on the policy agenda.

New Social Risks, Old Social Risks, and Pressures on Government

At the same time as the new risks derived from the transition to post-industrialism are confronting the citizens of European welfare states, the established structures designed to cope with the social needs generated by industrialism and centred on interruptions to the family wage are facing pressures from different directions. The crisis of the welfare state has been extensively analysed (e.g. Ferrera and Rhodes, 2000; Kuhnle, 2000; Pierson, 2001*a*, *b*; Scharpf and Schmidt, 2001; Taylor-Gooby, 2001, 2002). It involves three factors, operating simultaneously: rising demand, restricted resources, and constraints on the capacity of government to reconcile the two.

The most important pressure derives from population ageing as a result of rising life expectancy and lower birth rates. The proportion of the EU population aged sixty five and over rose from 13 to 17 per cent between 1980 and 2000 and is expected to rise to 27 per cent by 2040. The proportion of working age (15–64) increased slightly from 65 to 67 per cent in the earlier period but is expected to fall to 58 per cent in the latter (EU, 2002*a*; 30). Since spending on old age and survivors' benefits is far and away the largest proportion of welfare state spending (44 per cent for the European Union as a whole) and that on health care (which is mainly consumed by older people) is the second largest, at 22 per cent (EU, 2002*a*: table 2), and since provision for older people is financed mainly by the taxes and social contributions of those of working age, these changes in age structure imply substantial financial pressures.

Demands increase just as resources come under constraint. Drawing on the work of Baumol (1967), Rowthorne and Ramaswamy (1997), and Iversen and Wren (1998*a*, *b*), Pierson (2001*a*: 84) argues that the shift in the labour force from the manufacturing to the service sector in the post-industrial transition also involves a long-term trend to declining productivity. This has implications for economic growth. Productivity rates in the major economies fell through the 1970s, 1980s, and 1990s. Growth rates, which were between 2.7 and 4.6 per cent for the four largest European economies (France, Germany, Italy, and the United Kingdom) for the decade to 1973, fell to between 1.1 and 2.7 for the following decade, then to 0.4–1.7 per cent between 1989 and 1995. A rally in the late 1990s collapsed after the bursting of the dot.com bubble so that rates for 1996–2002 were between 1.4 and 2.6 per cent. The current outlook is one of weak growth (Calderon, 2001; OECD, 2001*d*, 2003: table A.1).

At the same time, governments' capacity to manage key aspects of their economies is weakened by the implications for tax and subsidy regimes of increasing capital mobility and the impact of high-volume currency speculation on exchange rates, so that demand-side approaches to unemployment have become less attractive to policy-makers (Scharpf and Schmidt, 2000: 51–68). For EU member states these effects are reinforced by the 'open market' policies of the 1986 Single European Act, the 1994 Maastricht Treaty, and the constraints on state borrowing of the 1997 Growth and Stability Pact. The fact that the working class is no longer organised through mass employment in manufacturing industry, the effect of greater income inequality (Esping-Andersen, 2002: table 2.2) and greater diversity in working lives, and the emergence of new political pressures in societies that have been enriched through continuing growth (involving age cleavages, gender interests, divisions over environmental issues, and other concerns) tend to erode the solidarity that supported and legitimated the traditional welfare state (Beck, 1992: ch. 2).

Pierson argues that welfare states, faced with growing needs and mounting pressures on resources, face a future of 'permanent austerity'. The loss of some of the levers by which national governments managed their economies and the limits to solidarity make the task of funding expensive state services more difficult. The services developed by the industrial welfare state to meet the needs associated with lack of access to market income (pensions, sickness, disability, and unemployment benefits and so on) are everywhere undergoing reform. Measures to constrain spending by curtailing entitlements, expanding the role of the private sector or setting more stringent eligibility conditions are widespread (Myles and Pierson, 2001: 312). Market-based systems are introduced to control spending on health services through competitive pressures (Rico, Saltman, and Boerma, 2003: 599–600; Rathwell, 1998; ch. 17). An indication of the impact of these policies is that average benefits for each person of pensionable age in the EU-15 fell by 2 per cent between 1994 and 1999; unemployment compensation per capita fell by one per cent a year between 1990 and 1994, accelerating to 2.5 per cent between 1994 and 1999 (EU, 2002a: charts 9, 10, and 11).

This approach stresses austerity as the overriding consideration in welfare reform. However, analysis of welfare state development must also include the societal changes of post-industrialisation that are creating a second set of demands and generating a second reform agenda in the context of the transition to post-industrialism. From the individual perspective these changes emerge as 'new social risks', concerned with access to employment and opportunities in work, and with managing the conflicting pressures of family life, social care, paid work, and career. From the welfare state perspective they present a shift in political economy which results in new constraints on and new opportunities for government and pressures to develop new policies to manage and meet them. We consider these levels separately.

Key Differences Between Old and New Risks

The Citizen's Perspective

The emergence of new risks has had a substantial impact on the range of people's social needs. Although circumstances vary between countries, the new risks share four characteristics from the perspective of the individual citizen:

1. Successfully managing new risks is increasingly important, particularly for the more vulnerable groups, since the risks themselves affect more people and because failure to cope with them successfully can have substantial implications for poverty, inequality, and future life chances. An exception is elder care, since most carers are middle-aged or older.
2. New risks tend to affect people at younger stages of their lives than do old social risks, since they are mainly to do with entering the labour market and establishing a position within it, and with care responsibilities primarily at the stage of family building, rather than with health care needs or retirement pensions. New risks in relation to long-term care and pension reform may become more significant in the future.
3. For those groups who successfully manage the transition into paid employment or develop strategies to meet care needs, new social risks cease to be so pressing. They represent more serious problems for minorities—those without access to adequate training or education, or who are unable to draw on child or elder care from the family or the state. Old social risks, to do with retirement and ill health, were more likely to form part of the continuing life-experience of the mass working class of industrial society. This has implications for the politics of new social risks.
4. They involve both labour market and family life, and thus extend demand for state intervention into areas of life that had been seen as private from an old risks perspective, redrawing the public/private boundary, and raising normative issues of where in the family the responsibilities for generating income and providing care lie.

New risks are significant but transitory and particular. They open up new issues about the moral assumptions behind welfare state policy-making.

The Perspective of Government

The new risks generate new constellations of interests, which cross-cut old social risk constituencies in complex ways. They bear particularly on women, on younger workers, and on those without relevant skills. One hypothesis is that new cross-class alliances will emerge to pursue welfare state restructuring in a more diffuse 'life-politics' (Giddens, 1994: 48–9). Those most affected are typically members of minorities and are intimately linked in families with partners and parents who do not face the pressures directly, which may explain why such groupings are only weakly developed.

The reform process is likely to involve groups other than the immediate risk-bearers, and the interests of groups such as employers in relation to child care may lead policy in particular directions.

Policy-making in the traditional welfare state essentially involved the design and implementation of programmes to meet needs that market incomes did not satisfy. The welfare states that developed operate mainly through horizontal transfer over the life cycle, with some vertical transfer to poor minorities. Such arrangements depend on intergenerational and (some) social solidarity. During the 'golden age' redistribution was relatively painless because the costs of transfers could be mitigated for the immediate losers by growth: higher incomes outweighed rising tax, an option unavailable in an age of 'permanent austerity'. Under current circumstances, the old risk politics of welfare is in large part about the gradual erosion of commitments to continue the expansion of state spending through processes of recommodification, retrenchment, recalibration, and rationalisation (Pierson, 2001: 455). The most important example is the adjustment of pension entitlements as schemes mature through such tactics as the raising of pension ages, increased stringency of payment calculations, a reduction in early retirement, and a greater role for the private sector (Hinrichs, 2001; Myles, 2002; Bonoli, 2003).

In this context, the zero-sum game of net tax-payer and net benefit recipient (or rather, those who believe themselves to be net payers and recipients) is particularly intense. This brings factors which inhibit reform to the fore—governments wish to avoid blame for unpopular reforms and interested parties seek to veto or delay change. Differences in institutional structures influence the extent to which these factors operate. An approach which places stress on new risks alongside the old risks of established welfare states must consider a modified agenda of political divisions and social values. From the perspective of government the main differences between new and old risks are as follows.

1. Old risk policies tend to involve financial commitments requiring substantial tax and social insurance contributions. For this reason, and because they involve mainly horizontal redistribution, they tend to require a politics of solidarity, for example through the notion of a 'generational contract', 'risk-pooling', or a state that provides 'cradle-to-grave' care or offers a 'people's home'. Since the overwhelming majority of the population of industrial societies thought they might need the services supplied, such solidarity could be mobilised. Virtually all attitude surveys (see, for example, Ferrera 1993; Kaase and Newton 1996;

Svallfors and Taylor-Gooby 1999; ch. 1; van Oorschot 2000) concur that pensions, health care and provision for disabled people—the major programmes to meet needs not met through the market—enjoy high legitimacy. Government in the transition to post-industrialism faces the problem of how to justify cut-backs and constraint in these areas while developing new risk services that tend to go to minorities. This involves the tactics of blame avoidance and cumulative change charted by Pierson (1994) and others, and is expressed in the enormous resilience of these services against change.

2. New risks affect particular subgroups at particular life stages most keenly. They involve political divisions that do not map easily onto the traditional class and party structures and are likely to involve alliances with other social actors interested in the expansion of the workforce and in enhancing national economic competitiveness. If old social risk welfare was often seen as the outcome of a 'democratic class struggle' (Korpi, 1983), new risk welfare programmes may be obstructed by the interests entrenched by the outcome of that struggle.

3. Old risk policies were designed primarily to support people at stages in their lives when needs were not met through the wage relationship. They thus involve substantial transfer expenditure and may be seen as an economic burden at a time of stringency. New risk policies are often concerned to help more people support themselves through paid work. They may form part of a national strategy to mobilise a greater proportion of the population and to enhance economic competitiveness in a globalised market, and open up particular agendas for business and unions. To the extent that policy focuses on these issues, labour market reform predominates and child care becomes a more important issue than care for older people. About 42 per cent of women of prime working age (between twenty and forty-nine) are involved in child care as against 6 per cent in elder care (Eurostat 2002a: table A.17).

4. New risk policies meet needs mainly by encouraging and enabling different choices and behaviour patterns rather than providing benefits. They are concerned with the engagement of the citizen in paid work and with changes in the pattern of family life. They involve issues of responsibility for providing income and for domestic care that cut across the boundary between public and private spheres. New risk politics directs attention to issues of legitimation and moral values.

5. Because new risks are less likely to involve the entrenched interests, major expenditures, and neo-Keynesian apparatus of interventionism that concern national governments and more likely to involve equal

access to employment, the balance of family and work and the issues of training and education that concern an open market in labour, the European Union is likely to seek a stronger role in this area than it has in relation to old risks. New social risk activity will also enable the European Union to intervene directly in citizen's lives and may help to repair the 'democratic deficit' (Richardson, 2001: p. xv).

The politics of old social risk policy-making concern the extent to which welfare states are able to resolve the tensions that emerge between different groups when governments seek to retrench or contain spending on highly popular policies. Interest focuses on the extent to which it is possible to construct agreements which allow the interests of labour, business, and welfare state service users to be reconciled and to contain the burden of financing provision (Pochet 1999; Rhodes 2001; Hemerijck 2002), and on examples of successful accommodation such as the 'Dutch miracle' (Hemerijk and Visser, 2000).

New risk welfare politics is concerned primarily with mobilising the population to enhance competitiveness and with expanding opportunities and changing behaviour and assumptions about responsibilities. While the mass services of the traditional welfare state generate their own constituency, new social risk cleavages are much more likely to cross-cut existing social divisions. At the same time, new possibilities for employers and for those trade unions which represent workers most affected by new risks to form alliances in response to the shifts in the labour market emerge. An important theoretical concern is with changing modes of economic regulation and social roles in the family. This raises questions of how public policy innovations are legitimated and of how shifts in the approach of policy-makers and of business and unions are to be understood.

Paradigms and the Legitimation of Policy Change

A convenient approach to the policy stance of a government is provided by the notion of policy paradigm. Borrowed from Kuhn's influential work on the development of core ideas shared by communities of natural scientists (1970), the notion of policy paradigm is used to sum up the shared core beliefs of a policy community. It includes ideas about the goals of policy; the identification of issues as problematic in relation to those goals; explanations of why problems arise; solutions to identified problems; explanations of why they will meet the problem; and definitions of the appropriate role for government and other actors (Hall, 1993: 279).

The Keynesian paradigm was dominant in industrial countries for much of the post-war period. This approach included an account of the workings of political economy and of why a market system might be subject to unevenness and shortfalls in growth through mismatch in the availability of capital and investment opportunities at particular times (leading to depression or inflation), together with a recipe for economic intervention that explained how government could intervene through manipulation of interest and exchange rates in order to stimulate or restrain the economy. In this context, the traditional welfare state was legitimated as intervention which redistributed to groups with a high propensity to consume, especially at times of demand deficit, and which enabled government to regulate demand through social programmes and social infrastructure projects. Meeting political pressures from the working class and other interest groups could thus be reconciled with policies which secured the conditions for continued economic growth.

After the oil crisis of the 1970s, policy-makers in many countries lost confidence in this paradigm as traditional approaches to economic management became more difficult to pursue. The internationalisation of financial markets reduced the capacity to manipulate interest rates and undermined governments' ability to dictate exchange rates; stronger international competition, reinforced by the growing importance of the European Union as a free trade zone, influenced the extent to which the return to labour in cash and social wage could be determined in response to internal political demands without regard to developments elsewhere (Scharpf and Schmidt, 2000: ch. 1).

Policy-makers sought for new paradigms. The chief response among economists was monetarism, which stresses neoliberal, anti-inflationary policies rather than employment or growth objectives. The fact that 'Germany's success with a pragmatic version of monetary policy that emphasized a strong and stable currency provided policy-makers with a powerful example to emulate' at the time, ensured that broadly monetarist approaches became the dominant paradigm in policy-making (McNamara 1998: 6). Monetarism enjoins governments to pursue the welfare of citizens by reducing economic intervention and containing inflationary pressures by manipulating the money supply as the primary tool of economic management, rather than working directly on the level of demand. Throughout Europe, political economic paradigms were increasingly influenced by the assumption that the objectives of the welfare state are best advanced by ensuring that the market works efficiently, rather than expanding the provision of benefits and services. Such an approach is implicit in the priority given to low inflation, low budgetary deficits and low public debt in the Maastricht treaty criteria for membership of EMU. As a recent President of the European Central Bank put it:

Greater flexibility in labour, product and financial markets together with sound fiscal positions and wage moderation will support the objective of maintaining price stability and will create stable conditions to foster employment creation. Such an interaction of policies . . . is the best possible way to enhance the long-term welfare of the citizens of the Euro area. (Duisenberg, 2002)

It is also reflected in the original guidelines for the European Employment Strategy, in which the four sections deal with increasing employability, developing entrepreneurship, encouraging adaptability, and strengthening equal opportunities policies (EU 1998, Annex), rather than reflation, job-creation, and passive benefits.

From this perspective new social risks, which direct policy-makers' attention to labour market change and issues surrounding women's greater involvement in paid work, offer opportunities which may fit the developing paradigms of social policy-makers more closely than the high tax/ high service spending approach of the industrial society welfare state. The paradigm-shift in economic policy also plays an important role in the legitimation of new developments in social policy.

New risk policy-making is bound up with new approaches to economic policy. We move on to consider new risks in the context of theoretical accounts of the welfare state.

Analysing New Social Risks: Welfare State Regimes

The regime categorisation of welfare states has proved remarkably durable in providing a framework for the analysis of social policy. It distinguishes Nordic social democratic welfare states, where entitlement is based on citizenship principles and where the objective is a high level of universal protection against social risks; Continental corporatist welfare states, based on social insurance systems, where levels of provision are generally high, but the social hierarchies of work are reflected in entitlement; Mediterranean welfare states where pensions, health care, and education are highly developed and other services are now catching up with average European Union levels and where the family plays a prominent role; and the liberal regime, where state provision is more limited and targeted and private market systems are encouraged to a greater extent. The regime categorisation also corresponds to distinctions in levels of welfare. Nordic regimes tend to have lower rates of poverty and inequality and better protection for vulnerable groups than corporatist or Mediterranean regimes, with liberal regimes faring worst (Esping-Andersen, 2002: table 2.3). The hierarchy of social opportunities follows a similar pattern (Korpi, 2000). Thus the regime framework applies both to policy mechanisms and to the outcomes achieved in welfare states.

This approach has provided the backbone for work focused primarily on old risks, whether globalisation and labour market shifts are seen as the chief problem (Scharpf and Schmidt, 2000), permanent austerity (Pierson, 2001a, b) or population ageing and the rigidity of existing systems (Ferrera and Rhodes, 2000). It requires some modification to analyse the emergence of new risks and the way in which welfare states address them. The regime perspective focuses on the way different social groups, mainly class-based, contest the allocation of the resources generated by economic growth, drawing on 'industrial society' and 'power resources' theories. The key concepts deployed are 'decommodification' (how far welfare provision reduces the domination of citizens' lives by market forces) and 'stratification' (how far class inequalities are modified by or simply reflected in the redistribution of resources by the welfare system—Esping-Andersen, 1990: 3).

Family and gender issues were relegated to a subsidiary role in the traditional welfare settlement, on the assumption that family provision for breadwinner husbands also met the needs of their wives (see, for example, Beveridge, 1942: 9–11). Policies to manage new social risks address the opportunities and burdens for women directly. Employment had previously been tackled via Keynesian economic policies and welfare had been largely concerned to reallocate market resources to those whose needs were not met through the market wage system. New risk policies are concerned strongly with meeting needs through the mobilisation of labour, with direct targeted interventions to support wages, where these are inadequate, and with the use of private services in areas formerly addressed via the state. 'Recommodification' and 'flexibility' emerge alongside decommodification and stratification as key concepts for analysing welfare reform. We now examine patterns of welfare state policy inputs and outcomes in relation to family and employment in more detail, to see whether regime categorisation needs modification to provide an adequate framework for understanding the emergence of policies to meet new social risks.

New Social Risks in Balancing Work and Family Life

State social policies differ in the assumptions implicit in them about women's activities and in the division of responsibility for waged work in the labour market and unwaged domestic work necessary to provide care for children and older people and maintain a home. Initial approaches to analysing this issue reflected the gender cleavages between the male productive and female reproductive and domestic spheres of ideal typical industrial society. Thus Lewis categorised European welfare states in the 1980s according to the extent to which policy assumes a gender division between male breadwinner and female homemaker (Lewis, 1993: ch.1). Similar approaches have been elaborated by Orloff (1993), Bussemaker and Kersbergen (1994), Rubery (1999), Knijn and Kremer (1997) and others.

More recent analyses point to the increasing recognition of women as workers in a number of welfare states, but indicate that social provision is in most cases ill-adapted to support mothers who also participate actively in paid work. 'Broadly speaking, states have tended to recognise women for the purpose of social entitlements either as mothers or as workers. In a rare case, like France, both . . . have been recognised. In Sweden in the late twentieth century, recognition as mothers has been grafted onto recognition as workers. Where the male breadwinner model still has major purchase, then women find that their position as paid workers is at best a matter of secondary concern (Britain and Germany) and at worst actively discouraged (Italy)' (Lewis, 1998: 15).

The chief input in this area is the level of state spending on services which relieve the care burden on the family and particularly on housewives from child and elder care. Outcomes are indicated by the extent to which women are able to participate in paid work alongside men.

Table 1.1 shows that the inclusive Nordic citizenship welfare states committed substantially more than any other group of European countries to care services for children and older people between 1980 and 1999, spending roughly three times the EU average on elder care and twice as much on family services. Care spending in the corporatist heartland of Europe has roughly doubled. The liberal-oriented states continue to rely heavily on market and family provision. Spending in the Mediterranean states has expanded rapidly from a low base and now exceeds the liberal group in family care. When the statistics are analysed on a national basis, France stands out through the level of spending on child care support,

Table 1.1 Trends in state spending on new social risks (% GDP 1980–99)

	1980			1999		
	Services for elderly and disabled	Services for families	Active labour market support	Services for elderly and disabled	Services for families	Active labour market support
Nordic	1.77	1.60	0.88	2.73	1.78	1.67
Corporatist	0.46	0.38	0.13	0.75	0.74	1.14
Liberal	0.53	0.29	0.28	0.59	0.33	0.74
Mediterranean	0.08	0.04	0.02	0.25	0.37	0.47
EU-15	0.65	0.55	0.25	0.98	0.83	1.00

Notes: Nordic: Sweden, Denmark, Finland; Corporatist: Austria, France, Germany, Belgium, Netherlands; Liberal: UK, Ireland; Mediterranean: Greece, Italy, Portugal, Spain. EU average is based on all fifteen members.

Services for elderly and disabled include: residential care, home-help services, day care, and other services in kind. Services for families include: formal day care, personal services, household services, other family benefits in kind. Active Labour Market Policies include: training, youth measures, subsidised employment, employment measures for disabled people, employment services.

Source: Calculated from OECD (2001a)

which at 1.23 per cent of GDP in 1999 is midway between the corporatist and Nordic groups. This pattern of spending on care is broadly reflected in the extent to which women with family responsibilities participate in paid employment.

Couples where both members are engaged in paid work may pursue one of four employment strategies—the 'dual earner' model, in which both women and men participate more equally in paid employment, the 'modified industrial' model, which casts the male as a full-time and the woman as a part-time worker, the 'dual carer', in which both work part time and share domestic care work equally, and the 'reverse industrial', in which the woman works full time and the man part time. The more flexible work and family roles of ideal typical post-industrial society are reflected in progress towards the dual breadwinner or dual carer models and in the extent to which social policy seeks to sustain this (Lewis, 2001; see also Daly, 2001). The European Labour Force Survey examines the employment patterns of dual earner households with and without dependent children. Nowhere do more than two per cent of working couple households follow the dual carer model with both partners in part-time work. Similarly, fewer than 2 per cent of working couples follow the reversed traditional pattern of female full-time, male part-time employment (Eurostat 2002b). For the vast majority, the division is between the modified industrial and the dual bread-winner pattern.

The proportion of dual earner households is rising across Europe, as part of the shift towards a post-industrial society, and accounts for at least 60 per cent of all couple households supported through work everywhere except in Greece, Italy, and Ireland, where it exceeds 45 per cent. In all cases, among working couples without children at least two-and-a-half times as many follow the dual earner as follow the modified industrial pattern. However, among those with children, there is a rapid shift to the modified industrial model, which predominates for this group in the United Kingdom, Germany, and the Netherlands, and is widespread in the other corporatist and liberal countries with the exception of France (Eurostat 2002b). Table 1.2 shows how motherhood reduces women's engagement with work to a very limited extent in Nordic countries, but has a much greater impact in the corporatist, liberal, and particularly Mediterranean context. In corporatist and liberal countries, mothers who remain in work are much more likely to do so part time.

More detailed analysis of trends between 1984 and 1999 in employment patterns in couple households with a young dependent child (under six) points to a wider impact of child care on women's paid work across the corporatist countries and the United Kingdom. Everywhere there is a trend away from the traditional model of man in full-time work, woman as full-time unwaged mother, which was dominant in 1984. However, in the Mediterranean countries the majority of those mothers who work do so full time, while in corporatist continental Europe and the United Kingdom, mothers tend to work part time. France with its extensive child support policies is again the exception (OECD 2001c: table 4.2). In relation to long-term care, a recent European study shows that midlife informal care is associated with 'reductions in work hours or exit from the labour force' which is not recovered after care responsibilities end (Spiess and Schneider (2002: 33).

Regime theory broadly corresponds to patterns of both welfare state inputs and of outcomes in relation to the balance of care and paid work for women and men. However, these outcomes are produced through different means as the following chapters show. In Nordic countries, state support

Table 1.2 Women's employment and child care

	% Women aged 25–55 in employment, 2000			Share of part-time employment for women, aged 25–55, 2001	
	No children	One child	Two children	All women	Those with a child under six
Denmark	78.5	88.1	77.2	20.8	6.1
Finland	79.2	78.5	73.5	n.a.	n.a.
Sweden	81.9	80.6	81.8	n.a.	n.a.
Austria	76.0	75.6	65.7	24.8	50.4
Belgium	65.6	71.8	69.3	33.4	45.0
France	73.5	74.1	58.8	23.8	36.7
Germany	77.3	70.4	56.3	33.9	57.1
The Netherlands	75.3	69.9	63.3	58.1	69.4
Switzerland	84.3	75.5	65.5	n.a.	n.a.
Greece	53.1	53.9	50.3	8.5	8.0
Italy	52.8	52.1	42.4	23.7	25.0
Portugal	72.6	78.5	70.3	14.3	11.0
Spain	54.6	47.6	43.3	16.6	19.4
Ireland	56.8	51.0	40.8	n.a.	n.a.
UK	79.9	75.6	64.7	40.8	66.4

Note: ILO definitions of employment and part-time employment used.

Sources: Calculated from OECD (2003) Social Indicators, 2002, SS4

enables high full-time participation by most mothers. In France, state provision, and in Mediterranean countries, strong family support, enables those mothers who work to do so full time. In the United Kingdom, the market emphasis leads to high rates of women's employment, but reliance on private provision means that mothers tend to shift to part-time work. Corporatist conservative countries have strong similarities in their reliance on social insurance, but differ markedly in orientation to women's opportunities to act as full-time paid workers, with substantial differences between France and Germany. Similarly liberal market regimes provide limited state support for decommodified child care. However, recommodification through entry into the labour market may be possible through reliance on private nurseries and day care, balanced by part-time employment, offering different opportunities to higher and lower earners.

Changing Labour Market Risks

The chief new social risks emerging in the sphere of paid work are three: problems in entering the labour market, problems in maintaining stable, secure, and reasonably well-paid employment and associated social security entitlements and problems in gaining adequate training in a more flexible labour market. Governments across Europe have devoted resources to active labour market programmes designed to increase the proportion of the population in employment and endorsed in the 1997 European Employment Strategy. Spending across the European Union on activation policies increased fourfold overall between 1980 and 1999 (Table 1.1). Nordic countries, which already had higher spending levels in 1980 remained in the lead, followed by corporatist, liberal, and Mediterranean regimes, who increased provision in the 1990s from a very low base. Table 1.3 gives information on activation spending and access to vocational training for employees on the input side and unemployment rates for young people and overall employment rates in relation to outcomes.

In general, Nordic societies have high levels of spending on labour market activation and maintain very high levels of engagement in paid work among their populations, which in turn supports the levels of taxation which are necessary to finance expensive welfare states. They have strong vocational training programmes. Unemployment among young people remains substantial despite high overall employment rates. Conversely, the liberal market-oriented United Kingdom spends much less on labour market policy and docs not provide statistics on vocational training, but maintains relatively high employment (with significant youth unemployment) in a much more flexible labour market. Among the corporatist countries, spending on activation has increased substantially in recent years from a low starting point, there is a strong commitment to training and the level of employment in general is moderate. Youth unemployment varies. Developing Mediterranean welfare states have lower levels of spending, less training, rather lower engagement in paid work, and much higher youth unemployment.

The divergent cases are Switzerland, where the high level of participation in work is achieved on lower activation spending, mainly through very high (88 per cent, OECD, 2003: table B) male employment, with much lower rates for mothers, consonant with the less extensive child care support noted in

Table 1.3 Labour market participation and active labour market support spending[a]

	ALMP spending (% GDP, 1999)	Employees in continuous vocational training (%, 2001)	Youth unemployment rate (15–24-year-olds as % labour force, 2002)	Employment rate (15–64, % population of working age, 2002)
Denmark	1.66	53	7.7	75.9
Finland	1.40	50	21.0	68.1
Sweden	1.96	61	11.8	73.6
Austria	0.44	31	6.8	69.3
Belgium	1.38	41	18.2	59.9
France	1.30	46	20.0	63.0
Germany	1.26	32	9.7	65.3
The Netherlands	1.32	41	5.2	74.4
Switzerland	0.51	NA	6.0	79.0
Greece	0.18	15	26.4	56.7
Italy	0.67	NA	27.2	55.5
Portugal	0.74	17	11.5	68.2
Spain	0.29	25	22.2	58.4
Ireland	1.16	41	8.0	65.3
UK	0.31	18[b]	12.1	71.7
EU15	1.00	38	15.1	64.3

Notes:
[a] Active Labour Market Policies include training, youth measures, subsidised employment, employment measures for disabled people, employment services
[b] The UK government statistics from CSO (2003: chart 3.18)

Sources: EU (2002*b*: chart 17 and table 9); EU (2003: annex); OECD Employment Outlook, July (2002*c*: tables B and C; OECD (2001*a*))

the preceding section and reflecting the high proportion of migrant workers; Portugal with a relatively strong commitment to paid work; the Netherlands, where high recent activation spending and high labour market participation reflect the policies associated with the 'Dutch miracle' and Finland where youth unemployment remains high in the context of relatively high overall unemployment, ineffective labour market management, and the economic shock of the break-up of the Soviet Union. The division between the two largest corporatist economies, France and Germany, noted in relation to gender and family policies, is also evident in relation to unemployment among young people, which is relatively high in the former case, in the context of barriers to labour market entry from high labour costs.

Those with low skill levels are particularly vulnerable to low-paid employment once they gain access to work—34 per cent of low-skilled workers in the European Union as opposed to 13 per cent of the higher-skilled workers are in jobs which pay more than 25 per cent below average national wages. Women and non-EU nationals are particularly likely to be in low-paid work. Low pay is particularly prevalent in liberal-leaning countries, the United Kingdom and Ireland (18 and 29 per cent of jobs) and scarce in Nordic countries (20 per cent or below) with the other regime clusters in intermediate positions (EU, 2003: table 37).

This brief review indicates that the regime categorisation provides a useful tool for approaching new social risk reforms, but needs to be modified to include the distinctions (which are most marked in relation to family policies) within the corporatist category and to analyse welfare goals in terms of recommodification and flexibility as well as decommodification and stratification. In general, Nordic countries secure higher labour market participation overall and among women and mothers; corporatist societies come next, followed by the Mediterranean societies. The liberal regime succeeds in activating some population groups but provides less support for women and young people. We now move on to consider the role of the European Union.

The European Union and New Social Rrisks

The growing importance of new risks opens up particular opportunities for the European Union in welfare policy-making, which we discuss in Chapter 8. Although the 1957 Treaty of Rome called on member states to cooperate to improve living standards and working conditions (article 117) and article 118 referred to 'close cooperation' in social security, attempts to develop a positive social policy, alongside economic policy, have met with limited success. These attempts are encapsulated in the rebuff to the 1993 Green Paper on European Social Policy (EC, 1993a: part III), which led to no positive policy proposals, while an Employment White Paper in the same year advanced a different set of priorities, promoting monetary stability and an open and decentralised labour market characterised by greater flexibility (EC, 1993b: 12–16). Economic policy co-ordination has enjoyed spectacular success in the creation of a common currency and an open market across much of Europe. Social policy has only progressed in areas directly relevant to economic issues, such as equal rights for women in training, education, employment and pay, or the use of structural funds to foster employment opportunities (Geyer, 2001: ch. 9).

The official summary of recent developments in employment policies highlights measures to address new risks:

Activation has become the main theme of labour market policy reforms . . . member states have sought to increase financial incentives to take up work . . . accompanied by increased pressure on those on benefits to participate in active labour market programmes, to intensify their efforts to look for work and to accept job offers. . . . In many parts of the Union, childcare support and parental leave arrangements have been improved to make it easier for women to take up paid employment. (EU, 2002a: 8–9).

Social inclusion policy is also directed primarily at the risks associated with access to employment:

A stable job providing a steady source of income is recognised as the key factor in preventing social exclusion . . . improvements in childcare and parental leave . . . are relevant social inclusion policies, especially when they focus on the vulnerable group of lone parents to help ease the difficult transition from benefits into paid employment. Some member states have sought to ensure equitable access to education and training, while a few have sought to enhance job opportunities for immigrants and ethnic minorities. (EU, 2002a: 7–8).

The EU social policy is at an early stage of development. However, it seems that attempts to intervene in relation to the 'old risk' areas of social insurance and taxation have not been successful. The chief social policy areas in which EU policies command consensus have been in relation to more equal opportunities in employment and in the use of the Open Method of Co-ordination to advance employability, entrepreneurship, and adaptability in the labour market. These policies address the new social risks of balancing work and family and gaining access to employment, and proceed by encouraging progress towards common goals rather than attempting to impose a legal harmonisation of national policy instruments. As the European Union develops, its capacity to support new risk policy-making may become stronger. This must be set in the context of the progress of EU economic policies which stress market freedoms. Open markets may expand the availability of jobs, but also increase the risks for more vulnerable groups and the need for further policy-development to deal with the problems that emerge.

The Emergence of and Response to New Social Risks

New social risk issues have entered the policy agendas of European countries at different periods and have met with varying responses. The pace of reform also differs. It is the regime frameworks, structured by old social risk policies, that are likely to exert the strongest influence on the recognition and experience of new social risks. In the Nordic context, the well-established care services and the active labour market policies mitigate the impact of the new risks. Citizens are well supported in balancing paid work and domestic care, and in gaining access to work. In this setting, the most pressing new social risks are likely to concern groups such as migrants who have weaker access to existing policies, or to derive from the expansion of private provision. In corporatist countries, the established compromises between social partners and government privilege the interests of core workers, and assumptions about gender roles delay the development of collective provision. New social risks are likely to emerge in an acute form and policy responses have to be deferred. The liberal model tends to offer market solutions to new social risk needs, so that access to care is unequal, and labour market policies prioritise limited and incentive-based approaches, excluding vulnerable groups. The Mediterranean context assumes a family basis for social care and more corporatist labour markets, with a large informal sector, so that new risks become pressing in relation to women's employment and the security of those unable to gain access to established jobs.

Second, the shifts in paradigm and policy discourse and in the recalibration of policy regime required by new risks will differ in different national contexts. Policy contests will be more intense and efforts to legitimate changes in policy assumptions and individual behaviour more marked where the divisions between social groups are most strongly entrenched in the existing welfare system, and where the resources of social solidarity to sustain new policies in the interests of minorities are weakest. Nordic countries with their established broad solidarity find it easier to develop inclusive new risk policies, and to pursue them through state interventions. In corporatist systems, where new risk issues cut across established insider/outsider labour market and public/private family divisions, redirection of policy provokes more intense conflict, and blame avoidance is significant. It is difficult to introduce new instruments, so policy typically modifies the existing settlement. In liberal countries, with their orientation towards private solutions, conflict will surround not so much the need to meet the new risks as the role of the state in doing so, but governments will find the strict regulation of private services in a flexible economy difficult. In Mediterranean countries, changes in women's involvement in paid work impose severe stresses on traditional patterns of family support and are likely to produce conflicts over whether and how far government should intervene in this area.

New social risks apply immediately to minorities. While opportunities to gain access to decision-making vary between countries, new risk minorities tend everywhere politically to be weaker than the established policy actors: trade unions, employers, and business. Those new risks which relate to the interests of actors who are more powerful than the immediate bearers of the risks (most importantly those which restrict the availability of workers and damage competitiveness) are likely to be most prominent on the political agenda. The risks which relate to the mobilisation of the working population will tend to attract most attention, followed by child care and then the care needs of older people. Thus new social risks will involve debates about public responsibilities in welfare that lead to different policy interventions in different regimes, with an overall emphasis on increased involvement in paid work.

A New Direction for European Welfare States

The welfare politics of new risks provides opportunities for the development of positive-sum policies which deliver gains to some groups without major penalties for others—for example, moderate-cost child care provision which enables more women to enter the labour market and reduces child poverty, or training programmes which assist those with obsolete skills to find work and aid national productivity. They also enable the formation of constellations of political interests more influential than the risk-bearers themselves, who may promote reform programmes that outflank the defensive and sometimes intractable attrition struggles of much traditional welfare policy-making. For these reasons, recognition of the significance of new risks alongside old risks adds an important rider to the bleak conclusions of work on permanent austerity. Pierson ends his influential study of *The New Politics of Welfare* (2001*b*: 456):

while reform agendas vary quite substantially across regime types, all of them place a priority on cost containment. This shared emphasis reflects the onset of permanent austerity . . . the control of public expenditure is a central, if not dominant consideration . . . the contemporary climate remains a harsh one for efforts to improve social provision . . . or to address newly recognized risks.

New social risks may involve policy developments that are significant and positive but which may not figure in traditional approaches to the study of welfare states, because they are not primarily concerned with issues of retrenchment and spending constraint. Instead they involve the problems of constructing constituencies of support across different social actors for new policy departures. A positive 'new politics' of welfare is thus possible to the extent that an adequate framework of policies to meet new risks can be justified and implemented within different welfare regimes and different polities. The responses to new social risks discussed in the following chapters demonstrate the continuing resilience and innovative capacity of European welfare states.

References

Baumol, W. (1967) 'The Macroeconomics of Unbalanced Growth', *American Economic Review*, 57(3): 415–26.

Beck, U., Giddens, A. and Lash, S. (1994) *Reflexive Modernisation*, Polity Press, Cambridge.

Beveridge, W. (1942) *Social Insurance and Allied Services*, Cmnd 6404, HMSO, London.

Bonoli, G. (2001) 'Political Institutions, Veto Points, and the Process of Welfare State adaptation', in P. Pierson (eds.), *The New Politics of the Welfare State*, Oxford University Press, Oxford 238–264.

—— (2002) *The Politics of New Social Risks*, presented at APSA, Boston.

—— (2003) 'Two Worlds of Pension Reform in Western Europe', *Comparative Politics*, July.

Bussemaker, J. and Kersbergen, K. (1994) 'Gender and Welfare States: some Theoretical Reflections', in D. Sainsbury (ed.), *Gendering Welfare States*, Sage, London.

Calderon, C. (2001) *Productivity in the OECD Countries: A Critical Appraisal of the Evidence*, Working paper no WP/01/99, IMF.

Cantillon, B., Ghysels, J., Mussche, N., and van Dam, R. (2001) 'Female Employment Differences, Poverty and Care Provisions' *European Societies*, 3(4), 447–69.

CSO (Central Statistical Office) (2003) *Social Trends 33*, HMSO, London.

Daly, M. (2000) 'Women's' Labour Market Participation', in Scharpf and Schmidt, *Welfare and Work in the Open Economy*, Vol. II, Oxford University Press, Oxford.

DFI (2003) *Balancing Work and Family Life*, HMSO, London.

DSS (1998) *Partnership in Pensions*, HMSO, London.

—— (2000) *The Changing Welfare State*, HMSO, London.

Duisenberg, W. (2002) 'Testimony before the Committee on Economic and Monetary Affairs of the European Parliament: Introductory Statement', Brussels, 21 May.

EC (1993a) *European Social Policy: Options for the Union*, com (93) 551, DG for Employment, Industrial Relations and Social Affairs.

EC (1993*b*) *Growth Competitiveness and Employment*, Bulletin of the EC, supplement 6/93, CEC.

—— (2001) *Employment in Europe 2001*, DG Employment and Social Affairs, EU, Luxembourg.

Esping-Andersen, G. (2002) *Why we need a new Welfare State*, Oxford University Press, Oxford.

—— (1990) *Three Worlds of Welfare Capitalism*, Polity Press, Cambridge.

—— (1999) *The Social Foundations of Post-industrial Economies*, Oxford University Press, Oxford.

—— Gallie, D., Hemerijk, A., and Myles, J. (2002) *Why we Need a New Welfare State*, Oxford University Press, Oxford.

EU (1998) *The 1998 Employment Guidelines: Council Resolution of 15.12.97*, Council of the EU.

—— (2000) *The Social Situation in the EU*, Office for the Official Publications of the EC, Luxembourg.

—— (2002*a*) *Social Protection in Europe 2001*, Employment and Social Affairs, Brussels.

—— (2002*b*) *Employment in Europe, 2002*, Office for the Official Publications of the EC, Luxembourg.

—— (2003) *Employment in Europe, 2003*, Office for the Official Publications of the EC, Luxembourg.

Eurostat (2000) *Persistent Income Poverty in the EU*, Statistics in Focus, series 3, no. 13.

—— (2002*a*) *The Life of Women and Men in Europe, 1980–2000*, Office of Official Publications of the EU, Luxembourg.

—— (2002*b*) *The Impact of Children on Women's Employment varies between member States*, News Release 60/2002.

Ferrera, M. (1993) *EC Citizens and Social Protection*, CEC, VE2, Brussels.

—— and Rhodes, M. (2000*a*) 'Recasting European welfare states' and 'Building a sustainable welfare state', *West European Politics*, 23(2): 1–10, 257–82.

—— and Rhodes, M. (2000*b*) 'Building a Sustainable Welfare State', *West European Politics,* 23(2): 257–82.

Gallie, D. (2002) 'The Quality of Working Life in Welfare Strategy', in G. Esping-Andersen *op. cit.*

George, V. and Taylor-Gooby, P (1996) *European Welfare Policy: Squaring the Welfare Circle*, Macmillan, London.

Geyer, V. (2001) *Exploring European Social Policy*, Polity Press, Cambridge.

Giddens, A. (1994) *Beyond Left and Right*, Polity Press, Cambridge.

—— (1998) *The Third Way*, Polity Press, Cambridge.

Goode Committee (1994) *Pensions Law Reform*, Cm 2342-1, HMSO.

Hall, P. (1993) 'Policy paradigms, Social Learning and the State: The case of economic policymaking in Britain', *Comparative Politics*, April 1993: 275–6.

Hemerijck, A. (2002) 'The self-transformation of European social models', in Esping-Andersen (ed.). *Why we need a new Welfare State*, Oxford University Press, Oxford: 173–214.

—— Visser, J. (2000) 'Change and immobility: three decades of policy adjustment in Belgium and the Netherlands' in M. Ferrera and M. Rhodes *West European Politics*, 23(2) (special issue): 229–56.

Hinrichs, K. (2001) 'Elephants on the move', in S.Leibfried (ed.) *Welfare State Futures*, Cambridge University Press, Cambridge.

Huber, E. and Stephens, J. (2001) *Development and Crisis of the Welfare State*, Chicago University Press, Chicago.

Iversen, T. (2001) 'The Dynamics of Welfare State Expansion', in Pierson (ed.), *The New Politics of the Welfare State*, Oxford University Press, Oxford, 45–79.

—— and Wren, A. (1998) 'Equality, Employment and Budgetary Restraint: The Trilemma of the Service Economy', *World Politics*, 50(4): 507–46.

Jenson, J. (2002) *From Ford to Lego : Redesigning Welfare Regimes*, paper presented at the Annual Meeting of the American Political Science Association, Boston, 29 August–1 September.

Jessop, B. (1994) 'The Transition to Post-Fordism and the Schumpeterian Workfare State', in R. Burrows and B. Loader (eds.), *Towards a Post-Fordist Welfare State?*, Routledge, London.

—— (2002) *The Future of the Capitalist State*, Polity Press, Cambridge.

Kaase, M. and Newton, K. (1996) *Beliefs in Government*, Oxford University Press, Oxford.

Kautto, M., Hekkla, M. Hvinden, B., Marklund, S., and Ploug, N. (1999) *Nordic Social Policy*, Routledge, London.

—— Fritzell, J., Hvinden, B., Kvist, J., and Uusitalo, H. (2001) *Nordic Welfare States*, Routledge, London.

Knijn, T. and Kremer, M. (1997) 'Gender and the Caring Dimension of Welfare States: Towards Inclusive Citizenship', *Social Politics*, 4(3) 328–61.

Korpi, W. (1983) *The Democratic Class Struggle*, Routledge and Kegan Paul, London.

—— (2000) 'Faces of Inequality: Gender, Class and Patterns of Inequality in Different Types of Welfare States', *Social Politics*, 7(2): 127–91.

Kuhn, T. (1970) *The Structure of Scientific Revolutions*, Chicago University Press, Chicago.

Kuhnle, S. (ed.) (2000) *The Survival of the European Welfare State*, Routledge, London.

Lewis, J. (1993) *Women and Social Policies in Europe: Work, Family and the State*, Edward Elgar, Aldershot.

—— (1998) *Gender, Social Care and Welfare State Restructuring in Europe*, Ashgate, Aldershot.

Lodemel, I. and Trickey, H. (2000) *An Offer You Can't Refuse. Workfare in International Perspective*, Policy Press, Bristol.

McNamara, K. (1998) *The Currency of Ideas: Monetary Politics in the European Union*, Cornell UP, Ithaca/London.

Myles, J. (2002) 'A New Social Contract for the Elderly?', in G. Esping-Andersen *op. cit.*

—— and Pierson, P. (2001) 'The Comparative Political Economy of Pension Reform' in Pierson 2001 *op. cit.*

OECD (2000) *Reforms for an Ageing Society*, OECD, Paris.

—— (2001a) *Social Expenditure Database*, 3rd edn., CD-rom.

—— (2001b) *Labour Force Statistics, 1980–2000*, OECD.

—— (2001c) *Balancing Work and Family*, Employment Outlook, June.

—— (2002a) *Economic Outlook*, no. 71, June.

—— (2002b) *Education at a Glance 2002*, OECD, Paris.

—— (2002c) *Employment Outlook, 2002*, OECD Paris.

—— (2003) *Economic Outlook 2003*, OECD, Paris.

Oorschot, W. van (2000) 'Who Should Get What, and Why', *Policy and Politics*, 28(1): 33–49.

Orloff, A. S. (1993) 'Gender and the Social Rights of Citizenship: The Comparative Analysis of Gender Relations and Welfare States', *American Sociological Review*, 58: 303–28.

Pierson, P. (1994) *Dismantling the Welfare State? Reagan, Thatcher and The Politics of Retrenchment*, Cambridge University Press, Cambridge.

—— (1996) 'The New Politics of the Welfare State', *World Politics*, 48(2) 143–79.

—— (1998) 'Irresistible Forces, Immovable Objects: Post-industrial Welfare States Confront Permanent Austerity', *Journal of European Social Policy*, 5(4): 539–60.

—— (2001*a*) 'Post-industrial Pressures on the Mature Welfare States', in Pierson (ed.), *The New Politics of the Welfare State*, Oxford University Press, Oxford, pp. 80–104.

—— (2001*b*) 'Coping with Permanent Austerity: Welfare State Restructuring in Affluent Democracies', in Pierson (ed.), *The New Politics of the Welfare State*, Oxford University Press, Oxford, pp. 410–456.

Pochet, P. (1999) *Monetary Union and Collective Bargaining in Europe*, PIE Peter Lang, Brussels.

Rathwell, T. (1998) 'Implementing Health Care Reform: A Review of Current Evidence', in R. Saltman, J. Figueras, and C. Sakellarides, *Critical Challenges for Health Care Reform in Europe*, WHO.

Rhodes, M. (2001) 'The Political Economy of Social Pacts', in Pierson (ed.) 2001: 165–96.

Richardson, J. (2001) *European Union*, Routledge, London.

Rico, A., Saltman, R., and Boerma, W. (2003) 'Organisational Restructuring in European Health Care Systems', *Social Policy and Administration, special issue*, in P. Taylor-Gooby (ed.), 37(6): 592–608.

Room, G. and Berghman, J. (1990) *The New Poverty in the EU*, Macmillan, London.

Rowthorne, R. and Ramaswamy, R. (1997) *Deindustrialisation: Causes and Implications*, Economic Issues paper 10, IMF.

Rubery, J. (1999) *Women's Employment in Europe*, Routledge, London.

Scharpf, F. and Schmidt, V. (2000) (eds.) *Welfare and Work in the Open Economy: Diverse Responses to Common Challenges*, Oxford University Press, Oxford.

Schmidt, V. (2002) *The Futures of European Capitalism* , Oxford University Press, Oxford.

Spiess, K. and Schneider, U. (2002) *Midlife Care-giving and Employment*, European Network of Economic Policy Institutes, WP9, February.

Svallfors, S. and Taylor-Gooby, P. (1999) *Responses to State Retrenchment: Evidence from Attitude Surveys*, Routledge, London.

—— (2001) 'Sustaining welfare in hard times', *Journal of European Social Policy*, 11(2): 133–47.

—— (2002) 'The Silver Age of the Welfare State', *Journal of Social Policy*, 31(3): 597–623.

Wilensky, H. and Lebeaux, C. (1958) *Industrial Society and Social Welfare*, Free Press, NY.

2

New Social Risks in a Conservative Welfare State: The Case of Germany

Andreas Aust and Frank Bönker

Introduction

The German welfare state is still in a state of transition (Bönker and Wollmann, 2000*a*). Given the weak performance of the German economy since the mid-1990s and the coming demographic challenge, the need for change is now broadly accepted. At the same time, institutional constraints and the breakdown of the traditional social policy consensus have complicated the initiation and consolidation of reforms, so that the contours of the new settlement are becoming visible only gradually. The reform debate has further intensified since the parliamentary elections in September 2002. The current term has seen hectic legislative activities in almost all fields of social policy.

In this chapter, we focus on one particular aspect of welfare state development in Germany, the emergence of, and the reaction to, new social risks. The German social policy tradition, structured to meet the needs of traditional breadwinners within an industrial labour market, faces sharp challenges from shifts in family roles and from the rise of non-standard employment (Esping-Andersen, 1999). The conservative welfare regime exerts a strong influence on the way in which new social risks emerge, and the policy-making framework with its multiple checks and balances imposes constraints on the response to them. We first examine how the interplay between the general socio-economic changes outlined in Chapter 1 and national welfare state institutions has shaped the emergence of new social risks. Then we turn to discourses and policy developments and

Thanks for useful comments on earlier drafts go to Hellmut Wollmann, Karl Hinrichs, Peter Taylor-Gooby, and other members of the WRAMSOC team.

analyse how the Christian-democratic led governments of Helmut Kohl (1982–98) and the red–green governments of Gerhard Schröder (since 1998) have responded to the new challenges. In the concluding section, we summarise our findings and put them into a broader perspective.

The Emergence of New Social Risks

As sketched out in Chapter 1, new social risks have been associated with three kinds of changes—changes in family and gender roles, changes in the labour market, and changes in the welfare state itself. In the following, we analyse to what extent these changes, and the resulting risks, have been shaped by the existing welfare state institutions and the conservative nature of the German welfare state.

New Social Risks Associated with Changes in Family and Gender Roles

Germany, like other OECD countries, has experienced 'a growing individualisation of social arrangements' (OECD, 1999: 18). As marriages have declined and divorces increased, the proportion of lone parents has risen and now stands at about one-fifth of all households with children (Statistisches Bundesamt, 2003: 26). The proportion of elderly living alone is among the highest among in the OECD and the European Union.

These changes in family structures have gone hand in hand with changes in gender roles. As the role of the housewife has lost its normative appeal, the share of women who regard paid work as a normal part of their life has risen. According to surveys, the share of West German women with 'modern' views on gender roles has increased from 32 per cent in 1967 to 61 per cent in 2000 (Statistisches Bundesamt, 2002: 533–40). Young women who have equal or better educational attainment than men are especially likely to share such views. About 80 per cent of women aged between eighteen and thirty favour female labour market participation and an equal partnership between the sexes. This compares to a mere 28 per cent (59 per cent) of women over sixty-five in the West (East).

The most important challenge raised by these changes in family structures and gender roles has been the reconciliation of paid work and family responsibilities. In the German case, the latter has been complicated by a notoriously weak infrastructure of social services (Bertelsmann-Stiftung, 2003). While personal social services have expanded substantially since

Table 2.1 The supply of child care facilities in Germany (1965–98, no. of places as % of the age-group)

Year	0–3 years		3–6.5 years[a]		6–10 years[b]	
	West	East	West	East	West	East
1965	n.a.	n.a.	33.0	n.a.	n.a.	n.a.
1982	1.4	n.a.	65.6	n.a.	3.6	n.a.
1990 (East: 1991)	1.8	54.2	69.9	99.3	5.0	50.9
1994	2.1	41.3	71.7	96.2	5.1	58.2
1998	2.8	36.3	86.8	111.8	5.9	47.7

Notes:

[a] 1965 figures are for children aged 3–6 years

[b] The 1994 and 1998 East German data for children from 6–10 years exclude Sachsen-Anhalt and Thüringen

Source: BMFSFJ (2002: 328); data for 1965: Alber (2001: table 9)

the 1970s, their overall level has remained meagre from a comparative perspective (Alber, 1995; Ostner, 1998). This applies particularly to child care (see Table 2.1). In the mid-1990s, child care facilities—most of them providing only half-time services—existed for less than three quarters for all children aged from three to six and a half years. Moreover, there were almost no kindergarten places for younger children and almost all primary schools operated only on a half-time basis.

The limited care facilities have been a major obstacle to the expansion of female employment. While female labour force participation has increased substantially and now exceeds the EU average, it is still significantly below the levels of the liberal welfare regime in the UK and the social democratic welfare regimes in Scandinavia (OECD, 2003: table B; see also Table 9.1 in Chapter 9). There is strong evidence that more women with caring responsibilities would like to enter the labour market, but refrain from doing so because of a lack of public social services (Bielinski, Bosch, and Wagner, 2002; Spieß and Büchel, 2003). The importance of service infrastructure is indicated by the fact that the difference in employment between women with and without caring responsibilities either for children or for older and other dependants is stronger in Germany than in most other EU countries (Eurostat, 2002: table A.20; see also Table 1.2 in Chapter 1).

Problems in reconciling paid work and family responsibilities have been an important determinant of poverty, especially among low-income households and lone parents (Bundesregierung, 2001: 104–17). The fact that, in 1998, almost 30 per cent of all lone parent households in West Germany received social assistance can partly be attributed to insufficient child care facilities.

Changes in relation to the family and to gender roles have also reduced the scope for family support in case of frailty, although this issue has received less attention than the issue of child care. Alongside increased life expectancy and the changing age structure, the eroding potential for family support has given rise to a growing gap between the need for care on the one hand and the availability of informal care on the other. The size of this gap is indicated by the estimate that, given the increasing number of frail elderly, the share of women aged 40–65 years engaged in informal elderly care would have to rise by about 200 per cent to maintain the current level of informal care in 2050 (Schulz, Leidl, and König, 2001). These developments have put considerable pressure on social services at the local level.

The weak service infrastructure is a deeply engrained feature of the German welfare state. Strongly shaped by social catholic thinking, the latter has rested on a traditional understanding of the family (van Kersbergen, 1995). The low degree of 'defamiliarization' has found its expression in the well-known principle of subsidiarity according to which the state should step in only when the family cannot cope. Several other factors have worked against an expansion of public provision. The experience of fascism in the past and GDR state socialism in the former East Germany has added to the reservations against public child care. In addition, the institutional setting has been unfavourable (Alber, 1995: 136–41). The competencies of the federal government in the field have been limited, as most legislation has rested with the states and provision with the municipalities and non-profit organisations. This institutional fragmentation has worked against an expansion of services by increasing the need for cooperation and provoking conflicts over competencies. Moreover, local governments have often lacked the resources to finance social services as they have enjoyed little autonomy in levying taxes and have been burdened by other commitments imposed on them by central government.

New Social Risks Associated with Labour Market Changes

Labour market changes have represented a second source of new social risks. As has been argued in Chapter 1, two changes stand out—the de-standardisation of employment and the weakening labour market position of the low-skilled. Germany has experienced both trends. As with changes in family structures and gender roles, the existing welfare state institutions have left their imprint on these changes and the resulting new social risks.

Owing to its strong industrial sector, highly regulated labour markets, and low female employment, Germany traditionally has been characterised by a high share of permanent, full-time employment. As the industrial sector has shrunk and as more women have entered the labour market, alternative forms of employment have gained ground (Hoffmann and Walwei, 2000; Klammer and Tillmann, 2001a). From 1988 to 1998, the share of employees with permanent, full-time employment contracts in the working population (in West Germany) fell from 67.4 to 62.1 per cent. Interestingly, the decline in the share of standard employment has not been associated with a shrinking number of permanent, full-time jobs. To put it differently, atypical employment has complemented rather than replaced standard employment.

The single most important type of non-standard employment has been part-time employment. The percentage of employees working part-time has increased from less than a twentieth in 1960 to about a fifth, and is now among the highest in the EU (European Commission, 2002: 22, chart 14). More than half of part-time employment takes the form of the so-called mini-jobs (*geringfügige Beschäftigung*), a German peculiarity. If working times and earnings do not exceed certain narrow thresholds, employers and employees have been allowed to opt for a special kind of employment contract. Before April 1999, these jobs were exempt from social insurance contributions and subject to a flat-rate income tax, to be paid by the employer. The exemption from social insurance contributions made the mini-jobs particularly attractive for groups such as married women, students, pensioners, or employees with a first regular job who enjoyed health insurance cover anyway. Employers benefited from the lack of bureaucracy associated with mini-jobs and the fact that many employees were ready to accept lower wages and waive part of their rights. The mini-jobs were the most dynamic segment of the German labour market in the 1990s. In the late 1990s, the number of employees with one or more of these jobs was estimated at between five and six million, up from four million at the beginning of the decade.

The expansion of part-time employment has been accompanied by increases in other forms of atypical employment. The share of employees with temporary contracts grew from 10 per cent in 1995 to 14 per cent in 2000 (European Commission, 2001: 20, chart 16). The 1990s also saw a sharp increase in dependent self-employment as well as in the number of those employed by agencies that specialise in temporary work (*Zeitarbeit*). The share of the self-employed without employees outside agriculture, a proxy for dependent self-employment, rose by about 50 per cent from 1988 to 1998 and reached about 4.5 per cent of the economically active population in 1998 (Hoffmann and Walwei, 2000: 3, table 2).

The de-standardisation of employment and its social consequences have been shaped by the entrenched institutions of the German welfare state. To start with, the strong increase in mini-jobs and dependent self-employment has been driven by the attempt of employees and employers to avoid Germany's high social security contributions. At the same time, the close nexus between contributions and benefits that has characterised the conservative German welfare state has increased the risk of inadequate social security coverage in the case of atypical employment (Pfaff, 1999; Bäcker, 2001; Klammer and Tillmann, 2001*a*, *b*: 189–200).

A second major change in the German labour market has been the weakening position of the low-skilled. It has manifested itself in a strong increase in low-skill unemployment rather than in a rising number of working poor. Since the early 1980s, unemployment among those with neither a vocational qualification nor a higher education qualification has grown substantially stronger than unemployment among the rest of the population. While low-skill unemployment exceeded average unemployment by 80 per cent in the first half of the 1980s, the low-skilled unemployment rate now stands at about 2.5 times the average unemployment rate (Hagen and Steiner, 2000: 90, Abb. 9). The increase in low-skill unemployment accounts for more than 40 per cent of the overall increase in unemployment from 1991 to 1997. EU statistics suggest that the German low-skilled unemployment rate has been above the EU average both in absolute terms and relative to the unemployment rate of the higher-skilled (European Commission, 2002: 24). The high low-skill unemployment, along with the high incidence of long-term unemployment in Germany, has raised fears of persistent exclusion from the labour market (see, for example, Alber, 2001: 16).

Many observers attribute the weakening labour market position of the low skilled to the limited adjustment of the German welfare state, with its relatively narrow wage differentiation, high social security contributions, generous benefits and limited 'activation' of the unemployed, to secular changes in the demand for low-skilled labour (Jochem and Siegel, 2000; Puhani, 2003). However, this interpretation has remained controversial. Comparative studies fail to show a clear-cut relationship between wage differentiation and low-skill unemployment (Freeman and Schettkat, 2000).

Other reasons for the high rate of low-skilled unemployment, such as weak overall economic performance, problems with integrating migrants, and various cultural and institutional barriers to an expansion of service employment can be identified (Bosch, 2003).

New Social Risks Associated with Welfare State Change and the Privatisation of Welfare

A final source of new social risks has been the move from state services to state-regulated, but privately provided services. In the German case, the role of such 'welfare markets' has for long been limited, as the conservative welfare regime has relied on the state and the family rather than on the market. This particularly applies to old-age protection where occupational pensions and private savings have played a small role and about 85 per cent of all retirement income have traditionally come from public pensions. More recently, however, the 2001 pension reform, by establishing a state-subsidised private pension pillar, has marked the first step towards a new public–private mix (Bönker and Wollmann, 2001: 86–9). While the red–green government refrained from its initial plans to make private pro-visioning mandatory, it has sought to make clear that in the future public pensions will no longer secure the maintenance of pre-retirement living standards and has introduced strong fiscal incentives to take out private pensions. With the move towards a new public–private mix, the regulation of the new private pension pillar has become a major political issue.

The situation has been more complex with regard to personal social services (Bönker and Wollmann, 2000a: 532–34, 2000b). As the bulk of personal social services traditionally has been provided by the so-called welfare associations (Wohlfahrtsverbände), non-profit organisations affiliated with the churches and the labour movement, one might speak of a tradition of state-regulated and state-funded, but privately provided services. Until the early 1990s, however, the welfare associations enjoyed far-reaching legal privileges, were closely interwoven with the state and behaved more like members of a cartel than market competitors. Like in the case of old-age protection, the rise of 'welfare markets' proper is thus a relatively recent development that has been brought about both by the entry of new private providers and by a more market-oriented regulation of service provision. The main engine of change has been the 1994 law on care insurance which, for the first time, explicitly put welfare associations and commercial providers on an equal footing and imposed major organisational reforms on the welfare associations.

Policy Debates and Developments

The emerging new social risks have not gone unnoticed. While the notion of 'new social risks' has rarely been used in German debates, the underlying trends have been invoked as arguments for reform. In the following, we give an overview of the major policy debates and developments. The policy trajectory has been influenced by the conservative tradition and the corporatist policy-making framework. The former delays reforms in the public provision of child care and ensures support for the informal sector in the care of older people. The latter has produced many problems in labour market policy. Not surprisingly the changes that have finally taken place have been much more substantial where there is strong support for reform (as in the case of child care) than where the constituency of those affected is weak (as in the case of the de-standardisation of employment), or where different groups are in opposition (as applies to policies designed to help low-waged workers). Our analysis focuses on the reactions to five different challenges—the difficulties in reconciling paid work and family responsibilities, the rising number of frail elderly people, the de-standardisation of employment, the weakening labour market position of the low-skilled, and the move towards 'welfare markets'.

Public Child Care and the Reconciliation of Paid Work and Family Responsibilities

Balancing paid work and family responsibilities has been an issue in Germany ever since the late 1960s when the new women's movement started to articulate women's interests (Schneider, 2002). SPD and Greens, both close to this movement, have always been sympathetic to increased female labour market participation. Emphasising the equality of sexes and the autonomy of women, both parties have been committed to a 'parallel' reconciliation of work and family and have argued in favour of expanding public social services to 'defamilialize' the German welfare state. In contrast, the position of the CDU/CSU has been more ambivalent. Traditionally committed to the male bread winner model, the party started to modernise its thinking and began to propagate a 'sequential' reconciliation of employment and family, with mothers working part time, in the 1970s. While the CDU/CSU has become less hostile to female labour market participation it has remained sceptical with regard to an expansion of public child care. Influenced by the papal encyclical *'laborem exercens'* of 1981, the party has emphasised the equal worth of paid work and care work at home. Accordingly, it has favoured a 'socialization' of the costs of child care by increasing transfer payments to caring mothers as well as by expanding pension credits for child rearing. These programmatic differences between the two camps have manifested themselves in substantial differences in government policies.

The reform flagship of the Kohl government was the overhaul of the parental leave scheme in 1986 (Bleses and Rose, 1998; Auth, 2002; Schneider, 2002). The old scheme, introduced by the then governing SPD/FDP coalition in 1979, had granted working mothers the right to four months of paid leave after birth. The CDU/CSU-FDP government slightly changed the provisions for working mothers and complemented them by introducing an income-related parental leave benefit (*Erziehungsgeld*) of DM 600 (307 euros) for all parents irrespective of their employment status. From 1986 to 1992, the maximum duration of the parental leave (*Erziehungsurlaub*) was gradually extended to three years. Parents were granted the right to work up to 19 h per week during their parental leave. In order to facilitate a reentry into the labour market, they also got an employment guarantee. Moreover, special labour market programmes were introduced with a view to supporting child-rearing mothers' return to paid work.

The introduction of the parental leave scheme represented a major innovation. For the first time in the history of the German welfare state, family duties, which had traditionally been regarded as a private matter, became the basis for benefit claims (Bleses and Seeleib-Kaiser, 1999). With regard to the balancing of paid work and family responsibilities, the reform of the parental leave scheme was ambivalent. While the chances of re-entering the labour market were only slightly improved, the universal allowance substantially increased the incentives to stay at home, thus tending to lure women out of the labour market and to reinforce the traditional division of labour between the sexes (Auth, 2002; Schneider, 2002). In doing so, the parental leave scheme has reflected, and strengthened, the familiaristic character of the German welfare state.

The Kohl government's explicit attempts to facilitate the 'parallel' balancing of paid work and family responsibilities focused on the promotion of part-time employment for mothers. By extending opportunities to reduce hours of work in the public sector and increasing the social rights of the part-timers, the government contributed to the strong increase in German part-time employment that has been reported above. By contrast, the improvement of public child care did not feature very prominently on the Kohl government's agenda. For one thing, this reflected the strong legacy of social catholic thinking with its emphasis on subsidiarity and its reservation against state involvement in child care. In addition, the federal government suffered from a lack of competencies in the field of child care. The powerful state governments opposed any attempt to curtail their own authority or increase their fiscal burden.

For these reasons, it took the reform of abortion law in the wake of German unification to bring about an expansion of child care facilities (Auth, 2002: 240–48). In order to forge a parliamentary majority for maintaining liberal provisions on abortion, a cross-party alliance of female MPs suggested combining reform of abortion law with the passage of various family-supporting measures including the introduction of a right to a kindergarten place for all children aged 3–6 years from 1996 onwards, a commitment to expanding child care facilities to children younger than three, the topping up of social assistance for lone mothers and some reforms of labour market policy aimed at supporting female re-entry into the labour market.

Although its implementation was eventually postponed to 1999 in order to reduce the fiscal burden on municipalities, the new right to a kindergarten place triggered a substantial increase of child care facilities in the 1990s. While kindergarten places existed for no more than 70 per cent of all children aged to 6.5 in 1990, the respective figure had jumped to 87 per cent in 1998 (see Table 2.1). There is some evidence that this expansion of child care facilities has contributed to the substantial increase in the employment of mothers with children between three and six years by 7.5 percentage points since 1996 (BMFSFJ, 2003a: 108–9).

Compared to the conservative–liberal government, the red–green coalition has committed itself more explicitly to the promotion of gender equality in society and economy (SPD and B'90-Die Grünen, 1998). The 1999 reform programme 'Woman and Profession' (*Frau und Beruf*) included several measures aimed at encouraging female employment and at facilitating the 'parallel' reconciliation of work and family for both sexes. Among the most important reform measures have been the introduction of a legal right to a part-time job in 2000 and the overhaul of the parental leave system (Fuhrmann, 2002; Klenner, 2002). As for the latter, the government increased the weekly period that parents on parental leave are allowed to work from 19 to 30 hours and made it possible for both parents to take the leave simultaneously. Moreover, it increased the incentives to shorten the interruption of employment by raising benefit size when the leave does not extend beyond one year. In addition the red–green government adopted the principle of gender-mainstreaming and updated the equality act for the public sector (Töns and Young, 2001). The initial attempt to adopt a similar act for the private sector failed because of resistance by employers. Instead, the government agreed to sign a legally non-binding agreement with the BDA—the employers' organisation—in July 2000 (Pfarr, 2001). The BDA promised to promote gender equality within enterprises and to bring about a 'significant increase of women's employment share'. Employers have continued to call for enhanced efforts to expand public child care facilities.

While measures to facilitate the reconciliation of paid work and family responsibilities featured prominently on the red–green agenda, the government initially did not launch any significant initiatives to expand child care facilities. This changed in the run-up to the 2002 elections. When the CDU/CSU came up with the plan to introduce a new and much more generous family benefit (*Familiengeld*), the red–green coalition finally responded by promising to support the expansion of public child care facilities (Ristau, 2003). In particular, the chancellor announced that the government would give an annual amount of 1 bn. euros for investment in all-day primary schools to municipalities over a period of four years (Schröder, 2002).

This move turned out to be highly popular and contributed to the surprising re-election of the government by helping the governing coalition to attract a majority of the female vote (Roth and Jung, 2002: 15). The popularity of the government's proposal was partly due to the fact that it was made shortly after the PISA study had revealed the bad shape of the German education system. It also documents the erosion of the traditionally strong reservations against public child care that has taken place in Germany.

The 2002 coalition treaty of SPD and Greens declared the expansion of child care facilities the most important target of family policy in the new term (SPD and B'90-Die Grünen, 2002). In addition, the government promised to ensure that child care facilities for at least 20 per cent of all children younger than three years will be in place by the end of its term of office. The required investments shall be financed by freeing 2.5 bn. euros per annum for local governments through the reform of the social assistance scheme. The implementation of these promises has run into difficulties. The federal government, the states and the local governments have haggled over the distribution of costs and competencies. Reacting to these conflicts, the government has already watered down its targets. With regard to children younger than three years, the promise now is that child care facilities, according to local need will be provided by 2010 (BMFSFJ, 2003*b*).

With its recent emphasis on the expansion of child care facilities, the red–green government is certainly trying to leave the traditional path of welfare development in Germany. However, much more resources would be needed to satisfy the demand for child care facilities and build a service infrastructure similar to France or the Scandinavian countries (Daly, 2000; DIW, 2001). It remains to be seen how these resources can be mobilised in the general context of fiscal austerity and budget consolidation at all levels of the German federal system.

Compared to the reconciliation of child care and paid work, the balancing of care for the elderly and employment has featured less prominently in Germany. In the debates that led to the introduction of the long-term care insurance scheme in 1994, the consequences of informal elder care for the labour market participation of carers played only a subordinate role (Götting, Haug, and Hinrichs, 1994). In contrast to child care, the major actors have shared a clear preference for supporting informal care arrangements.

Reflecting this preference for informal care, legislation on care insurance contained several measures aimed at encouraging informal provision (Behning, 1997). Frail elderly people can choose between the reimbursement of a certain level of formal care services, a cash benefit (*Pflegegeld*) that can be freely spent or a combination of both. As the cash benefit is supposed to be used to compensate carers, it provides a material incentive to look after frail relatives. A second set of measures is targeted on informal carers more directly. Under certain conditions, they are covered by the statutory accident and pension insurance scheme. Moreover, the care insurance scheme also provides relief for nurses when informal helpers are on holiday.

The effects of long-term care insurance on the balance of paid work and family responsibilities appear mixed. By providing benefits for the frail elderly and by contributing to an expansion of professional care services, the scheme has reduced the burden on caring relatives, thereby making it easier for them to reconcile family and work. At the same time, the substantial improvement of the situation of informal carers has created incentives to leave, or to stay outside, the labour market. This conflicts with the objectives of new risk policies in the labour market.

The Risks of Frailty and the Introduction of the Long-Term Care Insurance Scheme

The risks associated with frailty became a major issue in the 1980s. The debate that led to the introduction of an internationally unique long-term care insurance scheme in 1994 focused on the rising number of frail elderly people dependent on social assistance. In contrast, other issues such as the situation of caring relatives or the quality of care played a subordinate role (Götting, Haug, and Hinrichs, 1994). The focus on social assistance was favoured by the strong involvement of local government in the debate. As the tier of government in charge of financing social assistance, they were keen to reduce the rapidly growing spending on social assistance for people in need of care, which accounted for more than a third of the overall assistance budget in 1993. Various proposals to address the issue were floated. Some envisaged a solution within the health care scheme; others aimed at the introduction of tax-financed benefits or the creation of a separate insurance scheme or called for making private care insurance compulsory.

The Kohl government initially opposed comprehensive reforms. It argued that such reforms were likely to undermine readiness to provide informal care and to induce a switch from domiciliary to institutional care, thereby creating a high and unbearable fiscal burden. As the number of the frail elderly people grew, and the issue moved up the political agenda, the Kohl government eventually realised that reform would appeal to voters, and committed itself to the introduction of a new scheme in the run-up to the 1990 parliamentary elections. The passage of the reform was complicated by the fact that the business wing of the CDU/CSU and the FDP opposed it. Moreover, the government lacked a majority in the second chamber and had to make concessions to the Social Democrats. The interplay of both conflicts made the introduction of a long-term care insurance scheme a protracted process, which lasted until 1994 (Götting, Haug, and Hinrichs, 1994: 297–304; Meyer, 1996: ch. 6).

Long-term care insurance was established as a PAYG scheme financed through earmarked social insurance contributions and organised as a separate branch of social insurance (Ostner, 1998: 120–2). Benefits were not supposed to cover all expenses and were not indexed. Depending on the degree of care dependency and the type of care, they were set within a range of from 205 to 1,432 euros a month. In the case of domiciliary care, the frail elderly were granted the choice between cash benefits (*Pflegegeld*), the reimbursement of professional care and a combination of both.

The introduction of the long-term care insurance scheme has substantially improved the financial situation of the frail elderly and has made them less dependent both on their relatives and on social assistance. By increasing the purchasing power of the frail elderly and by reforming the structures of service provision, it has also contributed to an expansion of social services for this group. As a result, the new scheme has reduced the risks in case of frailty, including the risk of lack of family support. Meanwhile, however, the limits of the new scheme have become visible (Rürup-Kommission, 2003: 185–91; Deutscher Bundestag, 2002: 229–63). The gap between care costs and care benefits was greater than expected, and the proportion of frail elderly compelled to claim social assistance did not decline at the anticipated rate. In fact it fell between 1994 and 1998, but rose thereafter. The coexistence of the long-term care and the health insurance scheme has created high transaction costs for the frail and the service providers. These developments, together with a gradual deterioration of the fiscal situation of the long-term care insurance scheme and a controversial decision of the Constitution Court on the financing of the long-term care insurance scheme in 2001, have put major reform of the long-term care insurance scheme on the agenda.

Dealing with the De-standardisation of Employment

The de-standardisation of employment and the associated risk of insufficient social insurance coverage have been a prominent issue in German social policy debates since the mid-1980s. Some observers even argue that Germany is among the countries where this issue has featured most prominently (Alber, 2000: 542). Controversies have focused on two issues: first, whether to limit or to encourage the rise of atypical employment; second, how to adjust the welfare state to labour market changes.

While the expansion of regular part-time employment has been generally endorsed as a means to combat unemployment and to facilitate the balancing of paid work and family, the rise in other forms of non-standard employment has been more controversial. In the 1980s, trade unions and social democrats strongly opposed the easing of fixed-term employment by the Kohl government. In the mid-1990s, a huge debate on mini-jobs and on dependent self-employment developed. Trade unions, social democrats, the social insurance funds, and the labourist wing of the CDU/CSU blamed the increasing number of mini-jobs and the increase in dependent self-employment for contributing to the weak finances of the social insurance funds. However, the FDP and the business wing of the CDU/CSU blocked any change in the name of labour market flexibility.

In line with its earlier positions, the new red–green government initially committed itself to stopping the 'misuse' of mini-jobs and dependent self-employment. However, it did not agree on a clear approach to reform, and faced strong opposition not only by the employers, but also by some employees and self-employed people. As a result, the changes eventually adopted were modest. This applied particularly to the 1999 reform of mini-jobs (Bäcker et al., 2000: 187–89, 302; Dingeldey, 2000). This ruled out mini-jobs for employees with a regular first job and replaced taxes on mini-jobs with social insurance contributions, but left the income threshold untouched. Moreover, the change to social insurance contributions did little to improve the social insurance coverage of the mini-jobbers, as they have to top up contributions in order to acquire benefit claims.

The debate on the mini-jobs regained momentum in 2002 when the CDU/CSU, in their programme for the federal elections, called for an extension of the mini-jobs. The programme envisaged an increase in the income threshold from 325 to 400 euros and tapered insurance contribution rates between 400 and 800 euros. These suggestions were initially rejected by the Social Democrats. In late 2002, however, they became part of a compromise on labour market reform between the red–green coalition and the CDU/CSU led majority in the Federal Council. This compromise also reopened the mini-jobs for employees with a regular first job, thereby abolishing a centrepiece of the 1999 reforms of the incoming red–green government.

The ongoing de-standardisation of employment has also led to calls for adjusting the welfare state in order to limit the risk of insufficient social security coverage. The proposals under discussion have focused largely on the pension scheme and have included a full-blown transition to flat-rate pensions, the introduction of minimum pensions into the existing scheme, an extension of credits for times of economic inactivity and the inclusion of the self-employed in the public pension scheme. The consequences of the de-standardisation of employment for pensions have primarily been raised by the left. With the growing preoccupation with the demographic challenge in the 1990s, they have moved somewhat to the background.

The proposed reforms have met strong resistance. The adherents to the traditional pension scheme, centred around the social insurance funds, have warned against departing from the proven principles of Bismarckian social insurance. They have pointed to the legal problems of a transition to a flat-rate pension scheme and have argued that attempts at reducing the link between contributions and benefits are likely to undermine work effort and willingness to pay social insurance contributions (Rürup-Kommission, 2003: 110–14). As for extending membership of the social insurance scheme, the enthusiasm of those concerned has been limited. Most atypically employed tend to overestimate their pension rights or prefer to provide for old age outside the public pension scheme with its meagre 'returns'.

The de-standardisation of employment did not feature very prominently under the Kohl Government. Norbert Blüm, the powerful Minister of Labour and Social Affairs from 1982 to 1998, remained strongly committed to the existing pension system, and put heavy emphasis on maintaining a close link between contributions and benefits. In contrast, the 1998 coalition treaty of the red–green government, in line with earlier programmatic statements by the SPD and the Greens, emphasised the danger of inadequate pension entitlements resulting from labour market changes. It called for the inclusion of the self-employed in the public pension scheme and the creation of a minimum pension. However, these goals have only partly been met (Bäcker, 2001: 481–4). The government has so far refrained from extending the scope of the public pension scheme. Likewise, the initial plans to create a minimum pension have been watered down. Owing to fierce resistance by the CDU/CSU, the government retreated from its original plan to introduce a minimum pension within the framework of the pension scheme. Instead, the new minimum benefit (*Grundsicherung*), which was introduced as part of the 2001 pension reform, is now administered by the municipalities and is little more than a renamed social assistance. The main difference concerns the principle of subsidiarity. Only children with a yearly income of more than 100,000 euros are legally obliged to support their parents in contrast with 'normal' social assistance. Moreover, the government hopes that the renaming of the scheme and some organisational changes will increase the take-up of benefits by reducing the stigmatisation of recipients.

Low-Skilled Unemployment and Labour Market Policy

The weakening labour market position of the unskilled became a major economic policy issue in the mid-1990s. It has contributed to growing dissatisfaction with the traditional labour market policies and has been invoked as an argument for overhauling the German welfare state and for reforming labour market policy.

The traditional measures for improving the labour market position of the low-skilled have combined different elements: governments have sought to ensure the supply of a sufficient number of apprenticeships by a combination of subsidy and the moral suasion of enterprises. They have tried to prevent skill mismatch by updating curricula. Finally, the low-skilled have been seen as a key target group of active labour market policy.

With low-skill unemployment soaring, calls for alternative approaches have grown louder. A broad coalition of critics have argued in favour of complementing the concern about apprenticeships and the reform of vocational training by the promotion of low-skill employment through the creation of a low-wage sector (*Niedriglohnsektor*). Such proposals have come in different forms (Weinkopf, 2002; Steiner, 2003): On the one hand, employers and many economists have called for greater wage differentiation, for cuts in benefits and for restricting the rights of the unemployed to refuse job offers. On the other hand, various proposals to increase low-skilled employment by subsidising low-skilled employees and/or their employers have been made. Such proposals have aimed either at decoupling wages and total income by topping up wages by transfers or at decoupling wages and labour costs by subsidising employers.

The subsidy of low-waged jobs has been promoted by a heterogeneous coalition ranging from liberal economists to political scientists and sociologists with social democratic leanings such as Fritz Scharpf and Wolfgang Streeck . The opposition has been similarly diverse. The unions have feared the effects on the general level of wages; some economists have argued against subsidies for principal reasons and have warned that the intervention of the government might induce unions and employers to agree upon excessive wages; others have pointed to high fiscal costs and have doubted that the suggested measures are suited for reaching the long-term unemployed. Little progress has been made in the subsidy of low-waged employment, due to the strength of the opposition. The Kohl government only made timid attempts at promoting low-wage employment by subsidies. In December 1997, the government suggested a modest increase in committed earnings for social assistance claimants. However, this proposal was rejected by the Federal Council as the SPD-led states sided with local governments which feared an increase in the overall social assistance burden. In summer 1998, the Ministry of Labour and Social Affairs submitted a draft law which envisaged a new kind of wage-subsidy for long-term unemployed, but came too late to be adopted before the 1998 elections.

The red–green government also moved slowly (Heinze and Streeck, 2003). The subsidisation of low-wage employment had some prominent advocates within the government, including Bodo Hombach, the first head of the Chancellor's office. Moreover, the academic steering committee of the 'Alliance for Jobs', a tripartite body established after the elections, argued that employers' social security contributions for low-income earners should be subsidised. However, the proposals of the committee got a cool welcome from both unions and most economists. As a result, the government initially confined itself to experiments to test the effects of different schemes in four states.

The first results of the experiments were not very encouraging (Weinkopf, 2002; Steiner, 2003). Confronted with a deteriorating labour market situation and the approaching elections, the government in early 2002 nevertheless decided to extend one of the tested schemes (the Mainz model, a 'make work pay' scheme providing special state transfers to newly employed low-income earners) to the whole Federal Republic. The results were unimpressive. Only 9,260 persons were supported by the scheme between March and December 2002. The Mainz model was buried silently after the 2002 elections.

While few inroads have been made into the subsidisation of low-waged work, the low-skilled have been confronted with a general redirection of labour market policy since the mid-1990s. The shift towards 'activation' started under the Kohl government (Heinelt and Weck, 1998). Starting in 1993, the latter curtailed benefits, restricted the rights of the unemployed, and tightened requirements for benefit recipients to improve their employability and to carry out community related work. These measures were accompanied by cuts in spending on active labour market policy. During its first term, the red–green government refrained from further cuts in benefits and put more emphasis on improving job counselling and job placement (Blancke and Schmid, 2002). After the 2002 elections, the red–green government adopted a more neoliberal position and initiated substantial restrictions on benefits and the rights of the unemployed. Tighter rules on unemployment assistance were introduced in late 2002. In March 2003, Chancellor Schröder's 'Agenda 2010' proposed the reduction of the maximum period of payment for benefits for older unemployed people from thirty-two to eighteen months, the integration of unemployment assistance and social assistance and a further reduction in assistance payments to the unemployed.

These changes in labour market policy have been highly controversial. Benefit cuts in particular have been strongly opposed by the trade unions and, at least until 2002–3, most social democrats. As with the expansion of child care, German federalism has complicated reforms. States and local governments have lobbied against all changes in labour market policy which might increase the fiscal costs they faced. For both reasons, the Kohl and the Schröder government alike have been forced into concession and into limiting the proposed benefit cuts. Nevertheless, the adopted measures add up to a substantial transformation of German labour market policy. The effects on unemployment, especially among lower-skilled people, are not yet clear.

Coping with the Risks of 'Welfare Markets'

The new social risks associated with the move towards 'welfare markets' have only recently become prominent in debate. The introduction of the long-term care insurance scheme in 1994 has contributed to a new interest in the quality of care. As people have started to receive social benefits and to pay contributions, the sensitivity to service quality has increased. Regular newspaper reports on the dire situation in homes for the elderly and fraudulent service providers have helped to keep the issue on the agenda. While the public debate on the quality of care has focused on the size of long-term care insurance benefits and the lack of qualified personnel, there have also been concerns about an insufficient regulation of services.

The red–green government reacted to these concerns by amending the regulatory framework for institutional care (Deutscher Bundestag, 2002: 249–51). In 2001, it amended the law on nursing homes (*Heimgesetz*) and passed a separate law on the quality of care (*Pflege-Qualitätssicherungsgesetz*). According to the new laws, contracts between service providers, care insurance funds (*Pflegekassen*) and local authorities now must include more detailed provisions on service quality. The supervision of nursing homes has been strengthened. The government also raised the information requirements for service providers and extended 'consumer rights' in the case of misconduct. These provisions have so far been confined to institutional care.

More controversial than the new rules on institutional care has been the regulation of the new private pension pillar. The red–green government put heavy restrictions on the range of savings or investment plans eligible to state subsidies. Products must be certified to qualify for subsidies or tax relief. Certification requires the meeting of relatively strict criteria. Pensioners must get back at least what they put in and are not allowed to get access to their money until they reach sixty; providers must guarantee that benefits do not decline over the lifetime and have extensive responsibilities to provide information. The costs are spread over ten years, in order to make it less costly to switch to a new provider.

Not surprisingly, the financial services industry has protested about the constraints on individual choice and the costs of complying with the legal requirements. The CDU/CSU and the FDP also called for liberalisation of the regime. In the 2002 election campaign, they criticised the new 'Riester pension' (*Riester-Rente*) as a 'bureaucratic monster' and blamed the provisions for the disappointing participation in the scheme. Other critics have argued that the existing information duties are not sufficient to allow consumers to compare products (Tiffe and Reifner, 2002; Rürup-Kommission, 2003: 131–2). In an attempt to accommodate the dissatisfaction with the existing regulation, the red–green government announced a relaxation of provisions in October 2003.

Conclusions

In this chapter, we have dealt with one aspect of the ongoing trans-formation of the German welfare state, the emergence of, and the reac-tion to, new social risks. As our analysis has shown, there is strong evidence for an increasing spread of new social risks in Germany. Some of these risks seem to be even more prevalent than in other OECD countries. This applies particularly to the problems of reconciling paid work and family respons-ibilities, the risk of unemployment for low-skilled people and the risk of insufficient social security coverage. This chapter therefore supports the general view that the German welfare state faces a relatively great 'problem load'.

We have also found evidence that the incidence of new social risks has been influenced to a considerable extent by the conservative nature of the German welfare state. While it is true that most of the new risks can ulti-mately be related to overall socio-economic trends in family structures or in demand for low-skilled labour, our analysis suggests that the very size and the particular effects of these changes have been strongly mediated by the existing welfare state institutions. The weak infrastructure of social services has aggravated the problems of balancing paid work and family responsibilities. Strong reliance on social security contributions and the resulting high contributions rates have promoted the de-standardisation of employment and arguably exacerbated the weak labour market situation of the low-skilled. The strong link between contributions and benefits in the pension scheme has increased the risk that those employed in part-time or temporary jobs will have insufficient social security entitlement. Finally the traditionally dominant roles of the state and the family in welfare pro-vision have prevented the emergence of 'welfare markets' and have reduced the risks associated with an unfortunate choice of private provider.

Policy developments have substantially differed in the five fields under analysis. The framework for meeting care needs has undergone most change, with the introduction of the long-term care insurance scheme in

1994 and the strong expansion of child care facilities. In contrast, relatively little has been done about the consequences of the de-standardisation of employment and the weakening labour market position of the low-skilled. As for the regulation of 'welfare markets', an issue that has gained importance only recently, the Schröder government has taken a relatively tough stance.

With regard to the politics of new social risks, we have identified quite different patterns. In the case of child care and elderly care, where major reforms have been adopted, relatively broad reform constituencies have existed. Both the expansion of child care facilities and the introduction of the long-term care insurance scheme have been highly popular. The adoption of measures to cover the risks associated with frailty in old age has also been promoted by local government As for child care, further progress has been prevented by remnants of social catholicism, the fragmentation of competencies between the tiers of government and concerns over fiscal costs. In the case of long-term care, the main reform constraint has been the cost. Compared to the expansion of child care and the improvement of the situation of the frail elderly, there has been a much weaker reform constituency for tackling the risks associated with the de-standardisation of employment and the weakening labour market situation of the low-skilled. Those directly experiencing these risks have been relatively few and have not enjoyed much electoral clout. The measures discussed to improve the pension rights of the atypically employed have touched the 'identity' of the entrenched institutions and have thus provoked resistance by influential actors. Similarly, the subsidisation of low-wage employment has been opposed by the unions and has raised concerns about costs. These obstacles explain why the policy response to the new labour market challenges has been limited.

The policy developments reported in this chapter do not add up to a clear trend. First, they point into different directions. While the recent expansion of child care facilities has a Scandinavian flavour, the general changes in labour market policy look more Anglo-Saxon. Second, future developments are far from certain. In particular, it remains unclear whether the red–green government will be able to keep its ambitious promises with regard to child care and how far the provisions of Agenda 2010 will be implemented. Our analysis of new social risk policies thus lends further support to the general view that the German welfare state still finds itself in a state of transition. The demands made by new social risks on social provision are particularly hard to resolve in the context of fiscal austerity, a federal system and a conservative and corporatist tradition.

References

Alber, J. (1995) 'A Framework for the Comparative Study of Social Services', *Journal of European Social Policy*, 5(2): 131–49.

—— (2000) 'Sozialstaat und Arbeitsmarkt: Produzieren kontinentaleuropäische Wohlfahrtsstaaten typische Beschäftigungsmuster?' *Leviathan*, 28(4): 535–69.

—— (2001) 'Recent Developments of the German Welfare State: Basic Continuity or Paradigm Shift?' ZeS, ZeS-Arbeitspapier Nr. 6/2001, Bremen.

Auth, D. (2002) *Wandel im Schneckentempo. Arbeitszeitpolitik und Geschlechtergleichheit im deutschen Wohlfahrtsstaat, Leske + Budrich*, Opladen.

Bäcker, G. (2001) 'Flexibilität und soziale Sicherung in Deutschland: Bestandsaufnahme und Reformoptionen für die Alterssicherung', in U. Klammer and K. Tillmann (eds.), *Flexicurity: Soziale Sicherung und Flexibilisierung der Arbeits- und Lebensverhältnisse*, WSI/MASQT, Düsseldorf, 443–502.

—— Reinhard, B., Hofemann, K., and Naegele, G. (2000) *Sozialpolitik und soziale Lage in Deutschland. Band 1: Ökonomische Grundlagen, Einkomenn, Arbeit und Arbeitsmarkt, Arbeit und Gesundheitsschutz*, Westdeutscher Verlag, Opladen.

Behning, U. (1997) 'Richtungswechsel in der Sozialversicherungspolitik? Zur Anerkennung von nicht-professionellen häuslichen Pflegeleistungen durch das Pflege-Versicherungsgesetz', in idem (ed.), *Das Private ist ökonomisch. Widersprüche der Ökonomisierung privater Familien- und Haushaltsdienstleistungen*, edition sigma, Berlin, 103–17.

Bertelsmann-Stiftung (ed.) (2003) *Vereinbarkeit von Familie und Beruf*, Bertelsmann-Stiftung, Gütersloh.

Bielinski, H., Bosch G., and Wagner, A. (2002) *Wie die Europäer arbeiten wollen: Erwerbs- und Arbeitszeitwünsche in 16 Ländern*, Campus, Frankfurt, M. and New York.

Blancke, S., and Schmid, J. (2003) 'Bilanz der Bundesregierung Schröder in der Arbeitsmarktpolitik 1998–2002: Ansätze zu einer doppelten Wende', in C. Egle, T. Ostheim, and R. Zohlnhöfer (eds.), *Das rot-grüne Projekt: Eine Bilanz der Regierung Schröder 1998–2002*, Westdeutscher Verlag, Wiesbaden, 215–38.

Bleses, P., and Edgar, R. (1998) *Deutungswandel der Sozialpolitik. Die Arbeitsmarkt- und Familienpolitik im parlamentarischen Diskurs*, Campus, Frankfurt, M. and New York.

—— Martin S.-K. (1999) 'Zum Wandel wohlfahrtsstaatlicher Sicherung in der Bundesrepublik Deutschland: Zwischen Lohnarbeit und Familie', *Zeitschrift für Soziologie*, 28(2): 114–35.

BMFSFJ (Bundesministerium für Familie, Senioren, Frauen und Jugend) (2002) *Elfter Kinder- und Jugendbericht. Bericht über die Lebensituation junger Menschen und die Leistungen der Kinder- und Jugendhilfe in Deutschland*, BMFSFJ, Berlin.

—— (ed.) (2003a) *Die Familie im Spiegel der amtlichen Statistik. Lebensformen, Familienstrukturen, wirtschaftliche Situation der Familien und familiendemografische Entwicklung in Deutschland*, BMFSFJ, Berlin.

—— (2003b) Agenda 2010: Vorteil Familie. Bundesministerin Renate Schmidt zum familienpolitischen Profil der Reformen der Bundesregierung. BMFSF, Material für die Presse Nr. 84, Berlin.

Bosch, G. (2003) 'Sind Niedriglöhne der Motor für Dienstleistungen?' *Vierteljahreshefte für Wirtschaftsforschung*, 72(1): 36–50.

Bönker, F., and Wollmann, H. (2000*a*) 'Sozialstaatlichkeit im Übergang: Entwicklungslinien der bundesdeutschen Sozialpolitik in den Neunzigerjahren', in: R. Czada and H. Wollmann (eds.), *Von der Bonner zur Berliner Republik. 10 Jahre Deutsche Einheit*, Opladen Westdeutscher Verlag, 514–38.

—— and —— (2000*b*) 'The Rise and Fall of a Social Service Regime: Marketisation of German Social Services in Historical Perspective', in H. Wollmann, and E. Schröter (eds.), *Comparing Public Sector Reform in Britain and Germany*, Aldershot et al., Ashgate, 327–50.

—— and —— (2001) 'Stumbling Towards Reform: The German Welfare State in the 1990s', in P. Taylor-Gooby (ed.), *Welfare States under Pressure*, Sage. Thousand Oaks, London and New Delhi, 75–99.

Bundesregierung (2001) *Lebenslagen in Deutschland. Der erste Armuts- und Reichtumsbericht der Bundesregierung.* Bundesregierung, Berlin.

Daly, M. (2000) 'A Fine Balance: Women's Labor Market Participation in International Comparison', in F. W. Scharpf and V. A. Schmidt (eds.), *Welfare and Work in the Open Economy. Vol. 2: Diverse Responses to Common Challenges,* Oxford University Press, Oxford, 467–510.

Deutscher Bundestag (2002) 'Schlußbericht der Enquete-Kommission "Demographischer Wandel–Herausforderungen unserer älter werdenden Gesellschaft an den Einzelnen und die Politik" ', BT-Drs. 14/8800, Berlin.

Dingeldey, I. (2000) 'Das neue 630 DM-Arbeitsverhältnis: Impuls oder Illusion für mehr Beschäftigung?', in C. Schäfer (ed.), *Geringere Löhne—mehr Beschäftigung? Niedriglohn-Politik*, VSA, Hamburg, 92–113.

DIW (Deutsches Institut für Wirtschaftsforschung) (2001) *Abschätzung des Finanzierungsbedarfs für die Bereitstellung einer bedarfsgerechten Versorgung mit Kindertagesstätten Kurzgutachten für die Bundestagsfraktion B'90-Die Grünen,* DIW, Berlin.

Esping-Andersen, G. (1999) *Social Foundations of Postindustrial Economies*, Oxford University Press, Oxford.

European Commission (2001) *Employment in Europe 2001: Recent Trends and Prospects,* European Commission, Brussels.

—— (2002) *Employment in Europe 2002: Recent Trends and Prospects,* European Commission, Brussels.

Eurostat (2002) *The Lives of Women and Men in Europe, 1980–2000,* EU, Luxembourg.

Freeman, R. and Schettkat, R. (2000) Skill Compression, Wage Differentiation and Employment: Germany vs. the US. NBER, Working Paper 7610, Cambridge, MA.

Fuhrmann, N. (2002) 'Drei zu eins für Schröder. Bergmann muss im Hinspiel eine Niederlage einstecken', in K. Eicker-Wolf et al. (eds.), *'Deutschland auf den Weg gebracht'. Rot-grüne Wirtschafts- und Sozialpolitik zwischen Anspruch und Wirklichkeit*, Metropolis, Marburg, 187–212.

Götting, U., Haug, K., and Hinrichs, K. (1994) 'The Long Road to Long-Term Care Insurance in Germany', *Journal of Public Policy*, 14(3): 285–309.

Hagen, T., and Steiner, V. (2000) *Von der Finanzierung der Arbeitslosigkeit zur Förderung von Arbeit: Analysen und Handlungsempfehlungen zur Arbeitsmarktpolitik,* Nomos, Baden-Baden.

Heinelt, H., and Weck, M. (1998) *Arbeitsmarktpolitik. Vom Vereinigungskonsens zur Standortdebatte*, Leske + Budrich, Opladen.

Heinze, R. G., and Streeck, W. (2003) 'Optionen für den Einstieg in den Arbeitsmarkt: Ein Lehrstück für einen gescheiterten Politikwechsel', *Vierteljahreshefte zur Wirtschaftsforschung*, 72(1): 25-35.

Hoffmann, E., and Walwei, U. (2000) Was ist eigentlich noch 'normal'? Strukturwandel der Erwerbsarbeit. IAB, Kurzbericht Nr. 14, Nürnberg.

Jochem, S., and Siegel, N. A. (2000) 'Wohlfahrtskapitalismen und Beschäftigungsperformanz: Das 'Modell Deutschland' im Vergleich', *Zeitschrift für Sozialreform*, 46(1): 38-64.

Kersbergen, K. van (1995) *Social Capitalism. A Study of Christian Democracy and the Welfare State*, Routledge, London and New York.

Klammer, U., and Tillmann, K. (eds.) (2001*a*). *Flexicurity: Soziale Sicherung und Flexibilisierung der Arbeits- und Lebensverhältnisse*. WSI/MASQT, Düsseldorf.

—— and —— (2001*b*) 'Erwerbsbiographien als Mosaik – Längsschnittergebnisse zur Zusammensetzung von Erwerbsbiographien und ihren Veränderungen, zum Einkommenserwerb im Lebensverlauf und den Folgen für die Absicherung im Alter', in U. Klammer and K. Tillmann (eds.), *Flexicurity: Soziale Sicherung und Flexibilisierung der Arbeits- und Lebensverhältnisse*, WSI/MASQT, Düsseldorf, 141-223.

Klenner, C. (2002) 'Arbeitsmarkt und Gedöns. Rot-grüne Geschlechterpolitik zwischen Aufbruch und Frustation'. *Blätter für deutsche und internationale Politik*, 47(2): 202-10.

Meyer, J. A. (1996) *Der Weg zur Pflegeversicherung. Positionen—Akteure—Politikprozesse*, Mabuse, Frankfurt, M.

OECD (1999) *A Caring World: The New Social Policy Agenda*, OECD, Paris.

Ostner, I. (1998) 'The Politics of Care Policies in Germany', in J. Lewis (ed.), *Gender, Social Care and Welfare State Restructuring in Europe*, Ashgate, Aldershot 111-37.

—— Leitner S., and Lessenich S. (2001) Sozialpolitische Herausforderungen: Zukunft und Perspektiven des Wohlfahrtsstaats in der Bundesrepublik. Hans-Böckler-Stiftung, Arbeitspapier Nr. 49, Düsseldorf.

Pfaff, A. B. (1999) 'Veränderte Erwerbsbiographien und ihre Auswirkungen auf die Sozialpolitik', in W. Schmähl and H. Rische (eds.), *Wandel der Arbeitswelt. Folgerungen für die Sozialpolitik*. Nomos, Baden-Baden, 31-60.

Pfarr, H. (ed.) (2001) *Ein Gesetz zur Gleichstellung der Geschlechter in der Privatwirtschaft*. Hans-Böckler-Stiftung, Düsseldorf.

Pierson, P. (2001) 'Coping with Permanent Austerity: Welfare State Restructuring in Affluent Democracies', in idem (ed.), *The New Politics of the Welfare State*, Oxford University Press, Oxford, 410-56.

Puhani, P. A. (2003) A Test of the 'Krugman Hypothesis' for the United States, Britain, and Western Germany. IZA, Discussion Paper No. 764, Bonn.

Ristau, M. (2003) ' "Gedöns" als Chefsache: Wie Familienfreundlichkeit zum rotgrünen Überraschungsthema wurde', *Neue Gesellschaft/Frankfurter Hefte*, 50(3): 38-40.

Roth, D., and Jung, M. (2002) 'Ablösung der Regierung vertagt: Eine Analyse der Bundestagswahl 2002'. *Aus Politik und Zeitgeschichte*, 52(49-50): 3-17.

Rürup-Kommission (2003) *Nachhaltigkeit in der Finanzierung der sozialen Sicherungssysteme: Bericht der Kommission*, BMGS, Berlin.

Scharpf, F. W. (2000) 'Economic Changes, Vulnerabilities, and Institutional Capabilities', in F. W. Scharpf and V. A. Schmidt (eds.), *Welfare and Work in the Open Economy. Vol. 1: From Vulnerability to Competitiveness,* Oxford University Press, Oxford, 21–124.

Schneider, J. (2002) Die Vereinbarkeit von Beruf und Familie als Gegenstand der bundesdeutschen Politik. Eine Policy-Analyse. Master Thesis, Osnabrück.

Schröder, G. (2002) 'Familie ist, wo Kinder sind-Politik für ein familien-und kinderfreundliches Deutschland', Regierungerklärung von Bundeskanzler Schröder zur Familienpolitik. BT-Plenarprotokoll 14/22769–22775, Berlin.

Schulz, E., Leidl, R., and König, H.-H. (2001) Auswirkungen der demographischen Entwicklung auf die Zahl der Pflegefälle: Vorausschätzungen bis 2020 mit Ausblick auf 2050. DIW, Discussion Paper No. 240, Berlin.

Seeleib-Kaiser, M. (2002) 'A Dual Transformation of the German Welfare State?' *West European Politics*, 25(4): 25–48.

SPD and B'90-Die Grünen (1998) 'Aufbruch und Erneuerung—Deutschlands Weg ins 21. Jahrhundert. Koalitionsvereinbarung zwischen der Sozialdemokratischen Partei Deutschlands und Bündnis 90/Die Grünen vom 20. Oktober 1998', *Blätter für deutsche und internationale Politik*, 43(12): 1521–52.

—— and —— (2002) *Erneuerung—Gerechtigkeit—Nachhaltigkeit. Für ein wirtschaftlich starkes, soziales und ökologisches Deutschland. Für eine lebendige Demokratie. Koalitionsvereinbarung,* Berlin.

Spieß, C. K. and Büchel, F. (2003) 'Effekte der regionalen Kindergarteninfrastruktur auf das Arbeitsangebot von Müttern', in W. Schmähl (ed.), *Soziale Sicherung und Arbeitsmarkt*, Duncker & Humblot, Berlin, 95–126.

Statistisches Bundesamt (2002) *Datenreport 2002*. Bundeszentrale für politische Bildung, Berlin.

—— (2003) *Leben und Arbeiten in Deutschland. Ergebnisse des Mikrozensus 2002,* Statistisches Bundesamt, Wiesbaden.

Steiner, V. (2003) 'Beschäftigungseffekte einer Subventionierung der Sozialbeiträge von Geringverdienern', in W. Schmähl (ed.), *Soziale Sicherung und Arbeitsmarkt*, Duncker & Humblot, Berlin, 11–43.

Tiffe, A., and Reifner, U. (2002) *Die 'Riesterrente' aus Verbrauchersicht: Eine Analyse des Regulierungsrahmens*, Bertelsmann Stiftung, Gütersloh.

Töns, K., and Young, B. (2001) 'The case of Germany', in U. Behning and A. S. Pascual (eds.), *Gender Mainstreaming in the European Employment Strategy.* ETUI, Brussels, 129–56.

Weinkopf, C. (2002) Förderung der Beschäftigung von gering Qualifizierten—Kombilöhne als Dreh—und Angelpunkt? Friedrich-Ebert-Stiftung, Bonn.

3

The UK—A Test Case for the Liberal Welfare State?

Peter Taylor-Gooby and Trine P. Larsen

The most striking characteristics of the United Kingdom in the European context are its highly majoritarian system of government and its strong commitment to market principles. Despite limited devolution to Scotland and Wales in the late 1990s and the election of a centre-left New Labour government in 1997, it remains a centralised liberal welfare state. The British government is able to implement relatively swift reforms due to the absence of strong veto powers within the constitution (Lijphart, 1999: ch. 1). The dominance of the executive has been reinforced in recent years by the weakness of opposition parties and of trade unions. Because political power is centralised, the party of government has a relatively free hand in determining the direction of reform. Equally, opportunities to transfer the blame to other groups for policy failures are limited and the party of government must ensure that policy directions are acceptable to a sufficient proportion of the electorate to be confident that it will retain power (Rhodes, 2000: 261–2). In this context, as Schmidt points out (2002: 211), the communicative aspect of political discourse is particularly important, as the government seeks to convince the electorate of the value of its programme. Ill-organised minorities such as unemployed people and those on low incomes lack access to the political agenda.

The self-consciously market-liberal Conservative government from 1979–97 pursued a monetarist policy agenda which limited state interventions and sought to address new social risks in unemployment and access to paid work through market means. The political discourse associated with a commitment to monetarism, privatisation, and minimal state intervention proved highly attractive to the electorate and was sufficiently influential to be named 'Thatcherism' after the 1979–90 Prime Minister.

Papers by Anne Daguerre contributed to the chapter.

The new risks emerging in relation to work and family life were largely ignored, or addressed through exhortations to the private sector, for example, in the 1991 Employers for Childcare initiative. The chief opposition party, the Labour party, found it necessary to distance itself from its traditional interventionist social democrat approach in order to appeal to the electorate. It remade its policies during its long period out of office and succeeded in gaining power in 1997 on the basis of a radical programme that used market means to achieve welfare ends. New risk policy reforms played a major part in this programme. The central theme of the New Labour political discourse was that globalisation and increased competition rendered neo-Keynesian interventionism obsolete (Schmidt, 2002: 266). The centre left should therefore seek the mobilisation of as much of the population as possible into paid work, and the new policies sought to achieve this through highly targeted means with a strong reliance on market incentives.

New Labour pursues the traditional social democratic goals of reduced inequality, but aims at broader opportunities rather than greater equality of outcome and uses market means to realise its objectives. It is Janus-faced—a genuinely liberal, genuine welfare state (Taylor-Gooby et al. 2004). These policies reflect some aspects of EU policy-making—on the one hand an open market and a 'dynamic flexible knowledge-based economy', on the other awareness that 'social protection is . . . a productive factor . . . ensuring that efficient, dynamic, modern economies are built on solid foundations and on social justice' (European Commission, 2003). The United Kingdom may be seen as a test case of whether such an approach is viable at the national level.

In this chapter we review the emergence of new social risks in the United Kingdom, analyse policy discourse and policy development and provide an interim assessment of recent reforms. We conclude that the New Labour government has made considerable progress in relation to new social risks, but that contradictions between commitment to market liberalism and commitment to social welfare lead to problems that appear insoluble.

The Emergence of New Social Risks

The United Kingdom had been a leading manufacturing nation in the immediate post-war period, but its position declined from the 1960s. In 1960 value added by manufacturing accounted for 32.1 per cent of GDP, third among the major OECD economies after Germany and Japan. By 1980 at 21.4 per cent of GDP it had fallen behind all except Canada and was substantially below the EC average of 28.5 per cent (OECD, 1982: table 5.3). The repudiation of any elements of a neo-Keynesian strategy by the 1979 Conservative government (summed up in the blunt statement that 'public spending lies at the heart of Britain's economic difficulties'—PE white paper 1979) sharpened the impact of the transition. Job losses in manufacturing during the 1980s at an annual rate of 2.5 per cent were the highest in any of the twenty major economies surveyed by the OECD (1994: chart 11) and, by 2002 the sector accounted for 14.6 per cent of employment (ONS, 2003, table 4.12). The post-industrial transition affected work and family life and access to employment; welfare state reforms increased social risks for some groups.

Work and Family Life

Women's labour market participation in the United Kingdom is relatively high. Sixty-five per cent of women of working age were in paid work in 2001, well above the EU average of 55 per cent and the Stockholm target (OECD, 2003: table B). However, the weak provision of child and elder care leads many women to work part-time or leave the labour market. Only 32 per cent of women are in full-time work, well below the EU average of 41 per cent (OECD, 2003a, b). State support in this area has always been weak by European standards (see Table 1.1). Spending on family support services in fact fell back in comparison to GDP under the Conservative monetarist government, from 0.52 to 0.49 per cent between 1980 and 1999, while support for older and disabled people rose from 0.54 to 0.81 per cent (OECD, 2003b).

It is not surprising that, under these circumstances, dependent children have a sharp impact on women's participation in paid work (Table 1.2). This contributes to a curtailing of women's career opportunities and earnings potential. Women are over-represented compared to men in routine and semi-routine work and under-represented in managerial occupations—ratios of 140 and 72 per cent, respectively (GHS, 2003a: table 3.14). Women's earnings have amounted to between 78 and 82 per cent of men's throughout the 1990s (Bulman, 2002: chart 2). The 'wage gap' between women's and men's full-time earnings was higher in the United Kingdom than in any other European country except Ireland, Portugal, and Spain in 1997 (OECD, 2001b: 83).

Single parents find it particularly difficult to gain access to paid work, due to the high costs of child care. This group is particularly likely to be at risk of poverty. Single parents are over five times as likely to fall below a 60 per cent of median income poverty threshold as the members of the population in general—a greater risk than in any other EU country except Ireland, and exactly one and two-thirds times the EU average (Eurostat, 2002: table 1). Forty-seven per cent of single parents are in-work in the United Kingdom, compared with 59 per cent in the European Union, which accentuates the risk of social exclusion for these households. The living standards of single parent families average 60 per cent of those of families in general (Chambaz, 2001).

Access to Employment

The rapid economic shifts of the post-industrial transition created access-barriers to paid work, particularly for those without skills. High levels of youth unemployment have been identified as a problem throughout the past two decades. Unemployment among those aged 15–24 peaked at 21 per cent for men and 14 per cent for women in 1994, as a result of the recession of the early 1990s (EU, 2002a: 188). The immediate employment problems of young people are set in the context of persistent high levels of economic inactivity. The proportion of workless households in Britain (14.2 per cent) is among the highest in Europe, only exceeded by Belgium (16.5 per cent, Eurostat, 2003). Despite historically high employment rates, the number of economically inactive people increased from 7.5 to 7.9 million between 1986 and 2001 (ONS, 2002c: 71), chiefly as a result of increased early retirement and long-term sickness and disability among men. Approximately half of the disabled population in the United Kingdom are economically inactive compared with only 15 per cent of the non-disabled population (ONS, 2002b). Worklessness in general did not attract the political attention directed to youth unemployment until the late 1990s.

The market orientation of the United Kingdom leads to a situation in which educational qualification is more closely reflected in access to work than elsewhere and in which unemployment is particularly likely to lead to low income. The United Kingdom is the only EU country in which the unemployment rate of those with minimum educational levels is as high as four times the level of those with university level education—the EU average is two and a half times (OECD, 2002: table D). The UK government's own statistics show that 89 per cent of men and 85 per cent of women with university-level qualifications are in paid work as against 58 per cent of men and 45 per cent of women with no qualifications (ONS, 2003: table 4.11). Unemployed people are 4.2 times as likely as members of the population as a whole to fall below a 60 per cent of median income poverty threshold in the United Kingdom, a much greater risk than in any other EU member state, where the average is less than three times (1995 statistics, Eurostat, table 2). Low educational attainments also increase the risk of being trapped in low-paid and unskilled work and of persistent low income. Forty-two per cent of those with low literacy levels had low incomes, in comparison to 24 per cent of those with good literacy (DWP, 2002*b*: ch. 7; Sparkes and Glennerster, 2002: 180).

The Impact of Welfare Reforms on New Risks

The most important changes in the UK welfare state that increased the incidence of risk for more vulnerable groups were the pension reforms of the late 1980s. These cut back the contribution of the social insurance earnings related pension scheme to retirement incomes very substantially and encouraged people to take out lightly regulated private personal pensions. A series of scandals demonstrated the problems of regulation in the industry (Goode, 1994; Waine, 1995). During the 1990s and in the twenty-first century employers have cut back occupational pension commitments very substantially (IoA, 2002). The government has been unable to construct a pensions settlement that encourages the private sector or employers to provide adequate and secure pensions and preserves the commitment that the majority of pension cover should be provided by the private market.

The outcome has been a complex patchwork of state and private cover in which better-off groups tend to have access to a wider range of sources of income in retirement, while more vulnerable groups depend on diminishing state cover. The top fifth of pensioners relied on the state for only 19 per cent of income in 1999, receiving 40 per cent from private pensions, 26 per cent from investment and 19 per cent from earnings. The lowest fifth (on about 19 per cent of the incomes of the top fifth) received 85 per cent from the state, 9 per cent from private pensions and 5 and 1 per cent from investments and earnings (DSS, 2000). Retired people are at higher risk of poverty in the United Kingdom than in any other EU country except Greece and Portugal—one and a half times the EU average risk (Eurostat 2000: table 2).

A further change that affected vulnerable groups took place in formal long-term care provision. From the mid-1980s onwards, the number of publicly provided care beds fell and provision in the private sector correspondingly expanded. Social care for the elderly had in any case always been largely informal, but the net effect was to expand the role of the commercial sector and reduce public sector provision. In 1987, the state provided 124,000 beds and the private sector 115,000. By 2001, the corresponding statistics were 39,000 and 198,000 (ONS, 2000: chart 8.1, 2003: table 8.8). Local government social service departments operated means-tested fee-remission schemes that were brought into a national framework in the early 1980s, but the criteria for entitlements were constrained by the 1990 Health and Social Care Act, so that in most cases the costs of care fell on the individual or their relatives.

The liberal market orientation of UK welfare policy has produced a system of limited and highly targeted services and benefits with a strong role for the private sector. The new social risks resulting from the post-industrial transition were felt particularly keenly by the groups immediately affected. Welfare state reforms in the 1980s and 1990s were mainly cut-backs, stricter targeting, and privatisations that resulted in additional pressures.

Policy Discourses

The Conservative Government: 1979–97

The Conservative discourse of the 1980s and early to mid-1990s consistently stressed market forces and individual responsibility, so that state help should be targeted, the private sector encouraged and tax rates kept low: 'we want people to keep more of what they earn and to have more freedom of choice about what they do for themselves, their families and others less fortunate' . . . 'we will give people greater choice and responsibility over their lives', as the 1987 Manifesto (Conservative Party, 1987: 8, 27) put it. A series of denationalisations of state-owned industries (including telecommunications, energy, railways, and shipbuilding) took place. Much of social housing was sold to sitting tenants and the subsidised privatisation policies for pensions mentioned earlier were implemented. The issue of reconciling work and family life remained low on the political agenda. Child care was simply a private matter, although the government encouraged employers to provide day nurseries (but did not provide a subsidy) and launched a limited child care voucher scheme for working families in the early 1990s (Timmins, 1996: 493; Land and Lewis, 1998: xx). The question of finance of long-term care was discussed more in terms of the impact of costs on savings rather than the issue of whether care responsibilities damaged the labour market opportunities of informal carers (Parker and Clarke, 1998: 25).

Labour market policy also reflected the enthusiasm for a market approach by strengthening work incentives. The system of national insurance unemployment benefits was more tightly restricted and eventually, in 1996, a new time-limited benefit, Job Seeker's Allowance, was introduced for all unemployed people. Between 1983 and 1998 the value of unemployment benefits fell from 36 to 28 per cent of average incomes (Hills, 2002). By 1995, replacement rates in the United Kingdom were lower than anywhere in Europe, except the Mediterranean countries and Belgium (EC 1996: charts 36 and 37). Requirements to pursue job opportunities actively and to take any job that was available were progressively made stricter through the 1980s and early 1990s. The management of youth unemployment was pursued through a series of schemes with different degrees of compulsion, the most important being the Youth Training Scheme introduced in 1983 and strengthened through removal of benefit entitlement for all who did not participate in 1987. This scheme depended largely on the availability of training placements from employers, and it was impossible to find sufficient placements to cover all young people or to guarantee the quality of placements. In 1992, only 20 per cent of these gained a qualification at standard school-leaving level, rising to a third by 1997. Most trainees simply fail to complete their courses (ONS, 1999: table 3.23).

The privatisation of pensions followed from the market-centred policy agenda. Relatively large numbers of people switched from state to private pensions, as a result of the cut-back to entitlements from the former scheme and the subsidies to encourage take up of the private option, and by 1999, 29 per cent of the workforce had some personal pension entitlement (House of Lords, 1999). The problems that emerged were of two kinds, both to do with the issues of imposing regulation on an industry which the government wished to succeed in the private market. First, pension salesmen, paid on commission, had encouraged many people to transfer when this was against their interests. The problem is estimated by a government inquiry to affect nearly one million people, mainly older workers who were sold personal pensions by agents eager for commissions, although their contributions would have insufficient time to generate an adequate fund (OFT, 1997). The government was slow to respond and it was not until the end of 1996 that proceeding for unethical practices were taken against some companies. The Prudential, the largest company and the one most prominent in mis-selling was finally prosecuted in 1998.

The second issue concerned employers who invested occupational pension fund assets in their own business, brought to a head in 1991 when a leading newspaper owner, Robert Maxwell, misappropriated occupational pension funds to shore up a business which went bankrupt, dramatically cutting the pension entitlements of his former employees. Legislation in 1994 introduced some regulation and outlawed investment in the employers' own businesses, although employers remained in the majority on occupational pension boards. A solvency requirement for funds was introduced, and this led to a situation in which employers began to close funds since they were concerned that solvency could not be guaranteed against future demographic shifts without imposing a liability on themselves. At the same time as occupational pensions were being cut back, many individuals had lost confidence in private pensions as a result of the scandals and were reluctant to invest in schemes. The outcome was a gap between pension investment and the amount needed to provide adequate payments estimated at £27 billion (ABI, 2002: 2).

The market-orientation of the Conservative party, in tune with the liberal bias of the UK welfare state, was expressed in the assumption that care issues are primarily matters for the private citizen, the use of incentive policies to tackle labour market issues, the enthusiasm for the privatisation of pensions and the difficulties in imposing a satisfactory regulatory regime on the private sector in this area. The strongly centralised UK constitution enabled the Conservative government to carry forward its labour market and privatisation reforms rapidly. The Labour party took power in 1997 with a policy agenda that sought to combine the market approach that the previous government had found successful at the polls with a redirection of policy, to achieve the welfare ends previously associated with social democratic policies through liberal means.

New Labour Discourse

The UK Labour party had lost general elections in 1983, 1987, and 1992 when it had advanced a programme of expanded social spending paid for by tax increases that bore on better-off groups and a neo-Keynesian 'Alternative Economic Strategy'. It remade its approach to the welfare state as part of a painful process of restructuring from the Commission on Social Justice report (1994) to the 1997 election manifesto. The 1994 report argued that 'Britain needs to change if it is to find its place in a changing world' (1994: 91), and that a central part of that process must be a redirection of social policy effort to support economic competitiveness. The first paragraph of the 1997 manifesto set out the programme of 'building a modern welfare state, of equipping ourselves for a new world economy' (Labour Party, 1997: 1). The arguments to redirect state welfare to support economic success are striking because they conflict with a traditional left approach in the United Kingdom, which had seen the primary goals of social policy as redistribution across the life cycle, the promotion of high levels of employment and the provision of services to meet the social needs of citizens (Beveridge, 1942: 10–13, 301). The coherence of the new discourse contributed to New Labour's 1997 and 2001 electoral victories (in which the swing to Labour in middle-class areas at 12.1 per cent was slightly higher than that in working class areas—11.7 per cent, Butler and Kavanagh, 1997: appendix), and ensured an important position for social policy in its programme. It also imposed limits on the direction and scale of welfare interventions that resulted in a policy agenda at times much closer to those associated with right- rather than left-wing regimes. Social policy became the prisoner of the New Labour discourse.

The claim that a traditional approach to welfare policy is no longer tenable reflects a particular understanding of economic change that replaces the demand side interventions of neo-Keynesianism with the more market-oriented 'pragmatic monetarism' discussed in Chapter 1. Liberal welfare states, in Esping-Andersen's model (1990), are typically seen as poor relations, with less adequate standards of social provision. New Labour seeks to develop a *genuinely* liberal welfare state—genuinely liberal in the sense that welfare supports rather than obstructs the operation of a market system, genuinely a welfare state in the sense that the needs of citizens are effectively met.

In relation to welfare and citizenship, Tony Blair stressed four key values: the equal worth of individuals, equality of opportunity rather than equality of outcome, rights entail responsibilities, and the state as an enabling rather than a providing authority (1998: 3–4, see also 2003). These were the basis of a new 'Third Way' in welfare which provided a shift in centre-left assumptions about the role of government (Driver and Martell, 1998; Faux, 1999; Giddens, 2000). Rather than providing extensive passive benefits to meet the needs of its citizens as a whole, government should seek to empower people and equip them to take the opportunities available in a flexible modern economy—but the responsibility to seize the opportunities would ultimately lie with the citizens: 'Work for those who can, security for those who can't' as the DSS analysis of the *Changing Welfare State* (DSS, 2000: p.v) succinctly puts it. The approach seeks to achieve economic goals through the mobilisation of all citizens who can enter paid work and social goals by ensuring that they are in a position to pursue jobs and receive a fair return. Government is only responsible for providing welfare services where citizens are not able to do this through the market.

This implies a radically different approach to new social risks than that adopted by the Conservative government.

In pursuit of the idea that the state should play an enabling rather than a providing role, New Labour has placed greater emphasis on civil society institutions (Rhodes, 2000a, b: 269). This has led to consultations with sectoral interests—for example, the role of NGOs has been very pronounced in relation to issues of work-life balance and social care but relatively weak in comparison to that of business interests for active labour market programmes. At the same time, Government has strengthened mechanisms to direct spending departments and hold them to account (Butcher, 2002). A three-year cycle of Comprehensive Spending Reviews defines the programmes and allocates resources to spending departments and agencies which are then monitored through progress towards the targets contained in public sector agreements. In order to ensure transparency, the relevant information in relation to over 350 targets is available publicly via the Treasury website. Government seeks to involve a range of civil society groups in its policy-making, particularly with respect to service-orientated policies, but is careful to retain and enhance tight controls over implementation.

Policy Responses to New Social Risks

Work and Family Life

As we argued above, the fact that care had been seen chiefly as a private responsibility had led to very high levels of part-time working among women who take responsibility for dependants. The lack of affordable childcare in particular has a major impact on women's (and particularly single parents') work opportunities as places are available for only 34 per cent of children under three and 60 per cent of those between three and mandatory school age (OECD, 2001a, b: 144). Child care is also expensive: a nursery place for a four-year-old costs £135 per week in inner London and £90 per week in the Northeast (Daycare Trust: 2003a). In 2001, 29 per cent of single parents had difficulties finding a child care place (Strategy Unit, 2002). Similar problems arise with elder care: residential care fees are £240 per week, and can reach £340 per week for residential and nursing care home fees. (Baldock forthcoming; Lewis, 2001; Means et al., 2002; Henwood, 1999).

Labour stressed the goal of reconciling work and family life to enable more mothers to take paid jobs as part of labour market and poverty strategy (DfES, 1998; DWP, 2000; HM Treasury/DTI, 2003). The strategy was developed through extensive consultation with NGOs and other bodies and was also supported by unions, particularly those with mass membership in the service sector. It includes four elements: the inclusion of a child care element in the tax credit system; resources to enhance child care through the National Childcare Strategy and area-targeted Sure Start programme, extended rights for working parents and the National Carers Strategy to support families caring for an old or a disabled person. It was substantially modified after a review in 2001.

The main contributions of Working Families Tax Credit to women's employment are through enhanced incentives for those on low pay and through the child care element in tax credit, which provides resources to pay for day nursery or registered child-minder fees. The child care element initially covered 70 per cent of child care costs up to a maximum of £100 for low-income families with one child and £150 for those with two or more children (Rake 2001). Average full-time child care costs are considerably higher and entitlement rules stringent (Laing and Buisson, 2003 quoted in *Guardian* 6.05.03; Daycare Trust, 2003*a*, *b*). It is highly targeted and by 2002 only 167,000 families claimed the benefit—less than 3 per cent of all families with children (IFS, 2003*b*: 6).

The National Childcare Strategy provided over £300 million to expand day nursery provision. The government targets are free part-time (150 min per day) nursery education for all three- and four-year-olds by 2004 and the creation of 900,000 new nursery places for younger children. Day-care provision as a whole, however, remained stagnant. While the number of day-nursery places (almost entirely in the private sector) had more than doubled from 123,000 to 262,000 between 1992 and 1997, under the private market regime, it increased slowly to 304,000 by 2001 under the New Labour policies (ONS, 2003: table 8.21). Child-minder places which had risen from 277,000 to 369,000 in the previous period actually fell to 338,000, indicating that state policies were in effect transferring children from child-minders to nurseries rather than increasing overall supply. In addition, between a third and a half of child care for mothers who work is estimated to be provided informally (IFS, 2003*a*: table 7.2). The Sure Start programme (heavily influenced by Head Start in the United States in the 1960s) brought together health and education projects in highly deprived areas with a strong element of local initiative. The government initially intended to establish some 500 programmes by 2004 with a budget of £453 million (HM Treasury, 2000: ch. 24).

The National Carers' Strategy (1999) established a new charter on standards for long-term care and new powers to local authorities to provide services for carers and dependants. It includes provision to pay for carers' contributions to a state second pension as well as reductions in council tax. Lastly, a Carers' Grant was established with a £20 million budget in 1999 (DoH, 1999a, b). The 2000 Carers and Disabled Children Act streamlined these different measures.

Following an evaluation exercise in 2001–02, and the growing conviction by the Treasury that improvements in care were essential to the strategy of mobilising women as paid workers, the government improved the structure of support. The child care element of tax credit was incorporated into a new child tax credit, available to all families earning below £50,000 annually, and the care costs covered uprated to £135 per week for one child and £200 pounds for two or more children (HM Treasury/DTI, 2003). Investment in Sure Start was increased from under £200 million in 2000–01 to £1.5 billion by 2005–06 as the programme was expanded through the 2000 and 2002 Spending Reviews with the target increased from the most deprived fifth to the most deprived third of children (HM Treasury, 2000: ch. 24, 2002: ch. 6). This will support the creation of 250 thousand extra child care places in child care centres, which will bring together day care, social support, and help with early learning. In all, the child care programme plans to create 1.25 million extra places between 1997 and 2006—a substantial challenge, given current levels of provision and the fact that nearly all places are expected from private providers on the basis of government subsidy and assistance with fees. Maternity Pay was increased by a third to £100 a week and extended from eighteen to twenty-six weeks with greater unpaid maternity leave rights, two weeks paid paternity leave has been introduced and employers are required to consider requests for flexible working (HM Treasury/DTI, 2003: 1). Further expansion of tax credit and of the child care centres was promised in the Chancellor's 2003 Autumn statement (*Guardian*, 11.12.03).

Although the government focused mainly on child care, elder care was not completely neglected. A National Framework for older people was introduced, the budget for the Carers' Grant increased from £20 to £85 million and targets for the provision of home-based support services established (DoH, 1999, 2002; HM Treasury, 2000).

Overall, the current government is beginning to tackle issues of balancing work and family life, but child care remains a private responsibility for most families. The New Labour strategy is essentially to stimulate the expansion of the existing structure of private provision through extra resources and to target specific programmes on high priority groups (lone parents, low-income workers), again mainly to enable individuals to buy child care.

The government target of 70 per cent of lone parents in employment by 2010 is unlikely to be met unless the rate at which this group moves into paid work rises, and the continuing scarcity of affordable child care suggests that this is unlikely.

Issues of education and personal development have tended to be of secondary importance. The Treasury has maintained an approach which stresses the availability of mothers as paid workers, while the DfES has argued consistently that the chief merit of child care is the opportunity for enhanced education at an early stage. The Treasury view has dominated in the market incentives implicit in the tax credit system, but the educational strategy emerges in the expansion of school places for three- and four-year-olds. In relation to elder care, a market approach figures in the reduction of national care standards to encourage the provision of private places (*Guardian* 20.11.02). Whether the government will lower standards to promote the expansion of child care remains uncertain, but DfES is currently reviewing existing regulations to examine whether they deter market growth (Strategy Unit, 2002).

The debate on universal versus means-tested support is closely related to the tension between rights and responsibilities. The tax-credit system effectively means-tests support for child care. The government rejected the recommendation of the majority report of the Royal Commission on the finance of care for older people for free nursing care and retained means-testing (DoH, 2000). Devolution allowed the Scottish Assembly to introduce universal free personal care (LGA Briefing, 5/30/01), but the liberal commitment to targeted state intervention remains throughout the rest of the United Kingdom.

Active Labour Market Policies

The transition from an industrial to a service-oriented society accentuates the selectivity of the labour market. Low-skilled workers and other vulnerable groups, such as disabled and chronically sick people are particularly likely to suffer from long-term unemployment and poverty, as the OECD data on educational level and risk of unemployment discussed earlier showed. Worklessness is also more prevalent among these groups. Approximately half of the disabled population in the United Kingdom are economically inactive compared with only 15 per cent of the non-disabled population (ONS, 2002b). In addition, lone mothers are twice as likely as women in general to be economically inactive. Forty-four per cent of lone mothers are workless in Britain. (ONS, 2001).

Worklessness represents a major challenge for a government committed to workforce mobilisation and greater equality of opportunity. Under the free market policies of the previous administration, marginal workers found labour force entry difficult. Between 1979 and 1996, the number of households with no one in employment more than doubled, from 1.5 to 3.4 million (DSS, 1998: 3). Benefits for sick and disabled people represent one quarter of social security spending and related tax-benefits in 1999 (Emmerson and Leicester, 2000: 4). This explains why New Labour has recently emphasised the need to reduce incapacity benefit expenditure and to help all people on incapacity benefits who can to be economically active (DWP, 2002a).

New Labour's workforce activation policies concern those vulnerable to unemployment, especially young people, those the government wished to mobilise (chiefly lone parents and those affected by disability) and those in work but on low wages. These areas were linked through the endorsement of a 'make work pay' approach which enhanced work incentives by ensuring that the incomes of the low-paid in work were substantially higher than what was available through benefits. This differs from the previous Conservative approach through the use of much more extensive measures to increase the incomes of those in work as well as holding down benefits—carrots as well as sticks. Considerable efforts were devoted to enlisting the support of employers' groups for the programme. Some groups, especially those representing small businesses expressed concern about minimum wage policies, but became reconciled by the relatively low level of the wage adopted. Despite some initial opposition, trade unions endorsed the New Labour strategy and actively supported its later development. The policies developed in the first Labour term of office, from 1997 to 2001, were consolidated and developed during the second term.

The chief explicit activation policy was the New Deal, highlighted in the 1997 Manifesto, and aimed at those who found difficulty in entering the labour market. New Deal policies provided intensive training and work preparation programmes and slightly enhanced rates of benefit, and were targeted on specific groups of those out of work, most prominently young people and lone parents. In practice, the reforms were dominated by the 1997 manifesto pledge to move 250,000 young people into paid work by the 2001 election. The New Deal for Young People accounted for only 9 per cent of the total caseload but was by far the most resource-intensive programme, followed by the New Deal for Lone Parents, which set a target of 70 per cent of lone parents in employment by 2010, and then New Deals for partners of the unemployed, disabled people, those over their fifties and long-term unemployed (Evans, 2001: table 1). The New Deals for Young People and Long-Term unemployed people are compulsory and are effectively workfare schemes.

'Make work pay' policies have been pursued through three main mechanisms: the National Minimum Wage, Tax Credits to subsidise those on low wages and policies to hold down benefit levels for those out of work to enhance work incentives. Before the introduction of the minimum wage in April 1999, some workers were earning as little as £2 an hour or even less, often resulting in a poverty trap (HM Treasury, 1999: 32). Although initially set at a low level (£3.60 an hour) and increased thereafter at a slightly lower rate than average earnings, the minimum wage was expected to help two million people (HC, 1999b: 99/18).

The Working Family Tax Credit replaced the former government's Family Credit. It was a means-tested benefit paid through the wage-package at much more generous rates than the previous benefit. Some 1.4 million rather than 0.5 million families were estimated to be entitled (HM Treasury, 1999: 32). The benefit started to be withdrawn once net income reached £90 per week, with a less severe taper than Family Credit and included the help with child care costs described above (House of Commons, 1998). Following the Prime Minister's promise to reduce child poverty by 25 per cent by 2004 and 50 per cent by 2010 (Blair, 1999), the Working Families Tax Credit was expanded to incorporate a children's credit directed specifically at child poverty.

The policies of the previous government to hold benefit increases below earnings indices were continued, although the New Labour emphasis on supporting the incomes of the low paid above the rate of average living standards was distinctive. Income support, the most important assistance benefit, was paid at a rate equivalent to 29.5 per cent of median earnings in 1983 and had fallen to 22 per cent by 1997. It continued to fall to 19.5 per cent by 2001 (NPI/Rowntree, 2003).

In the second phase (2001–03), New Labour policies were mainly concerned with consolidation in order to meet employment and anti-poverty targets (HM Treasury 2002: ch. 4). Compulsion for job seekers was tightened and the administrative structure integrated to enable benefit claiming to be directly linked to searching and preparing for paid work. The level of targeted support available to low-income families was also enhanced. Since 2002, lone parents have been required to attend a work-focused interview and this condition has now been extended to incapacity benefit claimants (DWP, 2001: 79). A new Department for Work and Pensions incorporated the Department of Social Security and the job search component of the Department for Education and Employment, so that the management of all those claiming benefits who might enter the labour market was brought together into one agency. In April 2002. Jobcentre Plus incorporated the Employment Service—which was previously responsible for the job search aspect of claims for job seekers' allowances and the Benefit Agency, which administered benefits payments. Claimants were now required to pass through the 'single gateway' system (Butcher, 2002: 31). This includes assessment of benefit entitlement and of obligations to enter activation programmes, and counselling and advice about the impact of 'make work pay' benefits on incomes in work and the opportunities available on training schemes and in local labour markets, in order to reinforce the duties associated with the linkage of welfare state rights to citizen responsibilities.

Improved tax credits are the main vehicle to tackle poverty and inactivity traps. The Working Tax Credit, announced in the 2000 Budget, has been in operation since April 2003. This benefit extends in-work support to workers (aged twenty-five or over) without children or disabilities working 30 hours or more a week, and includes the enhanced child care element mentioned earlier (HM Treasury, 2003: ch. 4). The intention is to mobilise more mothers into paid work, to tackle poverty, reduce social spending and enhance economic competitiveness.

New Labour's labour market policies build on the basic liberal formula of negative activation by holding down benefits to make work pay and introducing compulsion for unemployed people to pursue work vigorously. They broaden the approach by enhancing low wages, providing more positive training programmes targeted on particularly vulnerable groups and developing the management of claimers to encourage behaviour more likely to lead to work.

New Social Risks and Pension Reform

New Labour adopted the previous government's long-term goal of enhancing private pension provision from the current 40 to 60 per cent by 2050 (DSS, 1998), while ensuring that pensions are adequate by strengthening assistance for pensioners. It has encountered problems in establishing a regulatory framework that will make private pensions adequate and secure but also profitable for providers, and in designing a means-tested minimum guarantee that both meets people's needs and does not encroach on the market for private pensions. The previous Conservative government had cut-back the developing state earnings-related pension from 1989, limited indexation of the other element of state pension provision—the basic pension—to price inflation—and vigorously promoted tax-subsidised private personal pensions (Waine, 1995). The problems encountered in regulating the sector were described above.

New Labour faced inadequate pensions for those on lower incomes and an ill-regulated private sector which failed to guarantee pension security for many members. Some aspects of the regulation of private pensions were dealt with by including them in the remit of the Financial Services Agency (established in 2001) together with provision for greater transparency, compensation, and disciplinary powers. The voluntary industry review of 'mis-selling' was strengthened, resulting in 1.7 million consumers receiving compensation totalling nearly £11.5 billion (FSA, 2002: 19). The traditional social democratic approach of a compulsory state earnings-related pension had been decisively defeated at the 1996 party conference and did not re-emerge. A proposal from a junior minister (Frank Field) for mutual 'stake-holder' pensions, chiefly managed by unions, was rejected, indicating the government's determination to do nothing that would damage the UK insurance industry (see *The Economist*, 1998: 39-41).

The government proposed three main policies (DSS, 1998): a higher assistance pension, indexed to earnings; a new contributory tax-subsidised State Second Pension, aimed at low to middle earners and providing blanketing in for disabled people and those with care responsibilities, subsidised from taxation; and new private Stake-Holder Pension (SHP) regime, aimed at middle earners and regulated through an enhanced and transparent regime with low management charges, strong transfer rights, and mandatory indexation up to a set rate.

These proposals were made in a context where occupational schemes (the most important forms of private pension) were in decline, and individual pensions stagnant. The falling stock market value of the funds that support occupational schemes and concerns about future demographic pressures have led the majority of companies to close or cut back occupational schemes, and crucially to reduce the contribution to them made by employers from an average of 11.1 per cent of salary to 5.1 per cent (GAD, 2002; NAPF, 2002). Concerns about the scandals in the 1990s led to a reluctance to invest in individual private pensions. Only 22 per cent of employees contribute to individual pensions and younger workers are starting to contribute later in life (PPI, 2003: 38–40). Average contributions fell slightly from 7.8 per cent of average earnings in 2001 to 7.7 per cent in 2002 (Hansard, 2002). The industry has proved reluctant to offer pensions under the government's new SHP rules since they constrain profitability. So far only 800,000 SHPs have been sold, as against some 10 million occupational pensions and over three million personal pensions (FSA 2002: 56).

The developments imply additional pressure on the means-tested minimum. The new assistance Pension Credit, introduced as a tax credit in 2003, effectively tapers assistance entitlement at 40 per cent against contributory pension income (from SSPs and small occupational or personal pensions) rather than removing it directly the means-tested threshold is reached. It is projected to have a substantial effect in reducing pensioner poverty from 11 to 6 per cent at the 60 per cent of household income standard (Clark, 2002: table 1). The numbers receiving the minimum will tend to rise over time, since the government's commitment is to uprate it at least in line with average earnings, while first-tier pensions are uprated with prices, so the gap between the two grows wider, further damaging the attractiveness of private pensions (Clark, 2002: 16–17). Official projections indicate an expansion of entitlement to assistance pensions from about half of today's pensioners to about two-thirds by 2040, while IFS modelling indicates growth to four-fifths (DWP, 2002c; Clark and Emerson, 2002).

Labour is finding it difficult to make progress towards its 60 per cent private provision target. One solution would be to introduce greater compulsion—the strategy introduced to enhance labour market participation—so that employers were compelled to provide schemes which pooled risks, or those with incomes to save privately. The government has commissioned reviews but so far failed to develop a policy in this area. The Sandler review (2002) recommended compulsory employer contributions—popular with the TUC, but ignored by government. A second review, headed by the former chair of the NAPF, the industry's main lobbying body, recommended relaxation of the regulation regime with the government providing for those who failed to gain adequate pensions (Pickering, 2002). This recommendation has not been followed.

The government's 2002 Green Paper (DWP, 2002c) was widely expected to contain proposals for resolving these problems. However, it simply endorsed attempts to spread best practice but held back from intervention and specifically ruled out state pension increases or the introduction of a compulsory occupational pension system. An inquiry to be headed by another senior industry figure, Adair Turner, will report by 2005, introducing further delay.

The unwillingness to commit to either expanded state or compulsory non-state provision indicates the problems that a government that wishes to secure adequate pensioner incomes in a liberal market-oriented setting faces. The outcome appears to be to drift towards the traditional liberal solution—extended means-testing.

New Labour's determination to use welfare to enhance competitiveness has focused attention on new social risks. The policy solutions in the areas of work and family life, access to the labour market and pension reform contain three characteristics: an emphasis on mobilising as many people as possible into paid work, heavily targeted state interventions, on a much greater scale than those pursued by the previous passive liberal conservative government, and use of private sector means to achieve policy goals wherever possible. We move on to evaluate the success of these policies.

New Labour's Genuinely Liberal Genuine Welfare State: An Assessment

New Labour policies have achieved some success, although they are unlikely to achieve the targets set by the government. The track-record also indicates that the project of pursuing welfare goals through market means has clear limitations.

Child and Elder Care Policies: A Mixed Record

The government's target for daycare provision is 900,000 new places by 2004 and an extra 250,000 by 2006 (HM Treasury, 2002b: Ch. 1). The 2004 targets seem likely to be met. However, most of the increase in provision is through part-time places for three- and four-year-olds in schools which is of little benefit to mothers seeking full-time employment. By 2003, 99 per cent of three-year-olds were attending school for part of the day, 88 per cent of them using free state school places. The Sure Start programme which is intended to provide coordinated children's centres in the most deprived fifth of urban areas, appears less likely to meet the target of 500 centres by 2004, although progress has been made. Only 260 centres were running in August 2002 (Sure Start National Evaluation, 2002). The allocation of extra funding to both Sure Start and the National Childcare Strategy in the 2002 Spending Review may help to reach the government's targets.

As indicated earlier, the most recent statistics available (for 2001) indicate that full-time day-nursery places are increasing slowly, and child-minder places are falling in number, so provision to enable women to work full time is limited. One important factor is cost. The independent Daycare Trusts 2003 survey shows the average cost of a child care place to be £125 a week

(Daycare Trust, 2003*a, b*). The 2003 tax credit reforms, which raised the child care element sharply, may have a substantial effect in stimulating the private day-nursery market. Claims for the benefit increased by 51 per cent in the first year and the average payment in practice is about £50 a week.

The long-term care target of 30 per cent of older people who receive social care help being supported in the community by 2006 (DSS, 2003*b*: Objective 2) seems unlikely to be achieved. The constant decline in the number of households receiving home care—a 23 per cent decrease between 1997 and 2002—and in the number of nursing and residential homes—a 10 per cent decline between 1999 and 2001—makes it difficult to reach the target (DoH, 2000, 2001). The current pattern is for more intensive service provision to fewer clients (ONS, 2003: tables 8.9–8.11). By far the greater part of the service is privately provided, and elder care is insufficiently profitable for the expansion envisaged to take place.

Access to Employment and Poverty Policy

Figure 3.1 shows that, after the downturn of the early 1990s, employment increased substantially in the United Kingdom for most groups, including those targeted by government policy, but in some cases fell back as growth slowed down after 2000. Since the mobilisation of all who can work into paid employment is at the heart of the government's economic and social strategies, success in this area is of great importance. A simple measure of success is provided by comparing employment rates with those of men

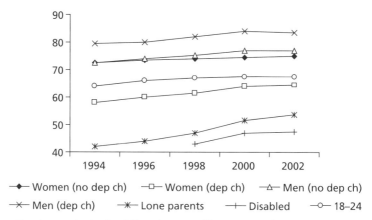

Fig. 3.1 Employment rates for different groups (%, 1994–2002)

Source: HM Treasury/DTI, Balancing Work and Family Life (2003: charts 2.4, 2.5); Labour Force Survey, ONS

with dependent children—the most substantial group and the one with strongest labour market engagement.

Government policies targeted specific groups—most prominently young people and lone parents through the two most resource intensive New Deal programmes and the support for child care for lower-paid people and, more broadly, women with dependent children, in the National Childcare Strategy. In addition, the 2002 Spending Review set the target of increasing the employment of disabled people in advance of general labour market trends. Employment among lone parents increased particularly rapidly, and continued to increase after 2000, indicating success in encouraging this group to enter paid work, although the rate of increase does not appear adequate to meet the ambitious target of 70 per cent (close to the rate for women without dependent children) by 2010.

The New Deal for Young People enjoyed some success and the headline target of helping 250,000 young people into paid work by the 2001 election was achieved, a much more substantial impact than in any previous UK scheme (DWP, 2001: 82). The National Audit Office, taking dead-weight and substitution effects into account, estimates that the scheme was responsible for a net reduction in unemployment by between 25,000 and 45,000, plus an increase in youth employment by between 8,000 and 20,000 a year during the three years: between 100,000 and 200,000 in all (NAO, 2002: 6). However, Fig. 3.1 indicates that the rate of increase in employment for this group has not been strikingly rapid compared with other groups. Employment among women with dependent children rose and converged slightly with that of men with dependent children, but the rate of convergence is slow. One factor is the currently limited scope of child care support, and the fact that government relies on stimulating private provision for the greater part of daycare. Employment for those with disabilities rose in the late 1990s but has only increased very slightly since.

More generally, although unemployment has fallen, economic inactivity among people of working age has changed little (from 21.6 per cent in 1994 to 21.4 per cent in 2002—ONS, 2004: 10) with the result that the proportion of workless households remains high at 16 per cent. The main reasons for economic inactivity with its attendant high risk of poverty are sickness and disability among men, and home responsibilities among women (ONS, 2002b: 69). While labour market opportunities for lone parents, women and young people have improved, success in relation to the welfare goal of relief of poverty must be qualified.

The Chancellor anticipated that the tax credit and minimum wage reforms would substantially reduce 'relative poverty' and, in particular, cut poverty among children (by the 60 per cent of median income threshold) by 1.2 million (HM Treasury, 2001: box 5.3). Despite the massive expansion of poverty benefits and credits, the reduction achieved was smaller than hoped. The number of households below the threshold after housing costs fell by 1.5 million from 13.9 to 12.4 million between 1996/7 and 2001/2. The largest components were working age adults—a fall of 0.3 million—pensioners—0.5 million—and children—0.5 million (DWP, 2003: 248, table 4.1). The most substantial fall was among workless households where the head was unemployed, explained mainly by a reduction in the overall size of the group from 2.3 to 1.1 million—in other words, by a move into employment (see Piachaud and Sutherland, 2002). For pensioners and children, reduction in the risk of poverty through better benefits played the chief role. However, despite the fall in unemployed workless households, the larger group of workless households where the head or spouse was not categorised as unemployed, but inactive for some other reason (such as sickness, disability, student status, or home responsibility) had in fact grown from 3.9 to 4.0 million.

The 2003 reforms, especially the new Tax Credits, will have a further impact, cutting child poverty by some 0.6 million. The government target of a reduction in child poverty by a quarter by 2004 may just be met, but the further target of a reduction by half by 2010 'as a contribution towards the broader target of . . . eradicating it by 2020' (HM Treasury, 2003: DWP public service agreement) will demand considerably more resources (Sutherland, Sefton, and Piachaud, 2003). The most important reason for the disappointing size of the fall is growing income inequality: a median income-based target recedes as inequality increases (IFS, 2003a: ch. 4, table 4.1). New Labour's policies to mobilise the workforce are impacting on low incomes by raising employment, but imply that the incomes of those without work will remain low, a problem that would become more serious in the context of economic downturn. Benefits targeted on groups such as children in poor families have achieved real improvements but require considerably more spending if they are to tackle inequality as incomes grow more unequal. The fact that poverty appears most intractable among those outside the labour force, and government has found it difficult to make an impact on this group, highlights a further problem for the liberal strategy: while that approach tends to focus on making the labour market deliver incomes through integration into paid work, post-industrial societies may well be developing in ways that leave greater numbers of people unable to enter paid employment.

The 2003 reforms, especially the new tax credit, are likely to reduce poverty among the lowest-income pensioners, perhaps halving current levels of pensioner poverty (Clark, 2003: table 1). Pension reforms have not met the liberal goal of substantial expansion of the private sector. The government has been unable to resolve the conflict between commitment to the expansion of the private sector and implementation of a regulation regime that would ensure strict regulation of that sector, and sharing of risks between different generations of pensioners or with employers, in a context where pension investment fails to rise.

Conclusion: The Limitations of the Liberal Welfare State

The New Labour government can claim success in relation to the expansion of part-time pre-schooling and child care centres in deprived areas, the mobilisations of lone parents and women with dependent children into paid work and the reduction of poverty, although it may not achieve the ambitious targets it has set itself. There appear to be real limitations in the overall expansion of child care on a scale which permits mothers to enter paid work full time, and thus for most women to attain opportunities in work approaching those of most men. The employment strategy has been unsuccessful in reducing the size of the workless population and pension policies have failed to produce an attractive private pension system which secures the support of employers, other private providers, and individual citizens. The genuinely liberal, genuine welfare state experiment has made progress towards welfare ends. It faces corresponding limitations, most importantly in stimulating and regulating private market provision (in child care, elder care, and pensions) and in managing the behaviour of private actors (in seeking to promote employment for workless groups) while it simultaneously pursues market freedom, so that regulation is limited and compulsion only deployed against politically weak groups such as young unemployed people.

   The United Kingdom is a highly centralised liberal-leaning system, in which the policy direction is dominated by the party of government and swift reform is possible. The Labour party in power has pursued an innovative agenda, underpinned by the New Labour policy discourse, which highlights policies to meet new social risks and seeks to integrate economic and social objectives by mobilising mothers, lone parents, disabled people, and others without work into employment in a flexible labour market in which the lowest wages are subsidised, to both reduce poverty and maximise competitiveness. The extension of private services both increases the profit-making sector and restrains state spending. The government has succeeded in ensuring that both employers' groups and trade unions continue to endorse the main aspects of the policy.

This approach is one interpretation of the EU's vigorous commitment to high levels of activation and pursuit of a 'dynamic, knowledge-based economy', but one which may only be feasible in a context where power is centralised in the executive. Social policy practice in the United Kingdom is bounded by a discourse that seeks to reconcile centre-left objectives with market-friendly means. It provides an example of a policy programme compatible with a liberal agenda that highlights new social risks but can only be partially successful in meeting them. It is, however, an approach with which a left-leaning party can win elections, and enlist the support of powerful interest groups, such as those representing business, in a majoritarian and market-oriented democracy.

References

ABI (2002) *What Makes People Save?* Occasional Paper, Association of British Insurers, London.

Age Concern (26/9–01) 'Free Nursing Care-Unworkable, Unfair and Unjust', Age Concern, London.

Baldock, J. (2003) 'Social Care in the UK' in A. Auttonen, J. Baldock, and J. Sipilä (eds.) *The Young, the old and the State*, Edward Elgar, Chettenham.

Beveridge W. (1942) *Social Insurance and Allied Services,* Cmnd 6404, HSMO, London.

Blair, T. (1998) *The Third Way*, Fabian Pamphlet 588, Fabian Society, London.

—— (1999) 'Beveridge Revisited: A Welfare State for the 21st century', in Walker R. (ed.), *Ending Child Poverty: Popular welfare for the 21st century?* Policy Press, Bristol.

—— (2003) 'Progress and Justice in the 21st Century', Fabian Society Annual Lecture, 2003.

Bulman, J. (2002) *Patterns of Pay*, Labour Market Trends, December, 643–52.

Butcher, T. (2002) *Delivering Welfare*, Open University Press, Buckingham.

Butler, D. and Kavanagh, D. (1997) *The British General Election of 1997*, Macmillan Cabinet Office (1999) *Modernising Government*, Cm4130, Stationery Office, London.

Chambez, C. (2001) 'Lone Parent Families in Europe', *Social Policy and Administration*, 35(6), 6: 58–71.

Clark, T. (2002) 'Rewarding Saving and Alleviating Poverty', IFS Briefing Note no 22.

—— and Emmerson, C. (2002) 'The Tax and Benefit System and the Incentive to Invest in a SH pension', IFS bulletin 28.

Commission on Social Justice (1994) *Social Justice: Strategies for National Renewal*, Vintage, London.

Conservative Manifesto (1987) 'The Next Moves Forward' Conservative Party Manifesto, London.

Daycare Trust (2003*a*) Press Release 11.9.03, Daycare Trust, London.

—— (2003*b*) *Evidence to the Work and Pensions Select Committee Enquiry into Childcare*, Daycare Trust, London.

DfEE (1998) Early Years Development and Partnerships—Planning Guidance 1999–2000 DfEE, HMSO, London.

DfES (1998) *Green Paper 'Meeting the Childcare Challenge'*, HMSO, London.

DoH (1999*a*) *Caring About Carers: A National Strategy for Carers*, HMSO, London.

—— (1999*b*) *Promoting Independence: Partnership, Prevention and Carers Grant—Local Authority Social Services Circular: Special Grant Reports*, Health and Social Care Joint Unit.

—— (2000) 'The NHS Plan—*The Government's Response to the Royal Commission on Long-term Care*, (7/11–02).

—— (2002) *Carers' Grant*, HMSO, London.

Driver, S. and Martell, L. (1998) *'New Labour Politics after Thatcherism*, Polity Press, Cambridge.

DSS (1998) A New Contract for Welfare, cm 3805, HMSO, London.

—— (2000) *The Changing Welfare State: Social Security Spending*, HMSO, DSS, London.

DSS Pensioners' Income Series 1999/00, HMSO, London.

DWP (2000) *Opportunity for All: Second Annual Report* cm 4865, HMSO, London.

—— (2001) *Family Resources Survey 2000–2001*, ONS, HMSO, London.

—— (2002*a*) *Opportunity for All*, Cm 5598, HMSO, London.

—— (2002*b*) *Households Below Average Income*, HMSO, London.

—— (2002*c*) *Simplicity, Security and Choice*, Cmnd 5677, HMSO, London.

—— (2003) *New Deal Evaluation Data Base*, 2003, HMSO, London.

EC (1995) *Social Protection in Europe*, DGESA, European Commission, Brussels.

The Economist (1998) *Field of Dreams*, 28 March, 39–41.

Emmerson, C. and Leicester, A. (2000) 'A Survey of the UK Benefit System', Institute for Fiscal Studies, London.

Esping-Andersen, G. (1990) *The Three Worlds of Welfare Capitalism*, Polity Press, Cambridge.

EU (1997) *Joint Employment Report*, European Commission, Brussels.

—— (2002*a*) *Employment in Europe, 2002*, DGESA, European Commission, Brussels.

—— (2002*b*) *Social Protection in Europe*, DGESA, European Commission, Brussels.

Eurostat (2002) *The Social Situation in Europe* 2002, Eurostat, Brussels.

—— (2003) *Population at Risk of Poverty in 1999*, Eurostat, News Release 43/2003, Brussels.

—— (2000) 'Social Exclusion in the EU Member States', Eurostat, News Release, 31 January, Brussels.

Evans, M. (2001) *Welfare to Work and the Organisation of Opportunity, Lessons from Abroad*, Centre for Analysis of Social Exclusion, LSE, London

Faux, J. (1999) 'Lost on the Third Way', *Dissent*, 4(2): 67–76.

FSA (2002) *UK National Strategy Report*, Financial Services Agency, London.

GAD (2002) *Occupational Pension Scheme* 2000, Government Actuaries Department, HMSO, London.

Giddens, A. (2000*)* *The Third Way and its Critics*, Polity Press, Cambridge.

Goode Committee (1994) *Pensions Law Reform*, Cmnd 2342–1, HMSO, London.

Griffiths, Sir Roy (1998) *Community Care: Agenda for Action—A report to Secretary of State for Social Services*, HMSO, London.

Guardian (12.3.2001) *Health and Social Care Bill—The Issue Explained*.

—— (12.3.2001) *Health and Social Care Bill: the Basics*.

Guardian (20.11.02) *Government Climbs Down on Care Home Standards.*

—— (20.11.02) *Ageism Charge.*

—— (6.12.02) *Alleged Abuse of Dementia Patients Investigated.*

—— (15.1.03) *U-turn on Child Tax Credit Gives Cash to Main Carer.*

—— (6.5.03) *Childcare Grows into £2.15 bn Business.*

—— (11.12.03) *Chancellor's Autumn Statement.*

Hansard (2002) 29 October, WA col 689, HMSO, London.

Henwood, M. (1999) *The Royal Commission on Long Term Care: A Vision of the Future*, Aged Care Conference, July.

Hills, J. (2002) 'Does the policy response change?' in J. Hills, J. Le Grand, and D. Piachaud (eds.), *Understanding Social Exclusion*, Oxford University Press, Oxford, 226–43.

HM Treasury (1999) *Tackling Poverty and Extending Opportunity: The Modernisation of Britain's Tax and Benefit System.* No.4. HMSO, London.

—— (2000) *Comprehensive Spending Review 2000*, Ch. 24, HMSO, London.

—— (2001) Budget Report, 2001, Ch. 5, HMSO, London.

—— (2002) *Comprehensive Spending Review 2002*, HMSO, London.

—— and DTI (2003) *Balancing Work and Family Life*, HMSO, London.

House of Commons (1998) 'Working Families Tax Credit and Family Tax Credit', HoC Research Paper 98/46, HMSO, London.

—— (1999*a*) 'Tax Credit Bills', HC Research Paper 99/3, HMSO, London.

—— (1999*b*) The National Minimum Wage, HC 99/18, HMSO, London.

Howard, M. (2001) *Paying the Price: Carers, Poverty and Social Exclusion*, Child Poverty Action Group.

IFS (2003*a*) *Green Budget*, Commentary 92, Institute for Fiscal Studies, London.

—— (2003*b*) How Can Childcare be Provided?, Briefing no 34, Institute for Fiscal Studies, London.

—— (2003*c*) *The New Tax Credits*, Briefing paper no 35, Institute for Fiscal Studies, London.

IoA (2002) *Press Release,* 16 November, Institute of Actuaries, London.

Jones C. and Novak, T. (1999) *Poverty, Welfare and the Disciplinary State*, Routledge, London.

Labour Market Trends, August 2002: *Labour Market Experiences of People with Disabilities.*

Labour Party (1997) *New Labour Because Britain Deserves Better: Election Manifesto*, Labour Party, London.

—— (2001) *Ambitions for Britain: Election Manifesto*, Labour Party, London.

Laing and Buisson (2003) *Report on Child DayCare*, (quoted in Guardian, 6-5-03).

Land, H. and Lewis, J. (1998) 'Care and the Change Role of the State in the UK', in J. Lewis (ed.), *Gender, Social Care and Welfare State Restructuring in Europe*, Ashgate, Aldershot.

Lewis, J. (2001) 'Older People and the Health-Social Care Boundary in the UK: Half a Century of Hidden Policy Conflict' *Social Policy Administration*, 35(4), 343–59.

LGA Briefing 234 (2.30.01) *Briefing on the Health and Social Care Act*, LGA, UK.

Lijphart, A. (1999) *Patterns of Democracy*, Yale University Press, New Haven.

Low Pay Commission (2003) *The National Minimum Wage, Fourth Report*, HMSO, London.

Means, R., Morbey, H., and Smith, R. (2002) *From Community Care to Market Care*, Polity Press, Bristol.

NAPF (2002) *Survey of Occupational Pension Funds*, National Association of Pension Funds, London.

National Audit Office (2002) *The New Deal for Young People* HCP 639 2001–2, HMSO, London.

NPI/Rowntree (2003) *Monitoring Poverty and Social Exclusion*, Joseph Rowntree Foundation, York.

OECD (1982) *Economic Outlook, January*, OECD, Paris.

—— (1994) *Jobs study: Facts, Analysis Strategies*, OECD, Paris.

—— (2001*a*) *Employment Outlook*, OECD, Paris.

—— (2001*b*) *OECD in Figures 2000*, OECD, Paris.

—— (2002) Employment Outlook, OECD, Paris.

—— (2003*a*) Employment Outlook, OECD, Paris.

OECD (2003*b*) *Socx- Social Expenditure CD-ROM*, OECD, Paris.

OFT (1997) *Director General's Inquiry into Pensions*, Office of Fair Trading, London.

ONS (2000) *Social Trends no 30*, TSO, London.

—— (2001) *Family Resources Survey 2000–2001,* DWP, TSO, London.

—— (2002*a*) *Living in Britain,* TSO, London.

—— (2002*b*) *NDLP*: *Statistical Release to September 2002*.

—— (2002*c*) *Labour Market Trends, August 2002*, TSO, London.

—— (2002*d*) *Social Trends no 32*, TSO, London.

—— (2003) *Social Trends no 33*, TSO, London.

—— (2004) *Labour Force Survey, 1984–2004*, TSO, London.

Parker, G. and Clarke, H. (1998) 'Paying for Long-Term Care', in P. Taylor-Gooby (ed.), *Choice and Public Policy*, Macmillan, Basingstoke.

Piachaud, D. and Sutherland, H. (2002) 'Child Poverty', in Hills, Piachaud and Le Grand (eds.) (2002), *Understanding Social Exclusion*, Oxford University Press, Oxford, 141–54.

Pickering, A (2002) *A Simpler Way to Better Pensions*, DWP, HMSO, London.

PPI (2003) *The Pensions Landscape,* Pension Policy Institute, London.

Rake, K. (2001) 'Gender and New Labour's Social Policies', *Journal of Social Policy*, 30 (2): 209–31.

Rhodes, M. (2000*a*) 'Social Democracy and the Third Way in British Welfare', *West European Politics,* 23(2), 178–79.

Rhodes, R. A. W. (2000*b*) 'Understanding the British Government: An Anti-Foundational Approach', in R. A. W. Rhodes (eds.), *Transforming Government*, Macmillan, London.

Royal Commission (1999) *With Respect to Old Age—Long-Term Care—Rights and Responsibilities*, CM4192-II, HMSO, London.

Sandler, J (2002) *Medium and Long-Term Retail Savings in the UK*, Treasury, HMSO.

Schmidt, V. (2002) *The Futures of European Capitalism*, Oxford University Press, Oxford.

Smith, M. J. (1992) *Pressure, Power and Policy*, Harvester Wheatsheaf, London.

Sparkes J. and Glennerster H. (2002) 'Education's contribution', in J. Hills, J. Le Grand, and D. Piachaud (eds.) *Understanding Social Exclusion*, Oxford University Press, Oxford, 178–201.

Strategy Unit (2002) Delivering for Children and Families, Report of the Inter-departmental Childcare Review, DfES, DWP, HM Treasury, Women and Equality Unit, Strategy Unit, HMSO, London.

Sure Start National Evaluation (2002) *Getting Sure Start Started*, National Sure Start Programme, DfES, HMSO, London.

Sutherland, H., Sefton, T., and Piachaud, D. (2003) *Poverty in Britain: The Impact of Government Policy Since 1997*, Cambridge University Press, Cambridge.

Taylor-Gooby, P., Larsen, T. P., and Kananen, J. (2004) 'Market Means and Welfare Ends', *Journal of Social Policy*, 33(2), forthcoming.

Timmins, N. (1996) *The Five Giants*, Fontana, London.

The Carers and Disabled Children Act, 2000, Chapter 16, HMSO, London.

The Economist (1998) *Field of Dreams*, 28 March, 39–41.

Waine, B. (1995) 'A Disaster Foretold?' *Social Policy and Administration*, 29, 4, 317–34.

4

New Risks—Are They Still New for the Nordic Welfare States?

Virpi Timonen

Introduction

The purpose of this chapter is to examine whether paying attention to new social risks makes a difference to our understanding of the Nordic welfare state, examined here in the light of the Swedish and Finnish cases. These social democratic, high-spending welfare states are often left out in discussions concerning new risks because it is assumed that new risks do not pose a serious challenge to the Nordic welfare state. It is frequently assumed that the Nordic welfare states have already been 'recalibrated' to deal with new social risks, and that these welfare states can therefore act as a model for other social protection systems that are not yet equipped to deal with new social risks.

The chapter seeks to answer the following central questions: are there any genuinely new risks in these welfare states, or have they been already addressed (thus making them old risks)? If new risks exist, are they being successfully addressed? Two main arguments are put forward. First, while they have already combated many new risks (which could therefore be called 'old' new risks), the Swedish and Finnish welfare states do face some genuine new risks that they have yet to address in a satisfactory manner. Second, while the extensive public sphere in the Nordic welfare states has enabled the state to respond to new risks more effectively than elsewhere in Europe (and has indeed prevented the large-scale emergence of some new risks), interests associated with old risks, as well as the perceived need to control public expenditure, put limits to the extent to which emerging new risks can be addressed within the existing welfare state and institutional framework.

Nordic Countries—Models of New Risk Management?

As Chapter 1 has shown, the Nordic welfare states appear to have invested considerably more in addressing new social risks than countries belonging to other welfare state models. The universalist, service-oriented and employment-oriented character of the Nordic welfare state appears to be well-suited to combating and addressing new risks. The Nordic welfare states spend more than twice the EU average on services for families, almost three times the EU average on support services for older people and people with disabilities, and considerably more than the EU average on active labour market policies (OECD, 2001). The Nordic countries also tend to be more advanced, in that the 'employment penalty' of having children or being the carer of an older relative or other dependants tends to be lower than in most other countries (Eurostat, 2002). The relative earnings of those with higher and lower levels of education also tend to be more equal than in countries outside Scandinavia: in other words, the 'low education penalty' is also less (EU, 2002; OECD, 2002).

These facts would seem to be rough indicators that the coverage of new social risks in the Nordic countries is on a considerably higher level than in countries belonging to the other models. In particular, the Nordic countries are seen as pioneers in the area of work–life balance and female employment as a result of the extensive care services infrastructure that enables both mothers and fathers to take up paid employment outside the home and reduces both the income and career costs of having children. The care needs of older people are much more extensively covered by the state than in most other countries. Active labour market policies are arguably a Nordic 'invention' and have a long-established role in combating entrenched labour market exclusion. However, in the rest of this chapter I hope to demonstrate both that new social risks have not ceased emerging in the Nordic countries and that old and emerging new risks are still calling for innovative responses from policy-makers in these countries.

The Emergence of New Social Risks

The Finnish and Swedish welfare states today face two main challenges (judged by the prominence of different policy areas in political debate): population ageing and achieving and maintaining high employment.

While these two main issues may appear at first to relate to old risks, they in fact encompass the new risks of increased need for service provision in old age (and reduced capacity to provide these services) and social exclusion resulting from long-term unemployment or atypical employment. In other words, the fact that the greatest structural challenges to the sustainability of the Finnish and Swedish welfare states originate in two very familiar problems should not blind us to the role and importance of new risks emerging in the areas of employment and service delivery.

Significant labour market-related new social risks are emerging for some groups, such as the older unemployed, those with low levels of education, and many recent immigrants. Innovative responses are called for as the Swedish and Finnish populations are ageing, the profile of older people becomes more diverse, demand for more individualistic solutions increases, and calls are made for more equal distribution of care work between mothers and fathers. New social risks brought about by welfare state changes (category 3 in Chapter 1) are as yet relatively small in Finland and Sweden because the role of private insurers and welfare service providers is relatively marginal: however, this area is increasingly important as private providers expand, particularly for pensions and care of older people. The preliminary conclusion reached in this chapter is that the relatively long history of addressing new risks puts these welfare states in a good position to deal with the emerging new risks.

Recent evaluations have established that the 'losers' during and in the aftermath of the 1990s recession in Sweden were young people, immigrants, lone parents, large families, and households that were dependent on social security transfers (SOU, 2001: 79; Government of Sweden, 2003). In other words, the reductions in welfare were concentrated on the young, recently arrived foreigners, those with poor anchoring in the labour market and some families with children (particularly families with only one parent). In Finland, the groups worst affected by poverty and social exclusion are the long-term unemployed, those living on basic security benefits (social assistance, basic sickness benefit, labour market support, housing benefits), and some families with children. A worrying trend is that deprivation appears to be increasingly concentrated in these groups (Kangas and Ritakallio, 2003). These findings match the description of risk groups in the theoretical literature on new risks. The increases in inequality, greater concentration of poverty among some groups, and the increased incidence of long-term social assistance dependence are causes for concern in these welfare states that pride themselves on being focused on finding employment for all and ensuring a high degree of equality through high employment levels and extensive redistribution (Penttilä et al., 2003).

This chapter argues that there are two types of new risks that the Finnish and Swedish welfare states have to confront: the new risks that have arisen very recently, and those that have been addressed by the welfare systems for some time, but have not disappeared or have become even more challenging with the passing of time. The remainder of this section will discuss the 'old' new risks and the 'recently emerged' new risks in the context of the Finnish and Swedish welfare states.

'Old' New Risks: Women's Labour Market Participation and the Service State

There are some new risks that in fact are 'old' ones from the perspective of the Scandinavian welfare state. The Scandinavian welfare states responded to these risks earlier and more thoroughly than other welfare states. Sweden and Finland both have extensive 'service states', that is, an extensive and elaborate framework of public services that are designed to remove care responsibilities from the spheres of the family and the private sector. Whereas in many European countries women's increasing labour market participation gives rise to new risks (the unmet care needs of children and older people and the precarious labour market position of women—see, for example, Timonen and McMenamin, 2002), in Finland and Sweden an extensive network of social and care services has responded to this need for several decades, making dual breadwinner families the rule rather than the exception.

Although care services for older people and children are firmly established in Finland and Sweden, there are emerging gaps in these services, and the future financing of services for older people in particular has become a subject of intense debate. While the question of care services for older people has arguably been the more burning issue over the last ten years, there is increasing concern in both countries over the position of families with children, and the related issue of work–life balance. Although home care benefits are available to Finnish parents who choose to look after their children at home, the benefit and service structures in both countries strongly favour and encourage the dual-breadwinner model. It is assumed that in most cases both parents are in paid employment outside the home, and such employment is encouraged through flexible and inexpensive public child care and through flexible working arrangements for parents.

Work–Life Balance and Women's Labour Market Participation

Employment rates in Sweden and Finland are higher among households with children than in childless households. Several recent policy statements in both countries confirm the commitment to the dual-earner model and the public services that help to create gender equality and welfare (see, for instance, Regeringskansliet, 2001 for Sweden and Speech by T. Filatov, 21.1.2003 for Finland). The programme of the Swedish Social Democratic Party declares that mothers and fathers have the right to be both an active parent and an active participant in the labour market (SAP, 2001). However, this commitment is not a guarantee against the new risks of work–life balance, because combining work and family life has become increasingly difficult due to greater efficiency requirements and uncertainty in the labour market (Ministry of Social Affairs and Health, Finland, 2003*a*). Parents working in the service sector in particular experience greater difficulties in combining work and family life as a result of increasingly irregular working hours (PAM, 2002).[1]

The unequal division of parental leave between mothers and fathers has also caused concern (not in the least among employers in female-dominated sectors of the economy). Changes in the parental leave system in Sweden appear to have contibuted to a more equal division of leave between mothers and fathers: the proportion of the parental leave used by men has steadily increased from 3 per cent in 1994 to nearly 14 per cent in 2001. Of the total amount of temporary parental leave (for those looking after a sick child), over 40 per cent was taken by fathers (Socialdepartementet, 2002*a*). The social democratic government in Sweden has plans for a further incentive for fathers to take parental leave by increasing the level of parental benefit for couples who share the leave equally. Following the Swedish model, Finnish fathers are now being encouraged to take parental

---

[1] At the end of the 1990s, a third of all Finnish children had a mother who was working in shifts, in the evenings, night-time or at the weekends, and over half of all Finnish children had a father who worked at such irregular times. Approximately one-quarter of the mothers and one-tenth of the fathers of children under eighteen were working part-time or on a temporary contract (Ministry of Social Affairs and Health, 2003*a*). Almost half of the parents of 5–11-year-old Finnish children feel that work is detrimental to their family life (Väestöliitto, 2002) A survey by STTK established that 42% of its members experienced difficulties in combining their duties at work and at home: this percentage had increased from 36% in a survey carried out in 1994 (STTK, 2001).

leave with the help of the 'father's month', a component of parental leave that is not transferable to the mother. Broadening of the partial care bene-fit (*osittainen hoitovapaa*) in Finland also improves possibilities for combin-ing work and family life. Care leave was extended to one or both parents of school children in grades 1 and 2, meaning that the parents of these chil-dren can work shorter days.

The new risk of women's precarious labour market position is also begin-ning to cause concern. Many central actors argue that it is important to monitor and enhance the quality, and not only the quantity, of women's employment. The Finnish Family Policy Strategy (Ministry of Social Affairs and Health, 2003a) acknowledges that short-term contracts, currently very common in the public sector, contribute to low fertility, and argues that they should be replaced by permanent posts. The Union of Service Sector Employees in Finland is concerned about the proliferation of short-term contracts, and is making the case for full-time, permanent jobs for women (including mothers).[2] The negative reaction of many unions to the proposal that part-time employment should be encouraged as alternative to unem-ployment (one of the proposals of the Working Group on Employment led by Raimo Sailas) is also telling, as is the unions' rejection of the suggestion that part-time employment suits older workers and young workers with families (Ministry of Labour, Finland, 2003). Finnish and Swedish trade unions resist all attempts to increase part-time employment on the grounds that part-time employees are likely to be women, which would lead to even greater wage inequality between men and women. In Sweden, concerns about the quality of women's employment in the public sector are the main motivation for the preparation of a 121-point programme on the duties of the state and municipalities as employers. The issue of women's employ-ment is therefore giving rise to new concerns and policy suggestions.

Child Care Services

Even in the apparently well-covered area of care services for children, new issues are emerging. The entitlement to public child care was expanded in a very determined manner in both Sweden and Finland during the 1990s, leading to the entitlement to this service becoming effectively universal. For instance, the number of Swedish children in some form of public child

---

[2] The labour market partners in Finland agreed in December 2001 that under 4-h days are not used unless the employee wants to, or the nature of the employment justifies it. The partners also agreed on guidelines for the use of temporary contracts and more effective monitoring of working hours.

care increased from 532,000 in 1990 to 720,000 in 1999 (SOU, 2001: 79, p. 96). In both countries it is believed that the moderate price of public child care encourages parents to take up paid work. The 'maxtaxa' reform in Sweden set a new upper limit to fees that can be charged from parents whose children are in public day care. The main purpose of the 'maxtaxa' reform in Sweden was to ensure that public day care remains popular among all income groups and that fees are never an obstacle to parents' employment or use of the child care facilities (SAP, 2002*a*). As the impact of increased work incentives is expected to be particularly strong among low-income parents and lone parents, the reform also serves the purpose of reducing dependence on social welfare among this group (Government of Sweden, 2002: 28).

However, the increasing demands of working life are leading to pressures to improve child care provision further, and to create new forms of child care that are better suited to evolving working lives. Longer and more irregular working hours and the proliferation of one-parent families mean that the traditional 9–5 day care model is no longer sufficient. Demand for morning and afternoon care services for young school children greatly exceeds the supply of such services (for situation in Finland, see Ministry of Social Affairs and Health, 2003*b*). In response to these demands, some interesting new innovations have been suggested and put to practice. Twenty-four-hour creches are operating in several cities in Finland, and demand for such ser-vices is increasing, particularly from parents who do shift-work. It has also been suggested that the school day should be extended to the length of the working day (so that children do not have to spend time alone at home) by incorporating into it various extra-curricular activities and hobbies. The Finnish Minister for Employment has also suggested (Speech by T. Filatov, 21.1.2003) that after-school care of young children should become a legally enforceable right and compulsory for the municipalities to organise. In Sweden, 2003 saw the introduction of *allmänna förskola* (access by all to pre-school). This means that since January 2003 all five- and six-year-olds will have had a right to 3 h free day care per day. From 1 September 2003 this will also apply to four-year-olds (Socialdemokraterna i Riksdagen, 2002). New arrangements like this are a reflection of the increased demands of working life on parents, and by extension, their children.

Care Services for Older People

While the availability and quality of services for older people are still comparatively good in Finland and Sweden, it is not excessively alarmist to consider them to be under a serious threat in the near future. The sustainability of services for older people poses a thornier problem than child care, as expenditure in this area is set to increase dramatically. In addition to the growth in their overall numbers, more and more older people are living on their own, and are therefore in need of both company and assistance with daily tasks.[3] The increasing diversity of the older population also poses a challenge: people with different socio-economic characteristics, family, and ethnic backgrounds, and lifestyles demand different kinds of services (Socialdepartementet, 2002b; Ministry of Social Affairs and Health, Finland, 2003b). Today's older people expect higher standards than previous generations and it is acknowledged that public services must be equipped to deal with different preferences and provide greater freedom of choice (SAP, 2001). This represents a major worry for those concerned with the future financing of the welfare state, and the increase in expenditure on older people is seen by some observers to threaten the sustainability of the entire welfare state model. According to some observers and reports, such as the report of the Finnish National Programme for Developing the Social Services, the quality and availability of care services for older people have already declined to a worrying extent as a result of inadequate central control and insufficient resources (Ministry of Social Affairs and Health, 2003b).

The share of older people receiving publicly financed home help services has declined in both Finland and Sweden (Socialstyrelsen, 2003a). An increasing share of the available resources has been devoted to serving the needs of the 'most deserving' clients of public services. This has meant that some of the responsibility for providing services to older people has shifted from the state to the private sector and families. In Sweden, this shift has had a definite socio-economic profile as better-off pensioners have turned to the private sector whereas the worse-off pensioners are increasingly reliant on their families (Trydegård 2000, 2003). The quality and availability of services for older people is also threatened by labour shortages that could occur in the care services sector once the baby boomer cohorts have retired and need care themselves. It has been estimated that the Swedish municipalities will need to recruit some 180,000 new care workers between 2001 and 2010 (Svenska Kommunförbundet, 1999). The final report of the Finnish Labour Force 2020 working group predicts that nearly 80,000 vacancies will need to be filled in the care services sector in Finland between 2000 and 2015 (Ministry of Labour, 2003).

---

[3] Sweden has the highest and Finland the second highest rate of older people (aged sixty-five and over) living alone in the European Union(Eurostat/European Commission, 2003).

The 2003 report of an expert working group on the state of the Finnish social services argued that greater national coordination is necessary in order to address three problems in the area of social service provision. First, the basic financing of these services must be ensured by increasing central state responsibility (such responsibility was gradually transferred from the state to municipalities during the 1990s). Second, the right to services must be reinforced and strengthened. Third, the minimum standards of social services must be defined at the central level. The report also proposed that labour legislation be changed so that employees are granted a right to temporary leave from work while arranging care for their elderly parents, and so that those looking after elderly parents can opt to work shorter hours. A moderate care guarantee is also proposed: this would mean that a person's need of care would be assessed within three days of requesting care and that a care and service plan be made in conjunction with this assessment. Through increasing the state grants to municipalities it is also hoped to increase the number of staff working in elder care services by 4,500 (the current estimated shortfall) (Ministry of Social Affairs and Health, 2003b). The fact that recommendations on such rather basic aspects of the care services for older people are necessary is illustrative of the inadequacies that are experienced in this area.

The costs of long-term institutional care have caused some concern, and in both countries more detailed regulations have been introduced, with the aim of ensuring that the payments do not exceed a level that is deemed reasonable.[4] In Sweden, both the maximum level of fees for care services (*maxavgifter*) and the minimum personal after-fees disposable income for older people in care (*förbehållsbelopp*) have been set by the state since 2001 (SAP, 2002b; Socialstyrelsen, 2003a). Legislation on the maximum level of fees may be introduced in Finland, too, if the proposals contained in a recent report are implemented (Ministry of Social Affairs and Health, 2003b). Some administrative reforms, such as the Ädelreformen in Sweden have been implemented with the view to reducing the involvement of many different levels of administration and ensuring that services are more user-friendly. In Sweden there are also plans to enhance quality control in care services through hiring officials (*äldreskyddsombud*) to monitor standards (Regeringskansliet, 2002).

Welfare services for older people are to some extent protected by the strong consensus among parties in both countries that tax cuts must not

---

[4] Before the maximum fees reform in Sweden, one in six over seventy-five-year-old refrained from getting help or requested less help than they needed for reasons of cost (Socialstyrelsen, 2002).

reach such proportions that they threaten the financing of services. In both Finland and Sweden social democratic politicians in particular have been keen to stress that services are more important than income transfers and that services will be spared where a choice has to be made between them and benefits. While some actors have proposed greater means-testing of services, left-wing politicians in particular have been quick to point out that this carries the risk, in the longer term, of reducing the legitimacy of public services among the general population and the middle classes in particular. The Swedish social democratic party has recently adopted a stance that is strongly critical of privatising the production and financing of services (SAP, 2001). Thanks to such attitudes, the risk of a serious short-age of care services for older people, and the risk that the private sector or families would have to take on a greatly expanded share of care-giving, are relatively small.[5]

'New' New Risks: Precarious Labour Market Status, the Working Poor, Immigrants, and Welfare State Changes

The policies discussed above were responses to 'old' new risks, that is, risks that emerged and were addressed in the Nordic welfare states at a relatively early stage. The most important 'old' new risks in the Nordic context were the increased care needs of children and older people created by the com-ing into existence of the dual breadwinner model. The above discussion emphasised that new risks continue to evolve and that addressing them is therefore not a short-term or one-off task. In fact, it is arguable that policies designed to address new risks give rise to demands for further or more com-plex policies as those risks evolve. For instance, the availability of child care has enabled labour market participation to become a norm for mothers, which creates pressures for more equal sharing of child care between par-ents, which in turn calls for leave and benefit arrangements that are acceptable for men. The needs of the people faced with these risks are also becoming more extensive and more difficult to satisfy. For instance, the above discussion showed how child care needs are becoming more com-plex as working life becomes more demanding, and how care needs of older people are also more difficult to satisfy as the profile of older service users changes.

---

[5] However, it has been acknowledged in both countries that the role of family carers may grow in the future (Socialstyrelsen, 2003*b*; Ministry of Social Affairs and Health, Finland, 2003*c*).

In addition to these 'old' but nonetheless constantly evolving risks, the Finnish and Swedish welfare states are also facing risks that could be described as genuinely new in that they have not existed at the same scale as today during the earlier, 'golden' years of the Nordic welfare state. The most important such new risks are lack of employment security (particularly for women) and long-term unemployment (particularly affecting the unskilled or those with obsolete skills, especially older workers). While 'the working poor' phenomenon is only incipient in Sweden and Finland (in the form of slightly increased numbers of people in employment receiving social assistance), many of the most heated social policy debates are currently focused on the trade-off between a relatively high degree of earnings equality and employment. Were these debates to result in policies that led directly or indirectly to increased wage differentiation, Sweden and Finland would probably see the emergence of greater numbers of employed individuals falling under the poverty line. Many of the difficulties faced by recent immigrants relate to the new risks of precarious employment and long-term unemployment, but the complex needs of many immigrants constitute a whole new risk category that these welfare states are not yet fully equipped to deal with. Privatisation and marketisation, which generate significant new risks in the liberal welfare states, are yet to assume significant proportions in the Nordic welfare states. However, the increased tendency to privatise service functions and the increased numbers of people taking recourse to private pension insurances indicate that this may be a new and growing area of new risks.

Precarious Labour Market Position and Long-Term Unemployment

The problem of high unemployment persists in Finland mainly due to shifts in labour market structures that have resulted from changes in technology and the structure of the economy. While the demand for workers with low skills has declined as a result of changes in work organisation, increased international competition and technological change, highly educated workers have emerged as the winners, particularly those employed in certain sectors where Sweden and Finland have gained comparative advantage (such as IT research and development, or telecommunications). The increased lack of employment security for unskilled and semi-skilled workers has emphasised the link between education and employment.

Sweden has been considerably more successful at combating unemployment than Finland, and for this reason the discussion here will focus on

Finland.[6] It has been suggested by many influential commentators that increasing wage differentials may be the only solution to the problem of unemployment in Finland. Against the argument that greater wage differentiation means a step towards a more unequal society, employer and business interests have argued that evening out wage inequality through central negotiations does not produce an equal society: it is more likely to produce high unemployment which is the most important cause of inequality and social exclusion. The counter-argument is that the majority of the unemployed in Finland will not find employment with the help of tax cuts and reduced indirect labour costs—rather, a variety of measures including intensive active labour market policies is required (Boldt and Laine, 2001).

Changes in production structure, the rise of the high-technology industry, and improvements in efficiency have led to the loss of many out-of-date jobs and to an increase in demand for highly qualified workers. In other words, there is a mismatch between the skills that employers are seeking and those that the job-seekers have to offer. The unemployment rate has decreased more slowly than the employment rate has risen. The structure of unemployment has become more problematic as the share of the long-term and repeatedly unemployed has increased. In 2002 almost 60 per cent of the unemployed in Finland were long-term or repeatedly unemployed. This 'hard core' of the unemployed comprised some 174,000 individuals in 2002. Unemployment is most persistent among the disabled, immigrants, and the older unemployed. Youth unemployment is also still very high in Finland: approximately 15,000 young people in Finland have major difficulties in entering the labour force. In 2002, there were still 140,000 fewer people employed in Finland than before the 1990s recession (Kantola and Kautto, 2002: 69). Sweden has been considerably more successful at integrating the 'most difficult' groups into the labour market: Sweden has the highest percentage in Europe of 50–64-year-olds in employment, and 'only' some 14 per cent of the unemployed in Sweden are long-term unemployed, that is, have been looking for work for more than twelve months (Government of Sweden, 2002: 38).

Addressing the problem of high unemployment and persistent long-term unemployment in Finland is made all the more difficult by the fact

---

[6] The relative success of Sweden in addressing the unemployment problem and in increasing employment levels is also reflected in the employment targets that have been set: in Finland, the aim is to increase the employment rate to 75% by 2010, but Sweden is considerably more ambitious in striving to reach 80% by 2004. The current rate in Sweden is approximately 78% and in Finland approximately 68% (Government of Sweden, 2003).

that the unemployed constitute a very diverse group of people. There are many older people, but also young people without education or work experience, people with disabilities and immigrants. However, over fifty-year-olds constitute an increasing share of the unemployed: whereas 20 per cent of the unemployed were over fifty in 1995, by 2001 their share amounted to one-third (Kantola and Kautto, 2002: 73). Very few older long-term unemployed manage to reintegrate into the labour market (Rajavaara, 1998; Viitanen, 2000), and they also constitute the most 'passive' group of job-seekers (Ervasti, 2003). Since 2000, there have been more determined attempts to involve the ageing long-term unemployed in activation measures, instead of assuming that they will retire after having received the maximum duration of unemployment benefits (Skog, 1999). These efforts have had only a marginal effect, although the share of the ageing long-term unemployed who found a job in the regular labour market increased slightly.

Many recent unemployment security reforms in Finland are designed to make it easier and economically more profitable for the unemployed to take up even short-term jobs (see, for instance, Statement by Minister of Social Affairs, M. Perho, 9.1.2002). There are also some experiments involving support of employers who hire a long-term unemployed person. The so-called combination support (*yhdistelmätuki*) is paid in Finland to employers hiring someone who has been unemployed for at least 500 days. While this is not strictly speaking a cut in employer social security contributions, it is nonetheless in most cases sufficient to cover such contributions. Trade unions are not opposed to measures such as the combination support, but they are concerned that employers may use it to replace 'regular' workers with 'cheaper' long-term unemployed employees.

The trend towards increased activation is likely to continue. The suggestions put forward by a recent Finnish working group on employment included limiting the duration of labour market support (*työmarkkinatuki*) to 500 days, which would be followed by a period of education or a work placement (currently labour market support is of unlimited duration). According to the working group the right to the support paid to employers should be broadened so that the support would become payable after unemployment had lasted for 200 days and in the case of young workers (under twenty-five-year-olds) after 100 days' unemployment. The report of the working group also recommended that employer supports be paid to those who hire workers in receipt of earnings-related benefits (at the moment the support is only paid to those who hire recipients of labour market support) (Valtioneuvoston kanslia, 2003).

Following the rapid reduction in unemployment in Sweden after the recession started to bottom out in the mid-1990s, active labour market measures have been focused on those with greatest difficulties in entering the labour market. The target is for 70 per cent of participants in active labour market measures to be in regular employment three months after the completion of their training. The actual proportion of participants who find employment within this time frame increased from 43 per cent in 1999 to 59 per cent in 2001 (Government of Sweden, 2002: 32). The largest active labour market programme is 'labour market training', and the second largest programme, 'on the job training' offers hands-on training at work places. The 'youth guarantee' programme is aimed at 20–24-year-olds who are offered work, training or education before they have been unemployed for 100 days. Some grants are available to employers who hire long-term unemployed persons: these cover 50–75 per cent of wage costs.

The so-called activation guarantee (*aktivitetsgarantie*) has become the main policy against long-term unemployment since its launch in 2000. This benefit is designed to help those who have been unemployed for a long time to find a new job or to take up studies/training. In addition to unemployed people, the guarantee is extended to those who are 'part-time unemployed' (working shorter hours than they would like to). The activity guarantee comprises a set of tailored measures to enable the jobseeker to enter the open labour market. The Swedish system of activation requires that jobseekers must broaden their search after 100 days of unemployment, both with regard to the occupation and geographical area. Those who decline offers of suitable work or labour market measures risk a cut in their unemployment benefit. In April 2002 nearly 38,000 people or 40 per cent of all long-term unemployed were participating in the activity guarantee. The activation guarantee has been criticised for being underfunded and therefore not working properly.

In addition to unemployment, 'atypical' employment has become a reality for more workers in Finland and Sweden. The number of people employed on short-term contracts (in contrast to permanent positions) has increased in both Sweden and Finland (SOU, 2001: 79, p. 10). The proportion of Finnish employees on short-term contracts remained at around 10 per cent until the end of the 1980s, but grew strongly during the 1990s and is now one of the highest in the European Union (Nurmi, 1999; Kauhanen, 2000; Lodovici, 2000), although it also varies between different groups of employees.[7] Fixed-term employees in Finland tend to be women, aged over

---

[7] According to a study by the Finnish trade union central organisation SAK (2001) around 25% of SAK members were on short-term contracts, in contrast to only one-seventh in 1995. According

thirty, well-educated and working in white-collar jobs. Fixed-term contacts are most common in the (female-dominated) fields of education, health-care and social work. Part-time employment (defined as usually working less than 30 h per week) has traditionally been lower in Finland than in the other Nordic countries but increased among both men and women in the course of the 1990s. Part-time employment also increased among Swedish men, but declined slightly among Swedish women. Nonetheless, part-time employment still constituted a higher proportion of total employment in Sweden than in Finland both at the outset and the end of the 1990s.

In both Finland and Sweden women are more often employed on a part-time and contract basis than men, and many women working on contract or part-time basis would prefer permanent, full-time employment (Government of Sweden, 2002: 18; and Nurmi, 1998: 107). The share of the involuntarily part-time and short-term employed increased as unemployment increased in the 1990s. Another negative dimension of the increase in atypical jobs is that people in this kind of employment have an increased risk of becoming unemployed (Parjanne, 1999). Increasing the number of part-time jobs was recently recommended by a Finnish working group as a part of the solution to the problem of high unemployment, but such suggestions have been met with fierce opposition by employee interest groups (Valtioneuvoston kanslia, 2003). By way of a positive development, the state pension systems in Finland and Sweden are now capable of taking into account even very small contributions made during short-term contracts.

As a result of the increase in the general level of education, the lack of (appropriate, marketable) education and training has become a greater risk than it used to be at a time when only a small proportion of the population had third-level education. Partly due to their commitment to equality, but also for economic reasons, the Nordic states have been active in promoting lifelong learning and 'second-chance' education for adults. Finland is following Sweden's example in setting up a national re-skilling and up-skilling programme in 2003. The main purpose of both the Swedish *Kunskapslyftet* and the Finnish *osaamisennosto-ohjelma* is to increase and update the qualifications of adults who only have a basic level of education and are therefore at a high risk of unemployment. The right to lifelong learning has been extensively discussed in Sweden, and incorporating this right into legislation and policy is one of the aspirations stated in the programme of the Swedish social democratic party (SAP, 2001).

to a survey carried out by the Finnish trade union central organisation for employees with third-level qualifications, as many as half of all under 30-year old female Akava members working full time were employed on a contract basis: of the membership as a whole, some 15% were contract workers (Akava, Summer 2001).

The Working Poor

While there is a possibility that the phenomenon of the working poor is too recent or as yet too subtle to be detected, there is no firm evidence of this problem in Finland or Sweden (Asplund, 2001; Ritakallio, 2000).[8] Labour legislation, relatively high minimum wages, solidaristic wage policies and the prominent involvement of trade unions in both wage bargaining and enforcement of employees' rights have together prevented large wage differentials emerging and ensured wage levels that can sustain a life above the poverty line. The principle that income from work must be sufficient to enable a benefit-free existence is deep-rooted in Nordic politics and popular opinion (e.g. SDP, 2003).

Despite the fact that income inequality is very low in Finland and Sweden in international comparison, there appears to be very little willingness among Finns and Swedes to allow such inequality to persist or to increase. According to a recent study by the Swedish central organisation for blue-collar workers (LO, January 2003), both blue-collar and white-collar employees in Sweden want smaller wage differentials, and also support increasing women's wages in relation to men's.[9] This opinion survey followed an earlier study by LO (December 2002) according to which wage differentials between white-collar and blue-collar workers in Sweden had risen. Between 1994 and 2001, wage increases were greatest for white-collar workers in manufacturing industry and in the private service industry (39 per cent). In comparison, increases for blue-collar workers in the municipal sector were around 25 per cent. Such trends, if they were to continue, would lead to greater wage differentiation and inequality, and hence possibly the emergence of the working poor.

The debate in Finland about the right recipe for curing the problem of persistently high unemployment has implications for the issue of inequality. While popular and (most) political opinion firmly reject benefit-subsidised low wages as the route out of unemployment, there have been some cautious recommendations that low-wage employment be stimulated through a 'package' of measures. For example, the recent memorandum by the SOMERA working group recommended that wages, taxes, indirect costs of labour (employee and employer social security contributions) and social security payments be 'fitted together' in such a way as to enable job creation in

[8] However, a recent survey by STAKES in Finland found out that in November 2001 one in every ten social assistance recipients was also earning income from work, which was interpreted as a worrying trend.

[9] The study (of 7,000 employees between the ages of eighteen and sixty-four) established that four out of five Swedes think wage inequality is too great.

the low-wage sector (Ministry of Social Affairs and Health, 2002). A recent Finnish working group on employment emphasised that unemployment is particularly high among unskilled and semi-skilled workers as a result of the relatively small number of low-skilled, low-productivity (service sector) jobs in Finland. Somewhat less explicitly, the group also argued that many long-term unemployed persons could most successfully be re-integrated into the labour market through private service sector jobs. It is also implied in the group's report that a 'calm' approach to wage increases is necessary in order to stimulate demand for workers in low-productivity sectors of the economy: it is not 'meaningful' to seek any supplementary wage increases for those on low wages (Valtioneuvoston kanslia, 2003). Instead of higher wage increases for the lowest earners, low wages should be supplemented with the help of income tax cuts. While the majority of politicians in Finland are still wary of endorsing extensive tax cuts, the argument that labour costs have to be reduced has been gaining popularity. Even social democrats now argue that cuts in employer social security contributions would promote the creation of low productivity jobs and therefore alleviate structural unemployment.

The suggestions on increasing the supply of low-wage employment are resisted by some powerful interests because they pose a danger of creating the problem of the working poor. Trade unions resist all attempts to increase wage inequality, to control increases in the lowest wages and to promote part-time jobs: extensive cuts in employer contributions, income tax cuts, and some forms of employment creation (subsidising employers) are also mostly viewed negatively. Governments also remain concerned about their ability to finance social protection if taxes and employee and/or employer contributions are cut.

While radical action to increase employment in the 'low-wage, low productivity' sector has not been taken, some innovative mechanisms have been developed to prevent poverty among those who work less than full time. In Finland, the so-called adjusted unemployment benefit (*soviteltu päiväraha*) is designed to help those who have been seeking work and found a job that involves working 28 h per week or less. These workers receive adjusted unemployment benefit in addition to the income from work for a maximum duration of thirty-six months.[10] A similar arrangement (*a-kassa på deltid*) is in place in Sweden, but the entitlement to it is likely to be restricted (Regeringskansliet, 2003). There are plans, however, to introduce

---

[10] A number of trade unions are currently working to ensure that the duration is made unlimited in order to ensure that these workers do not leave employment or become reliant on unemployment benefit once the maximum duration of thirty-six months is exhausted.

a similar support to employers who hire long-term recipients of sickness benefit.

The adjusted unemployment benefits are an example of social security that complements earned income, and as such they are broadly similar to the earned income tax credits that have been introduced in liberal welfare states such as the United States and the United Kingdom. A recent Finnish working group on employment has recommended that over fifty-five-year-old unemployed persons should have the opportunity to take up part-time employment without losing their benefits. In other words, the unemployed should be provided with an incentive to seek work and to take up even part-time work with the help of benefits that supplement earned income: this principle is in conflict with the deep-rooted belief that full-time work should be the norm and that earned income from such work should always be sufficient for living above the poverty line. However, this kind of combination of earned income and benefit income has not yet been recommended for full-time employees, which is at least partly a reflection of the relatively high level of the lowest wages in Finland and Sweden. The Finnish working group on employment did point out, however, that increasing the tax-free proportion of incomes would enhance the attractiveness of low earned incomes in relation to benefits (Valtioneuvoston kanslia, 2003). Recommendations such as this can be interpreted as an acceptance of low incomes supplemented with the help of taxation and benefits as a means of combating high unemployment.

Immigrants

Concerns have been raised in Sweden that immigrants are in the process of becoming the new Swedish underclass (Arbetslivsinstitutet, 2002). The employment rate among immigrants (with less than ten years' residence in the country) plummeted by 33 per cent during the 1990s, in contrast to an 8 per cent drop among native Swedes. The study established that the poverty among immigrants from ex-Yugoslavia, Africa, and Poland was approximately five times higher than among Swedes. Evidently, even in a highly interventionist welfare state such as Sweden, immigrants from outside the European Union are caught in vicious circles that are difficult to break. Recent research has shown, however, that the employment situation of immigrants has improved in Sweden every year since 1997, partly as a result of intensive cooperation between the authorities such as employment offices, educational institutions and the municipalities (Integrationsverket, 2003).

Immigration into Finland increased in tandem with the worsening employment situation during the 1990s recession. A study of immigrants who arrived in Finland between 1989 and 1993 found that only 5 per cent of them had been working throughout their time in the country. Some 60 per cent had precarious labour market positions, and 28 per cent had been unemployed throughout their stay in Finland (between four and eight years). Between 1991 and 1992, unemployment among immigrants nearly doubled, and it peaked in 1994 at over 50 per cent (Forsander, 2001).

The employment situation of immigrants in Finland improved after the end of the recession, largely thanks to the economic upturn but also due to training and special labour market integration measures. In some cases, persistent unemployment is explained by special circumstances and characteristics of refugees. For instance, very high unemployment among the 'quota refugees' is partly due to the humanitarian criteria that is used in selecting them: it takes a long time to train and adjust them to the Finnish labour market. In addition to suffering from high unemployment, immigrants are over-represented in the marginal labour force in Finland, characterised by short-term and insecure employment that is strongly influenced by economic currents (Forsander and Alitolppa-Niitamo, 2000). Training and work experience acquired abroad is generally considered to be of little value by Finnish employers, who require qualifications and experience gained in Finland. There is a considerable risk that immigrants will remain at entry level jobs, that is, unskilled and semi-skilled jobs in the service sector (cleaning, restaurants). This in turn threatens social cohesion and stability. Children in immigrant families are also at a high risk of child poverty as they often live in workless households with many children.

Duration of stay in the country has a strong impact on, among other things, the need for social assistance among those born abroad: immigrants who have lived in Sweden for twenty-one years or longer have, by and large, the same income level as people born in Sweden (Government of Sweden, 2003). In order to prevent social exclusion among immigrants, individual 'settling-down plans' have been made and a law on a new means-tested benefit for immigrants of retirement age will come into effect in October 2003 in Finland. Here, again, Finland appears to be emulating Sweden where a similar replacement of social assistance for immigrants (*introduktionsersättning*) has been in existence since 1993 for those immigrants who have been granted residence permits and who are undergoing a 'programme of introduction' to Sweden. Other special initiatives in Sweden include supplementary vocational training, more stringent rules against discrimination, validation of qualifications gained abroad and language training (Government of Sweden, 2002: 21). The Finnish payment will be paid to over sixty-five-year-old immigrants and to immigrants who are unable to work and have lived in the country for at least five years, and would be otherwise dependent on social assistance for long periods of time (Ministry of Social Affairs and Health, 2003*b*).

While the Nordic welfare states have during their lifetime proved to be effective in promoting equality and equal rights among their native populations, integrating non-EU immigrants and refugees represents a novel challenge for them. There has been a 'visible' number of immigrants in Finland only for the last ten years or so, and while Sweden has a longer history of immigration (including large-scale immigration from Finland during the 1960s and 1970s), it is evident that neither country is fully prepared for dealing with the challenge of labour market and social integration of immigrants.

Welfare State Reforms

As was pointed out above, the importance of welfare state changes in generating new social risks is as yet relatively small in Finland and Sweden: the risks generated by privatisation and exposure to the markets, significant in many liberal welfare states, are not yet felt. However, this may become an area of crucial importance for these welfare states, particularly in the area of pensions and care services for the growing numbers of older people. For instance, the number of private pension policies in Finland increased from 10,000 in 1985 to 200,000 in 2000, and the fact that many of these policyholders belong to the youngest age groups is a sign of a possible future trend towards increased reliance on private pension provision (Suutela, 2000). Another interesting development that may have significant long-term ramifications is the introduction by SACO (trade union central organisation for employees with third-level qualifications) of an unemployment insurance for its members, designed to cover loss of income up to a considerably higher threshold than the public unemployment insurance does.

A new risk may be posed by the fact that pensions in Sweden are now linked to economic growth. They are designed to be financially viable in the face of demographic and economic change. The size of pensions is determined by the general earnings trends, so that favourable developments in earnings result in higher pensions, and vice versa. The fact that the average life expectancy of age cohorts is going to influence the size of pensions may also be said to constitute a new risk, in combination with the impact of fluctuations in economic growth. The role of private provision, and consequently the new risks posed by privatisation, is still rather small in the area of social insurance. In Sweden, fixed contributions to pensions amount to 18.5 per cent of pensionable income, of which 16 per cent is used to pay for current pensions (PAYG). 2.5 per cent of the contribution is deposited in individual accounts which will yield the pre-funded or premium pension, equivalent to personal pensions saving. This may in future lead to smaller pensions for those who did not invest this premium in the optimal way, but the very small size of the premium pension means that this is unlikely to become a serious problem. However, it is possible that the share of individualised, funded elements in the pension systems and the popularity and importance of private pensions will grow, which will lead to a greater exposure to the market forces. In Finland, too, employment and earnings records are more decisive in determining future pensions following the pension reforms over the last ten years, which may in future lead to increased popularity of private pensions in securing retirement incomes (Hinrichs and Kangas, 2003).

The Politics of New Risk Policy in the Nordic Context

Different welfare states create different obstacles to addressing the new risks that they face. For instance, in liberal welfare states the reluctance to increase taxes sets a limit to how much state intervention there can be in the area of child care, however important such provision is considered from the point of view of women's employment and prevention of poverty among lone parents.

In the context of the Nordic welfare states, the sheer popularity of existing social policy arrangements can be a very powerful obstacle to reform. For instance, in the light of recent opinion surveys, over 80 per cent of Finns consider the welfare state to offer good value for money (taxes) (Kantola and Kautto, 2002: 18). However, popularity alone may not be a sufficiently powerful motive for reforming or expanding the welfare state: yet, expansion or reallocation of funding is required if the new social risks are to be adequately addressed. At the practical level, reallocation of funds is more likely than expansion through higher taxes, given that taxes are already at a comparatively high level in Finland and Sweden (although an increase in the employment rate would allow a reallocation of funds both towards new and old risks).

The thorny question that arises is: should resources be diverted away from 'traditional' risks towards the new risks? For instance, it could be argued that many Finnish and Swedish pensioners do not 'need' the large pensions that they are entitled to, and that this money could be better spent on, say, the long-term unemployed or families struggling to balance work and care responsibilities. Benefits covering 'old risks', especially pensions and unemployment benefits of the insured workers, are solidly defended by well-organised and politically influential groups such as trade unions and pensioners (Kangas, 2000, 2002; Timonen, 2002). The former are powerful organisations that are involved in economic and political decision-making in both Finland and Sweden, and the latter are a large and growing constituency of voters. If further investment in training for the socially excluded and long-term unemployed, in services for immigrants and in further support of the so-called work–life balance must happen at the expense of unemployment insurance and pensions, the battle is likely to be a bitter one, and one where the new risks are in a weak position. Unions remain strongly committed to old risk policies such as earnings-related social security benefits (and earnings-related unemployment benefits in particular) to the extent that they are reluctant to allow increases in other programmes (such as basic flat-rate unemployment benefit and labour market support) unless they are extended to the earnings-related component (Lehtonen et al., 2001: 120). They have also been fairly successful recently in campaigning for reversals of the changes in earnings-related unemployment benefits that took place during the 1990s recession.

Some groups are confronted with both new and old risks. For example, a family may face both the new risks of inadequate care services for children and older relatives and precarious employment for the working parents, and the old risk of sickness or unemployment. Similarly, an older person may have unmet care needs (a new risk) and concerns about the value of their pension. At the level of individuals, new risks are therefore mixed with old ones, and it would be desirable for both to be addressed. However, politically and economically this is likely to be extremely difficult or impossible, depending first and foremost on the development of public finances and employment levels.

As in other countries, the politics of new social risk management in Finland and Sweden involves divisions that do not map easily onto the traditional class and party structures. Interest organisations that represent new social risk categories are yet to emerge, and may never come into existence due to collective action problems. 'Old' interest groups have taken divergent positions regarding new risks. For instance, some unions are actively promoting policies to counteract new risks, while others are opposed to or indifferent towards such policies (e.g. support for part-time workers who were previously unemployed). There is evidence of old interests making new risk coverage conditional on improvements in their old risk benefits. However, opposition by old interests is strong only if proposed policies represent a major departure from underlying principles of the welfare settlement (expansion of low-pay service sector jobs) or if new risk policies are introduced at the cost of increased costs for old risk categories (better paternity leave shifting costs from female-dominated to male-dominated sectors of the economy).

There is some evidence of new alliances emerging around new social risk issues: for instance, representatives of the Church and service-sector trade unions are opposing increased flexibility and irregularity in private service sector jobs. Employer–employee coalitions have also been constructed over issues such as enhanced flexibility of women's employment. Employer interests can be highly supportive of new risk policies while simultaneously being anti old risk policies. For example, service-sector employers are actively backing extensions to paternity leave but oppose improvements in unemployment benefits. The precise division of loyalties regarding new social risks among existing interest groups remains to be seen: discussion of appropriate responses and policy solutions is as yet undeveloped. However, it seems that conflict is not always necessary and positive-sum solutions are possible, particularly if achievement of high employment levels enables the generation of extra tax revenue.

Conclusion: The Impact of New Risks on the Nordic Welfare Settlement

The Nordic welfare states have responded to new social risks earlier and more effectively than most other welfare states. The most frequently discussed examples of policies to deal with new risks are usually found in countries outside the Nordic regime, again because they represent qualitatively new and sometimes radical departures for those countries.

However, as this chapter has shown, we cannot simply state that the Nordic welfare states have already successfully addressed the issues: they may be pioneers in this area, but they have not invented a magic formula against new social risks, nor are they immune against new forms of new risks emerging as their economies and societies become increasingly post-industrial, diverse and exposed to the forces of globalisation in the form of immigration and competition with low-wage and low-tax economies. Furthermore, the role of new social risk policies themselves in generating further risks cannot be ignored. This chapter has drawn a distinction between areas where new risk policies have been in place for a long time, and areas where new risks have only recently emerged and are only now beginning to be addressed. Examples of 'old' new risks are care services for older people and children: while these have been in place for several decades, demand continues to grow and the needs of new risk groups are becoming increasingly complex, while services are in some cases being scaled back. Examples of more recent new risks that these welfare states are currently faced with include persistent long-term unemployment that affects unskilled and older workers in particular, increases in atypical employment, and integration of the immigrant population into the labour market and society at large. While there is relatively little evidence of new risks generated by welfare state changes and of the 'working poor' phenomenon, this chapter has emphasised the importance of monitoring trends that may become more pressing in the future.

The great challenge that the Finnish and Swedish welfare states now face is the continued combination of economic growth and the relatively high degree of equality that they have managed to create. Increasing economic growth and employment levels at the expense of income equality fits ill with the Nordic model. However, it appears that the capacity to tackle some of the new risks that these welfare states face depends on higher growth and employment. Some groups argue that this can only be achieved through allowing income inequality to increase. This issue is certain to be pivotal for the future of the Nordic welfare state. Another issue that is crucial for the future shape of the Nordic welfare state is the continued quality and legitimacy of public services: this issue is also closely linked to dealing with the new risks of work-family balance and service needs of groups such as older people. If middle- and high-income earners become dissatisfied with these services, their willingness to finance them will decline, thus posing a major challenge to the long-term sustainability of these service states. As always, in dealing with new risks, the greatest challenge for the Finnish and Swedish welfare states is to ensure widespread legitimacy by creating high-quality benefits and services, as 'only the best is good enough for the people'. The examples discussed above show that they continue to be relatively successful in fulfilling this aim.

References

Arbetslivsinstitutet (2002) *Platsförmedling för arbetslösa invandrare (Job-seeking assistance for unemployed immigrants)*, Arbetsmarknad & Arbetsliv, 2002: 04. Arbetslivsinstitutet, Stockholm.

Asplund, R. (2001) *Koulutus, palkkaerot ja syrjäytyminen (Education, wage differentials and exclusion)*, Memorandum to the Working Group of the Economic Council (muistio talousneuvoston työryhmälle), October 2001.

Boldt, P. J. and Laine P. (2001) *Joustavuus, työmarkkinarakenteet ja työttömyys (Flexibility, Labour Market Structures and Unemployment)*, SAK Tutkimustieto 1/2001. SAK, Helsinki.

Ervasti, H. (2003) 'Kuka haluaa töihin? Aktiivisten ja passiivisten työttömien profiilit (Who wants to work? Profiles of active and passive jobseekers)', in Ritakallio, Veli-matti (ed.), *Riskit, Instituutiot ja Tuotokset. Esseitä hyvinvointitutkimuksesta professori Olli Kankaan täyttäessä 50 vuotta (Risks, Institutions and Outcomes. Festschrift for Professor Olli Kangas on His 50th Birthday)*, Society for Research on Social Policy, Study No. 59, Painosalama, Turku.

EU (2002) *Social Protection in Europe*. DG Employment and Social Affairs, Brussels.

Eurostat (2002) *The Impact of Children on Women's Employment Varies Between Member States*, News release 60/2002.

Eurostat/European Commission (2003) *The social situation in the European Union 2003*. Office for Official Publications of the European Communities, Luxembourg.

Forsander, A. (2001) 'Kenelle ovat aukeavat? Maahanmuuttajat ja työllistymisen ehdot (Who are the doors open to? Immigrants and employment requirements)', *Työpoliittinen Aikakauskirja*, 2: 28–38.

Forsander, A. and Alitolppa-Niitamo A. (2000) *Maahanmuuttajien työllistyminen ja työhallinto—keitä, miten ja minne (Immigrants' Integration Into the Labour Market and Labour Market Administration—Who, How and Where)*. Työhallinnon julkaisu 242, Työministeriö: Helsinki.

Government of Sweden (2002) *Sweden's Action Plan for Employment 2002*, May 2002.

—— (2003) *Sweden's Action Plan Against Poverty and Social Exclusion*, July 2003.

Hinrichs, K. and Kangas, O. (2003) 'When is a Change Big Enough to be a System Shift? Small System Shifting Changes in German and Finnish Pension Policies', *Social Policy & Administration*, 37(3) 573–91.

Integrationsverket (2003) *Rapport Integration 2003 (Report on Integration 2003)*. *Integrationsverket, Norrköping*.

Kangas, O. (2000) 'Why are Some Welfare States more Robust than Others? Potentiality for Changes', Paper Presented at Aalborg University, 6 April 2000.

—— (2002) 'Muutos ja pysyvyys: miksi toiset sosiaalipoliittiset järjestelmät ovat pysyvämpiä kuin toiset?' in Blomberg, H., Hannikainen, M. and Kettunen P. (eds.), *Lamakirja. Näkökulmia 1990-luvun talouskriisiin ja sen historiallisiin konteksteihin*, Kirja-Aurora, Turku, 233–54.

—— and Veli-Matti R. (2003) 'Köyhyyden monet kasvot: suomalainen köyhyys 1990-luvulla (Finnish poverty in the 1990s)', in Kangas O. (ed.), *Nousun huuma ja laman jäljet*, Kansaneläkelaitos, Helsinki.

Kantola, A. and Mikko, K. (2002) *Hyvinvoinnin Valinnat*. Suomen malli 2000-luvulla. Edita, Helsinki.

Kauhanen, M. (2000) *Määräaikaiset työsuhteet ja sosiaaliturvajärjestelmän kestävyys (Limited-Term Contracts and the Durablity of the Social Protection System)*, Sosiaali- ja terveysministeriö, Selvityksiä 9, STM, Helsinki.

Knijn, T. and Ostner, I. (2002) 'Commodification, De-Commodification, Re-Commodification', in B. Hobson, J. Lewis and B. Siim (eds.), *Contested Concepts in Gender and Social Politics*, Edward Elgar, Cheltenham.

Lehtonen, H. et al. (2001) 'Did the Crisis Change the Welfare State in Finland?' in Kalela, J. et al. (eds.), *Down from the Heavens, Up from the Ashes. The Finnish Economic*

Crisis of the 1990s in the Light of Economic and Social Research, *VATT Publications* 27: 6. VATT, Helsinki.

LO (2003) *Kort om röster om facket och jobbet. Synen pålönesättning och löneskillnader (Views on Wage Determination and Wage Differentials).* Landsorganisationen i Sverige, Stockholm.

Lodovici, M. (2000) 'The dynamics of labour market reform in European countries, in: G. Esping-Andersen, and M. Regini (eds.), *Why Deregulate Labour Markets?* Oxford University Press, Oxford, 30–65.

Ministry of Labour, Finland (2003) *Työvoima* 2020. Osaamisen ja täystyöllisyydem Suomi (Labour Force 2020: Finland of Skills and Full Employment), *Ministry of Labour, Helsinki.*

Ministry of Social Affairs and Health, Finland (2002) *Sosiaalimenojen kehitystä ja sosiaaliturvan rahoituksen turvaamista pitkällä aikavälillä selvittäneen toimikunnan mietintö (Report of a Working Group on Social Expenditure).* Sosiaali- ja terveysministeriön monisteita, 2002: 4.

—— (2003*a*) *Sosiaaliturvan suuntan (Developments in Social Protection).* Ministry of Social Affairs and Health, Helsinki, 2003: 6.

—— (2003*b*) *STM:n talousarvio vuodelle* 2003 (Ministry's budget for 2003). *STM:n tiedote* 210/2003.

—— (2003*c*) *Ikääntyminen kansainvälisen ja kansallisen toiminnan kohteena (Ageing as a focus of national and international initiatives),* Ministry of Social Affairs and Health, Helsinki.

Nurmi (1998) *'Se pieni ero' hyvinvointivaltioiden koulutus- ja työmarkkinoilla. Tutkimus koulutus—ja työmarkkinoiden sukupuolijaoista kahdessatoista OECD-maassa.* Turun yliopiston julkaisuja C 140.

—— (1999) 'Changes in Women's and Men's Labour Market Positions in the EU', in O. Kangas and R. Myhrman (eds.), *Social Policy in Tandem with the Labour Market in the European Union,* Ministry of Social Affairs and Health, Helsinki.

OECD (2001) *Society at a Glance; OECD Social Indicators,* OECD, Paris.

—— (2002) *Employment Outlook, 2002,* OECD, Paris.

PAM (2002) Sovitellun työttömyyspäivärahan enimmäisaika poistettava, Letter to Maija Perho, Minister for Social Affairs and Health, Helsinki 12 March 2003.

Parjanne, M.-L. (1999) 'Määräaikaiset työntekijät—joustava työvoimapuskuri (Short-Term Contract Workers: A Flexible Labour Reserve)', *Työpoliittinen aikakauskirja* 41(2), 3–10.

Penttilä, I., Kangas, O., Nirdberg, L., and Ritakallio, V.-M. (2003) *Suomalainen köyhyys* 1990-luvulla—väliaikaista vai pysyvää? (Finnish poverty in the 1990s: temporary or permanent), *Ministry for Health and Social Affairs, Helsinki,* 2003: 7.

Rajavaara, M. (1998) *Työtä, eläkettä vai työttömyyttä? Ikääntyneiden pitkäaikaistyöttömien palvelutarveselvityksen seurantatutkimuksen osaraportti* 4 *(Employment, pension or unemployment: service needs of the ageing long-term unemployed).* Sosiaali- ja terveysturvan tutkimuksia, Kansaneläkelaitos, Helsinki.

Ritakallio, V.-M. (2000) 'Tuloerot ja köyhyys kansainvälisessä vertailussa 1980–1995 (Income Inequalities and Poverty in International Comparison, 1980–1996), in M. Heikkilä and J. Karjalainen (eds.), *Köyhyys ja hyvinvointivaltion murros,* Gaudeamus, Helsinki, 17–42.

Regeringskansliet (2001) 'Social Insurance in Sweden', Fact sheet, Ministry of Health and Social Affairs, No. 1, March 2001.

—— (2002) 'Faktablad "Budget 2003" ', Socialdepartementet. October 2002.

—— (2003) *Vårbudget* 2003 *(Spring Budget 2003).*

SAK (2001) *Jäsenkysely, kevät* 2001 (Survey of Members, Spring 2001), *SAK, Helsinki.*

SAP (2001) *Party Program of the Social Democratic Party*, Social Democratic Party, Stockholm.

—— (2002*a*) *Maxtaxa (Maximum Childcare Fees).* Socialdemokratiska Arbetarepartiet, Stockholm.

—— (2002*b*) *De äldre (Older People).* Socialdemokratiska Arbetarepartiet, Stockholm.

SDP (2003) *Varma Vaihtoehto (Secure Choice).* Election Manifesto of the Finnish Social Democratic Party.

Skog, H. (1999) 'Työhallinnon toimintatavoissa ravistus (Radical Change in the Labour Market Administration)', *Työeläke* 4: 13.

Socialdemokraterna i Riksdagen (2002) *För ett barnvänligare Sverige (For a More Child-Friendly Sweden)*, Välfärdslaget/Rapport, Riksdagen, 13.2.2002.

—— (2002*a*) 'Swedish family policy', Factsheet No. 5, April 2002.

—— (2002*b*) *Hur står det till med hälso—och sjukvården och äldreomsorgen?* Report 2002–04–26, Ministry of Social Affairs, Stockholm.

Socialstyrelsen (2002) *Vårdens värde—vad får vi för pengarna I vården och omsorg?* National Board of Health and Welfare, Stockholm.

—— (2003*a*) *Socialtjänsten I Sverige (Ch. 9: Vård och omsorg om äldre).* National Board of Health and Welfare, Stockholm.

—— (2003*b*) *Framtidens anhörigomsorg*, National Board of Health and Welfare, Stockholm.

SOU (2001) 79. *Välfärdsbokslut för* 1990-talet.

Speech by T. Filatov, Minister for Employment, at a seminar organised by the European Social Fund, Helsinki, 21.1.2003.

—— in Hämeenlinna, 16.11.2002.

Speech by Matti Vanhala, Director of the Bank of Finland, at a Seminar hosted by Palvelutyönantajat, titled 'Financing the Welfare State', 21.5.2002.

Statement by Minister of Social Affairs, Maija Perho, 9.1.2002, PTK 176/2002 vp, SKT 224/2002 vp.

Suutela, A. (2000) *Vapaaehtoinen vakuutus osana Suomen kokonaiseläkejärjestelmää (Voluntary Insurance as Part of Finnish Pension System).* Unpublished Masters Thesis, Department of Social Policy, University of Turku.

Svenska Kommunförbundet (1999) *Vår framtid. Äldres vård och omsorg inför 2000-talet.* Svenska Kommunförbundet, Äldreberedningen, Stockholm.

STTK (2001) *Toimihenkilöbarometri (Survey of White-Collar Employees)*, STTK, Helsinki.

Timonen, V. (2002) 'Intressit ja hyvinvointivaltion puolustus: ay-liike työttömyysturvan leikkauksien vastustajana', in H. Blomberg, M. Hannikainen and P. Kettunen (eds.), *Lamakirja. Näkökulmia* 1990-luvun talouskriisiin ja sen historiallisiin konteksteihin, *Kirja-Aurora, Turku*, 255–80.

—— and McMenamin, I. (2002) 'The Future of Care Services in Ireland: Old Answers to New Challenges?', *Social Policy and Administration*, 36(1): 20–35.

—— (2003) *Restructuring the Welfare State. Globalization and Social Policy Reform in Finland and Sweden*, Edward Elgar, Cheltenham and Northampton.

Trydegård, G.-B. (2000) *Tradition, Change and Variation: Past and Present Trends in Public Old-Age Care*, Stockholm University, Department of Social Work.

—— (2003) 'Swedish elderly care in transition: Unchanged national policy but substantial changes in practice', Paper presented at the ESPAnet conference, Copenhagen 13–15 November 2003.

Valtioneuvoston kanslia (2003) *Työllisyystyöryhmän loppuraportti (Final report of the working group on employment)*. Valtioneuvoston kanslian julkaisusarja 5/2003.

Viitanen, M. (2000) *Ikääntyneiden pitkäaikaistyöttömien työllistyminen ja työnhakuaktiivisuus (Employment Situation and Jobseeking Among the Ageing Long-term Unemployed)*, KELA, Sosiaali-ja terveysturvan tutkimuksia, 54 137–161.

Väestöliitto (2002) *Perhebarometri (Survey of Families)*, Väestöliitto, Helsinki.

5

France: A New World of Welfare for New Social Risks?

Bruno Palier and Christelle Mandin

The French social protection system is divided into a number of different sectors, structured to respond to old social risks in five main areas: health care, old age, family, unemployment, and poverty. The main components of the system clearly reflect the Bismarckian tradition of social insurance: entitlement is related to employment status and is conditional upon contribution record; most benefits are earning-related; financing is provided mainly by employers' and employees' contributions; and the social partners are heavily involved in management.

During the 1980s, this way of organising welfare appeared more and more unable to deal with new social problems: social exclusion, which affects those without access to the labour market and thus to social insurance benefits; the growing number of frail elderly people; changes in the labour market, which generate unemployment 'traps' due to difficulties in creating low-paid jobs; the eviction of older workers from the labour market before retirement age, which reduces pension entitlement; and finally the still difficult reconciliation of paid work and family responsibilities for women, although this issue is not seen as a new one in France.

Public debates developed about these different issues in the 1980s. They are seen as 'new', because the Bismarckian institutions are unable to cope with them. The solutions developed in France to deal with these new problems usually involve sharp policy reorientations, since they create new kinds of benefits which are flat-rate, financed by taxes, and managed by the state. In this sense, one can speak about the development of a new world of welfare for new social risks. All the characteristics of these new social policies imply a path-departure from the Bismarckian institutions, which is particularly difficult to implement. Indeed, the French social welfare system is often seen as one of the most 'immovable objects' among European welfare states (Pierson, 1998: p. 558, note 8). Its particular characteristics help to explain the obstacles hindering major reforms and adaptations: a highly popular but fragmented social insurance system, financed mainly by social contributions; numerous trade unions particularly keen to maintain their position in the system since they are weak in industrial relations; and a state relatively weak in this field and thus obliged to negotiate with the other social actors.

However, some changes have been introduced in the Nineties under European pressures and in a context of economic recession (Palier, 2001). Policies of retrenchment of the welfare state have become possible thanks to the conjunction of three factors: negotiation with trade unions (who should be considered as veto players); the realignment of one of the trade unions (the CFDT), which rebalanced the distribution of powers; and a political quid pro quo, which distinguished insurance (financed by contributions) and solidarity (financed by taxes—Bonoli and Palier, 1996). To make retrenchments acceptable to the unions, the state has increasingly accepted responsibility for non-contributory benefits, and for financing any kind of new social measures. As a consequence, the most striking change of the last two decades is that the non-contributory, tax-financed element of the system has grown considerably, leading almost to a two-tier welfare state. The implementation of new policies aimed at coping with new risks should be understood in the wider context of this dualisation of the French welfare state. Because new social risks are partially a consequence of failures of social insurance, and because a specific politics is associated with the reform of social insurance, policies to cope with new social risks have required new kinds of institutions, separate from the traditional social insurance system.

The Emergence of 'New' Social Problems as Consequences of Bismarckian Social Insurance

In France, two main problems have been perceived explicitly as new social risks: social exclusion and dependency in old age. In the 1980s, the question of new poverty and social exclusion emerged and became more and more important. Debates highlighted the reappearance of poverty, and the theme of the new social risks became a real challenge, since it revealed the loss of efficacy, and consequently of legitimacy of the traditional social insurance schemes. Insurance rights are acquired through work, so that those socially excluded from the labour market are also excluded from social protection. In the 1990s, the second main challenge was the development of dependency in old age. In this case also, social insurances appeared not to be the best way to deal with frailty in old age.

Other problems usually recognised as part of the new social risks (such as the poverty trap, low employment rate of the elderly, balancing family and working life) are much less prominent both in the French debate and on the political agenda since benefits are relatively generous and there is an established tradition of child care. However, these problems are gaining attention, and their appearance in France is also based on an understanding of the negative consequences of social insurance-based welfare. The insurance system, because of the way it is financed, is also perceived as preventing the emergence of new (low-paid) jobs, thus creating unemployment traps. To preserve the family wage (Esping-Andersen, 1996), various strategies of early exit from the labour market have long prevailed in France as in other Bismarckian countries, which have eventually become problematic. Finally, if French social policies have sought for a long period to help women combine family and working life, this objective has always been pursued in an ambiguous way, and has tended to divide women by social status.

Social Exclusion

At the end of the 1970s, the social effects of the economic crisis begin to be felt, especially 'structural unemployment'. Unemployment rose from 4.1 per cent of the active population (900,000) in 1974 to 10.5 per cent by 1987, fell slightly in the late 1980s, but then rose to 12.5 per cent by 1997. Long-term unemployment also increased. In 1974, 16.9 per cent of the unemployed were jobless for more than one year, 2.5 per cent for more than two years. These proportions had risen to 42.7 and 21.0 per cent by 1985. The average length of unemployment was 7.6 months in 1974, 15 months in 1985, 16 months in 1998, and 14.8 months in 1999 (L'état de la France, 2000).

In the 1980s, new ways of understanding social problems emerged. These are reformulated in terms of first 'new poverty', and then social exclusion. In 1974 two important books highlighted the defects of the French social protection system. Storélu (1974) suggested that the social question of poverty remains topical even in countries where the welfare state is well developed. Lenoir (1974) underlines the variety of the situations in which people are not protected by the social insurance system: handicapped, unemployed, 'maladjusted persons', and so on. Between 1978 and 1981, several government reports confirmed this new perception of problems within the administration and policy communities responsible for social policy.[1] By the end of the 1970s, poverty has been rediscovered in France.

During the 1980s, attention was drawn to 'new poverty' by the media and groups from civil society. Paugam argues that the media enhanced the visibility of the new poverty by denouncing the incapacity of socialist governments to face the new social problems, and by supporting organisations (associations, social movements taken up by show-business) which promoted solidarity. Personalities from civil society like Abbé Pierre (well known for his struggle for the housing of poor people in the 1950s), Père Wresinsky (founder of the association *Aide à toute détresse quart monde*) or Coluche (the humorist who founded the *'Restos du Coeur'*) play an important role in the formulation of the problems and in the orientation of politics towards poverty and exclusion.

'Structural unemployment', 'new poverty', the reformulation underlines the novelty of these social problems, and indicates that they cannot be dealt with by the social protection system. The social protection system, designed for circumstances of full employment, requires a period of work before one is entitled to social benefits. In a period of economic crisis, it cannot protect those who are without work or who lack a work record that gives access to adequate social security, who are the very groups who are increasing in number and who need help the most. The Wresinski report, *Grande pauvreté et précarité économique et sociale*, published in 1987, suggested that some 400,000 people were living in France without social protection.

Furthermore, the social protection system is accused of reinforcing the mechanisms of social exclusion, because of the gap between the 'insiders' included in the labour market and who can rely on the insurance system, and the 'outsiders' who obtain a much lower level of protection although they need it the most. The social protection system is also criticised for its opacity and its complexity. The organisation of the social security system in separate sectors is also called in question, since impoverished people cumulate different problems—housing, unemployment, sickness, and so on. At the beginning of the 1980s, the issue finally enters the political agenda, leading to the introduction of 'insertion policies' to fight social exclusion. Social exclusion is framed as a problem of lack of support rather

---

[1] For example, the Péquignot Report (1978) which described new poverty, or the Oheix Report (1981) which proposed new policy directions and a minimum income (the 'minimum de soutien social').

than lack of work, and requires a response in terms of social rights, rather than labour market reform. It is only more recently that developments in the labour market have also been perceived as problematic.

New Social Risks Linked to Labour Market Changes

In the 1990s, two main issues are highlighted: first, the development of unemployment traps; second, the need to reverse the trend to early exit from the labour market. Again, these developments are perceived as a consequence of Bismarckian welfare institution, especially the way in which the system is financed.

In the late 1980s the problem of unemployment traps emerged, partly linked to the functioning of the welfare institutions. Social contributions, which are the main way of financing welfare expenditure in France as in other Bismarckian systems, are understood to have a negative impact on employment, especially for low-paid jobs. Furthermore, globalisation exerts pressure especially on those low-paid jobs which are vulnerable to international competition (Esping-Andersen, 1996: 258). The countries of continental Europe are particularly affected by these socio-economic changes, because the financing of the social protection system by social contributions increases the cost of labour (Scharpf and Schmidt, 2000). During the 1990s, a debate developed about this issue in France and led to discussion of policies by both right and left to cut social contributions for the low-paid.

Related to this problem, a 'working poor' phenomenon emerged afterwards, because a growing proportion of workers have part-time jobs, or occupy a full-time job but for a limited period with interruptions of work and periods of unemployment. This development tends to increase the proportion of those without a sufficient work-record to obtain adequate social protection. The proportion of working poor (being full or part time) rose from 11.4 per cent in 1983 to 15.1 per cent in 1997 (Concialdi and Ponthieux, 1997: 12), and increased thereafter. 1.3 million people worked for less than 533 euros a month in 2000 (OECD, 2000). Recognition of this issue has led to the development of in-work benefits.

Another specific policy associated with Bismarckian welfare institutions, early retirement, has more recently been called into question. In France, as in many other industrialised countries, early labour market exit has been an essential tool for adapting to economic and social change. Indeed, it appeared to be an efficient and easy way of managing the workforce in a context of unemployment, and one supported by an implicit social and intergenerational consensus, since it creates opportunities in the labour market for young job-seekers (Guillemard, 2002). This strategy of 'welfare without work' was especially used in the 1980s in continental Europe (Esping-Andersen, 1996). This type of policy was termed the 'social treatment of unemployment' in France. In 2001, six different early exit schemes were still available (ASFNE, ARPE, CATS, CFA, ACA, ASA), and apply to some 550,000 people. On average, workers cease work at fifty-eight and the activity rate for men between fifty-five and sixty-four years is about 32 per cent.

The early exit strategy started to be questioned by the late 1990s, first, because of its huge cost, second, because it conflicted with pension policies. In this sense, welfare without work policies made a major contribution to the development of a new social risk (being out of work before the legal age of retirement). In 1993, the contribution-period required for entitlement to a full pension was increased from 37.5 to 40 years for private sector employees (extended to the public sector in 2003) while the effective length of the working life diminished. As a result, more and more workers will find it difficult to obtain a full pension. Current plans will increase the contribution period further. Pension policy reforms may lead to the development of a new social risk for older workers: if they are unable to work until retirement age, they risk cuts in their pension entitlement. Two main alternatives, which may also be complementary, are under discussion: encouraging people to work longer, and developing pension savings funds 'à la française' to compensate for lower pensions.

Frailty in Old Age

The third issue that appears explicitly as a new social risk in the 1990s is frailty in old age. As in other European countries the proportion of older, and particularly very old, people has increased, and traditional informal caregivers—younger and middle-aged women—are more likely to be in full-time paid work. Although France developed strong child care services from the 1970s, much less has been done for older people.

Between 1950 and 2003, life expectancy for men rose from sixty-three to seventy-five years, and for women from sixty-nine to eighty-three years (Palier, 2003: 30). The number of over seventy-fives (most vulnerable to frailty) rose from 3.8 to 7 per cent of the population over the same period, and is projected to increase to 10 per cent by 2020 (DREES, 2000b). Women outnumber men by two to one among the frail elderly and are most likely to live alone (DREES, 2000b: 94). According to opinion polls, the great majority (72 per cent) of French people still believe that children should be responsible for meeting the care needs of their parents (CREDOC, 1995). Women, who are most likely to be caregivers, are increasingly involved in the labour market and suffer a double burden (DREES, 2001*a*). The situation is likely to deteriorate as the numbers needing care continue to rise and the size of the younger generation falls (DREES, 2002*a*).

Frailty in old age has thus emerged as a new social risk. The French debate has highlighted social divisions (it is lower-income people who tend to enter residential accommodation while the better-off pay for support at home—DREES, 2001*b*). It has also stressed the problem of 'dependence'— loss of autonomy—and a new benefit has been proposed to promote care at home. This has two objectives: to contain the costs of population ageing and to improve the quality of life of older people.

Women's Access to the Labour Market: Balancing Paid Work and Family Responsibilities

The issue of balancing paid work and family responsibilities does not appear as a specific new risk since women have been heavily involved in paid work in France since the 1960s. However, the theme of 'conciliation' between paid work and family responsibilities reflects an ambivalence. In 2002, the employment rate of women was 62.4 per cent, 73 per cent of them working full time (INSEE, 2002). However, even those women who do paid work remain the principal caregivers for their children. Seventy per cent of domestic tasks (housekeeping, cooking, child care) are done by women. Men devote 2.30 hours each day to these activities, whereas women devote on average 5 hours each day (INSEE, 2000). A similar ambivalence emerges in family policy: some benefits subsidise day nurseries and facilitate the women's access to the labour market, while others encourage mothers to stop working to care for young children. Whatever the solution, 'conciliation' is still an issue for women, who are considered as the main caregivers (Commaille, Strobel, and Villac, 2002: 68). In France, the male breadwinner model, where the social rights of women depend on their husband's rights, is almost obsolete. The dual breadwinner model, in which men and women take equal responsibility for child care and for earning a living has not yet emerged (Lewis, 1992). One reason for this is that French family policy has been traditionally concerned with pronatalism rather than with women's opportunities in paid work.

If the balancing of paid work and family responsibilities does not appear as a new risk in France, societal changes have produced other issues, which could be considered as new social risks. The increasing proportion of divorces and separations leads in many cases to financial difficulties which particularly affect mothers. Some 85 per cent of lone parent families are female-headed and face an increased risk of poverty (see Chapter 1).

New Policies for New Social Risks

The theme of new social risks developed continuously in public debates since the early 1980s. However, they have received less attention in welfare state reform than the old risk problems of financing and sustaining the industrial welfare state in the face of rising demand. As in other countries old risk policies affect more people. The entrenched role of employers and unions in relation to old risk welfare in France also focuses political attention on these issues. Policy-makers have introduced new benefits to respond to the new issues. Since the new problems are interpreted as negative consequences of the former (Bismarckian) social policies, the new policies are inspired by another repertoire of social protection than the traditional one. These changes are leading first to 'a second world of social protection' composed of flat-rate benefits, financed by taxes and managed by the state, and second to new make-work-pay incentive strategies.

The Construction of a Second World of Social Protection

In France, a new set of 'insertion' policies has been created for those who were not covered by the social protection system (the long-term unemployed, single parents, older people, the disabled, and on), and who were suffering from social exclusion, the main new social risk in France. The aim was to enhance social cohesion between the 'insiders' included in the labour market and 'outsiders' (more often women, young people, and long-term unemployed). Nevertheless, the multiplication of minimum income benefits created a new world of social protection, and favoured the emergence of a neoliberal rhetoric that denounced disincentives and underlined the need to make work pay. These residual benefits are financed by taxes and managed by the decentralised state (local authorities and family insurance institutions). Support for these benefits was initially broad-based, since they can be understood both in terms of the established tradition of social inclusion on citizenship solidarity, and also in terms of a more liberal agenda of targeting and of regulating the poor. This led to some ambiguity in the extent of compulsion to work. It also opened up divisions between those on the left who pursued a modernising agenda, and those committed to a more traditional defence of high-quality passive benefits.

The Basic Income

In 1989, the creation of a new basic income support, *revenu minimum d'insertion* (RMI), represented a fundamental step in the development of the 'insertion policies'. During the 1980s, the French social protection system was criticised for not providing the poorest with decent social support. In the 1980s, attempts to develop minimum incomes have been proposed in several cities, and emergency plans to address 'vulnerability to poverty' (*pauvreté-précarité*) have been launched since 1981. After 1986 additional resources (*compléments locaux de ressources*) were given to people who had a part-time job in a city hall or an association. Since the 1980s, a series of reports proposed the creation of a minimum income means-tested benefit, to adapt the social protection system to the new social and economic conditions.

The multiplication of minimum incomes (for old-age people, handicapped and disabled, wives, single parents, long-term unemployed) was not sufficient to cope with the problem of social exclusion. During the campaign of 1988, Mitterrand proposed a minimum income to guarantee livelihood for those 'who don't have anything' and 'who cannot do anything' (1988). The proposal was accepted unanimously by right and left.

The RMI is not only a minimum income: social and employment inclusion is seen as a 'national imperative'. The 'minimum income of insertion' is one element in a global mechanism to fight poverty and suppress all forms of exclusion, especially in the fields of education, employment, training, health and housing. RMI also has a re-insertion dimension, in the form of a contract between the recipient and 'society'. Recipients must commit themselves to take part in a re-insertion programme, stated in the contract and signed by the recipient and a social worker. Such a programme can be either job-seeking, vocational training, or activities designed to enhance the recipient's social autonomy. Receipt of benefit is not conditional upon participation in the insertion contract. The notion of inclusion remains an ambiguous one. For most beneficiaries, the action plan is more important in providing access to social than to directly work-related activities.

The RMI functions as the final safety net, missing in the social insurance system. It is available to each person who lives in France, who is over twenty-five and meets the means-test conditions. The benefit amount is 411.70 euros for a lone person in 2003. It is financed by the state, through taxes paid by those with the highest incomes, and is managed by the family benefits institutions. The number of beneficiaries increased from

300,000 initially to a peak of over one million in 1999. It then fell slightly, but by 2003 the benefit supported 3.2 per cent of the French population, 1.07 million recipients, with a further million family members.

Besides RMI, there are seven other minimum incomes in France. By 2000, 3.4 million of households, or 6.1 million people, (more than 10 per cent of the population) depend on one of these benefits. Benefit levels remain low at between 20 and 40 per cent of the average wage. If overall cost is relatively small (only 11.5 per cent of all social spending) they symbolise a qualitative change and the introduction of new mechanisms in the French welfare system. In contrast to the Bismarckian tradition, these benefits are residual, targeted, and means-tested. They are financed by taxes and managed by the state (central and local). In the development of this new world of social protection, the creation and expansion of minimum income was the first step (relatively late compared to other welfare regimes). The second step involved new employment policies aimed at pushing people back to work.

From Passive to Active Labour Market Policies

The problem of unemployment has been understood and dealt with in two different ways in France since the late 1970s. In the 1980s, and early 1990s, it has been perceived as an unavoidable consequence of new economic policies and thus treated passively (especially through the development of minimum income benefits, early retirement schemes and welfare without work policies). In the early 1990s, in the face of continuing high levels of unemployment especially among young people, governments started to change their policies to improve job-creation by reducing insurance contributions on low-paid work. After 1998, the Jospin government introduced explicit 'make-work-pay' strategies to reduce the risk of unemployment traps for socially excluded people. The most important measure is the *prime pour l'emploi* (PPE). As in other Bismarckian countries, successive governments have used early exit from work to cope with rising unemployment since the 1970s, and now face the need to reverse this trend in the context of population ageing. A policy change is being implemented to close early exit schemes and to encourage people to work longer.

Making Work Pay

A first strategy for creating incentives to take jobs has been to try to make work pay, first by decreasing non-wage costs (especially employers' social contributions) and then by developing negative income taxes. In general, these policies have been supported by the political right, employers' groups and most of the left. They have divided trade unions, with the modernising CFDT supporting change and joining with the employers' associations in a call for a *refondation sociale* at the end of the 1990s, but other unions tending to oppose or express reservations about the changes. From the *Loi Quinquennale* in 1993, (extended in 1995 and 1996) various measures designed to reduce the labour costs for unskilled workers were implemented through progressive exemptions from employers' social contributions. Exemptions from family benefit and health insurance contributions were merged in 1996, for those earning below 1.33 times the minimum wage, and the amount of contribution relief available was increased to 12.4 per cent of labour costs in 1988. Relief was proportional to the number of hours worked so as not to unduly favour part-time work, which was covered by a separate flat-rate relief. The scheme was believed to have had a positive impact on job creation. It has been extended by the socialist government, who meanwhile tried to reduce the poverty-traps caused by massive hiring of low-paid, part-time working employees. Further increases in the social contribution rebate were implemented in the second 35 h law in 2000 approaching a level of 1.8 times the SMIC.

The impact of these measures is difficult to assess. The digressive relief on low wages is expected to permit the creation of somewhere between 80,000 and 280,000 new jobs by the end of four years according to the OECD. The wage ratio between skilled and unskilled workers, after rising continuously in the mid-1980s, was significantly reduced by the introduction of employer contribution relief on low wages, and the share of unskilled labour in total employment has stabilised since 1993 (OECD, 2000). Another study indicated that 460,000 jobs were created or protected between 1994 and 1997 through reduction of social charges (INSEE, 2001). This work was criticised by left-wing representatives on the grounds that it fails to take account of economic growth during the period. A less controversial study puts the number of jobs created at some 200,000 (DARES, 2001).

The labour costs of low-paid jobs have been reduced and the incentives for low-skilled workers to enter the labour market increased. In 1998, legislation against exclusion set out the mechanisms of the make work pay strategy for beneficiaries of the different minimum incomes (ASS, AI, RMI, and API). The aim is to guarantee access for all people to social rights in the field of health care, housing, and culture, and to prevent exclusion. The law allowed those receiving the insertion, single-parent, and widows benefits to draw both income support and wages for up to a year, and modified existing rules for other benefits, to encourage re-entry into the labour market. Beneficiaries thus retain housing allowances, free access to health care, and other benefits linked to minimum income when they return to work, even if only for a short period (Daguerre and Palier, 2001). In 2000, a fifth of ASS and 14 per cent of RMI beneficiaries were covered by such schemes (PNAE, 2001).

Policies which combined minimum income and wages were inadequate to make work pay, and experts recommended the introduction of a negative income tax. Employers' representatives and the CFDT supported this change on the grounds that it enhanced labour market activation, but it was opposed by the other unions. In 2000, a worker would lose entitlement to RMI at a wage level of half the minimum wage. The benefit is in fact worth 80 per cent of earnings and carries additional benefits (especially for children) which at least make up the difference. The Pisani-Ferry report (2000) argued that the state should enhance the income of low-paid workers by a benefit of 289 euros a month to make up for the loss of RMI or ASS. In other words, existing make work pay strategies did not reduce the risk of unemployment traps.

The government sought to encourage low-paid employment through the adoption of a special subsidy for low-income households, the PPE, effective since 2001. It consists of a state bonus proportional to earned income, which increases to a maximum for a full-time employee on the minimum wage, and thereafter decreases to be extinguished at 1.4 times the minimum wage. The amount of the PPE will take into account the resources and the charges of each household (Daguerre and Palier, 2001). PPE is inspired by a neoclassical analysis of the disincentives to work resulting from social benefits, but was promoted during the 2002 electoral campaign as an instrument to increase consumption in a neo-Keynesian way. It was increased twice by the socialist government to support consumption and attract electoral support from low-income households (Palier, 2002: 317). Raffarin, the new Prime Minister also committed himself to keep this measure and it was supported by those in favour of the *refondation sociale*.

Active Ageing

Activation measures have also been implemented to increase the activity rate of older workers. A new early retirement scheme was established in 2000, restricted to workers who had difficult working conditions (fifteen years of successive shift work or production line service, more than 200 nights shifts a year over fifteen years, or disability). The measure reflects the political objective of restricting and targeting early exit, by replacing the different old schemes by this new scheme. Indeed, to limit access to the Special National Employment Fund programme, which supports most early exit programmes, the contributions paid by firms were raised in 2001, increasing the direct costs for all schemes. The early exit scheme for civil servants was closed in 2002, and another scheme, the Job Substitution Allowance Scheme, terminated in 2003.

The closure of early exit schemes does not compel older workers to stay in paid work. The slight reduction in the number of beneficiaries from early exit schemes has been largely offset by the increase in those claiming exemption from seeking employment, a category that now represents 70 per cent of all inactive workers aged fifty-five and above (Jolivet, 2002). The use of these benefits is justified by the difficulties in reintegrating older job-seekers. This group is generally the last to benefit from a declining unemployment rate. In 2001, the number of job-seekers fell by 17 per cent overall, but by only 12 per cent among those over fifty (COR, 2001).

Specific measures for reintegrating older workers in the labour market are currently under discussion. The Pension Steering Committee, created in 2000 to prepare the ground for the next pension reform, stressed that the main strategy required to solve the pension problem was to encourage people to work until the legal retirement age of sixty. It proposed an active employment policy targeted on workers over fifty to include an information campaign, lifelong learning, the restriction of early exit schemes and the development of gradual retirement and pre-retirement schemes (COR, 2002).

The new activation policies seem marginal compared to other main welfare state reforms in France (especially those in pension and health care). They indicate a new trend but do not constitute the core social policy agenda of French governments. Dependent elderly people have also attracted interest from policy-makers in the late 1990s.

From the Prestation Spécifique Dépendance to the Allocation Personnalisée d'Autonomie: The Progressive Recognition of the Risk of Dependence

Before 1997, frail elderly people could receive either social assistance or benefits for handicapped people. The main benefit was *l'allocation compensatrice pour tierce personne*, introduced in 1975 for those who needed help in daily tasks. This benefit was intended for handicapped people. However, by the 1990s, frail elderly people represented 70 per cent of the beneficiaries

(Huteau, 2001: 358). The benefit was criticised because it was not adapted to the specific problem of frailty in old age and did not meet the actual costs of long-term care. A series of reports drew attention to the problems as the number of elderly people rose. Reports by Théo Braun in 1987 and Pierre Schopflin in 1991 argued for a specific allowance for the frail elderly.

Various unsuccessful attempts to pass legislation were made in 1994 and 1995 (Join-Lambert, 1997: 493). Finally, the Juppé government created the *prestation spécifique dépendance* in 1997, to relieve the pressure on local authorities who were responsible for the costs of existing benefits to meet old age dependency. This means-tested benefit was available to those over sixty, and was based on the degree of dependence. It was paid through vouchers and was managed by the local authority. As in the case of the social inclusion policies, this new benefit was not included in the social security system, but was considered as part of national solidarity. Between 1997 and 2001 394,000 old people received the PSD, about half living at home, and four out of five females (DREES, 2002*b*).

A series of reports criticised the benefit (*Livre noir de la PSD, Livre blanc pour une prestation autonome*). Jean-Pierre Sueur (a socialist MP) denounced the inefficacity of the benefit for three reasons. First, only one-fifth of those theoretically entitled actually received the benefit due to means test conditions, fear of loss of inheritance, or lack of information. Second, local government and pension insurance schemes shared responsibilities, and the services provided by the latter were inadequate. Third, local authority management meant regional differences in assessment criteria (Rapport Sueur, 2000: 7–8). Finally, the benefit was insufficient to finance the real cost of long-term care (DREES, 2001*a*). The Sueur report proposed a new benefit, available as a social right and designed to preserve the auto-nomy of the elderly, through a personalised evaluation of their needs. The costs of these services should be determined by the state at the national level. The state would also contribute to the financing of the benefit (Sueur Report, 2000: 11).

The Jospin Government established the '*allocation personnalisée d'autonomie*' (APA) in 2001. This is a national means-tested benefit for those over sixty, with the same conditions in all regions, with the amount based upon degree of autonomy as assessed by a GP. It is paid in cash, as a subsidy to a residential home or as vouchers to a carer. It is still managed by the local authorities and mainly financed by the regions, with a subsidy from a specially created tax-financed national fund (Palier, 2002).

In 2002, 600,500 people received the APA, half of them living at home and half in residential homes. By the end of 2002, the average amount of the benefit reached 516 euros. More than 80 per cent of the beneficiaries were over 75 and 75 per cent were women (DREES, 2003). The principal advantage of this benefit is that, unlike the PSD, it is not reclaimed from inheritances. However, the costs have been attacked by the Raffarin government in 2003, which faced a shortfall of 1.2 bn. euros in the fund. Legislation to increase the contribution of the frail elderly living at home was adopted in 2003, supported by the right with a large majority.

The difficulty of creating a new benefit in an era of permanent austerity may partly explain the debates that developed since the early 1990s and the evident difficulties in producing an inadequate benefit for the frail elderly, although the need is well recognised. The debate and the response show that in France, as in other continental European countries, care for the elderly is understood as a task for the family, although the state may provide some financial support. Policies in this area thus have implications for women's capacity to enter the labour market.

Balancing Paid Work and Family Responsibilities: Unequal Access to Work?

In 2000, most French women aged between twenty-five and forty-nine-years-old were in paid work. However, the rate of labour market participation decreases with the number of children: 80 per cent of women with one or no children are in work, falling to 60 per cent for those with two children and 50 per cent for those with three (Gauvin, 2001). A number of policies encourage mothers and particularly lone parents to enter the labour market, but family benefits also reflect socio-economic inequalities in access to work.

In France, free pre-schooling is available from the age of three, and an increasing proportion of two-year-olds also attend school. For those under three, only a quarter have access to day nurseries or child-minders, half being looked after by parents and the remainder cared for by informal minders or relatives (DREES, 2000a).

Two main benefits exist to improve mothers' access to the labour market: an allowance for a child-minder in the parents' home (established in 1986) and an allowance to pay a child-minder in their own home (1990). The latter was intended to promote the employment of skilled child-minders supported by local authorities, and is available for those with children under six. The numbers receiving the benefit rose from 190,000 in 1992 to 468,000 in 1998 (Huteau, 2001: 396). However, low or middle income families find difficulty in paying for child-minders, and these benefits tend to support women on higher incomes. In 2000 a means test was introduced.

Other policies pursue a contrary direction, and tend to encourage women not to engage in paid work. The *allocation parentale d'éducation* (APE) is available to families who have a second child younger than three years old. It is paid if one of the parents, who has worked for at least two years in the past ten, gives up work. In 2001, the benefit was made available for the first two months of paid work, to encourage women to find a job.

This benefit, created in 1985, was initially available to families with three or more children. It was not very generous and was used by middle-class women who were confident they could return to work, and by unemployed women. Take-up was low. In July 1994 it was extended to families with two children. By 1996, 65,000 women were claiming the benefit. The employment rate of the group entitled fell, for the first time for 30 years, from 70 to 44 per cent between 1994 and 1995 (Maruani, 2000: 76). This trend continues: 80 per cent of women in the group worked before this benefit was available, falling to 57 per cent in 1998 (Afsa, 1998). Most of these women seek jobs when their child is three but often encounter difficulties (DREES, 2000a).

The Jospin Government tried to reverse this trend. In 2000, a new benefit to help women returning to work (*aide à la reprise d'activité des femmes*, ARAF) was introduced. This benefit is available to unemployed women, who receive assistance and have at least one child under six. It subsidises low wages or supports vocational training or setting up a business. The government also introduced a two-week paternity leave at full pay in 2002. This seems to have been successful and have been taken up by about a third of fathers (DREES, 2003).

The duality in French family policy reflects conflicting policy discourses. Bodies such as MEDEF and women's organisations have advocated for measures that include enhanced child care facilities to promote women's employment, while the family association UNAF fear that private child care will be a problem for low-paid women as they would not have access to these services (interviews with MEDEF and UNAF officials). In addition, policy-makers and interest groups also dispute the role of family benefits in enabling women to stay at home and provide child care. Conservative policy-makers argue that such policies support families, and primarily women, to reconcile work and family life. For unions such as CGT the main purpose of these benefits is to reduce rising unemployment rates (interview with CGT official). The conflict is exacerbated by the fact that working mothers, unlike those who leave the labour market, no longer receive a pension bonus. Similarly, dual-earner families receive reduced family benefits, compared with families consisting of one earner and one carer (CGT interview).

Conclusion: The Impact of New Risks Policies on the Welfare Settlement

Besides the five main 'old' risks (health care, old age, family, unemployment, and poverty), the French governments have also had to cope with the emergence of new social problems since the early 1980s. The most important are 'new' poverty and social exclusion, unemployment traps, the increasing number of frail elderly people, and problems in combining work and family life, which all reveal weaknesses in existing Bismarckian institutions.

France has a strong tradition of promoting child care and encouraging women to take part in paid work (Lewis, 1992). Response to the other new social risks presents more problems. In the case of frailty in old age and social exclusion, governments have had to deal with problems which were not foreseen by the welfare institutions. According to the male bread-winner model, wives and daughters are considered as the principal care-givers for their frail relatives, something which no longer corresponds to the current situation in which most women are employed. Social exclusion cannot be covered by the logic of insurance, since those concerned do not have access to the labour market and are unable to contribute and gain entitlement to insurance benefits. In addition, strategies of 'welfare without work' (Esping-Andersen, 1996a,b) were pursued during the 1980s and early 1990s, as in other Bismarckian countries. These are no longer viable in the context of the population ageing.

In comparison with the difficulties facing 'old' risk policies—the financing of the healthcare system, increasing unemployment or the threat of the population ageing for the pension system—the new social risks may seem less important and lower on the policy agenda. However, condemnation of the new social problems, especially by the media, has facilitated the emergence of these issues as was the case for social exclusion in the early 1980s. The need to cope with these new social risks has become more pressing for an increasing proportion of the population. Indeed, new social risks may no longer be perceived as marginal, as the 'success' of APA for the frail elderly demonstrated, or in a context in which a sixth of French households receive an income support benefit. An increasing proportion of the population may be seen as 'socially vulnerable', especially among those with low qualifications, young people, and lone mothers. The introduction of new benefits to respond to the social new risks (RMI, APA, PPE, API) has often been presented as an important social progress. These benefits improve the lives of many people, but may result from logics which are not always sources of social progress.

The creation of these benefits led to the development of a second world of social protection, totally separate of the insurance social protection system, sometimes termed the domain of 'national solidarity'. All the benefits are means-tested, targeted, financed by taxes, and managed by the state. Recent governments have chosen to target these benefits to achieve social efficacy (giving more to those who have the least) but also for budgetary efficacy (making the best use of scarce resources). 'National solidarity' bows to budgetary preoccupations. Since social contributions may only finance contributory benefits, the state becomes responsible for the non-contributory expenses.

This took place in the context of a new politics of social welfare. The initial development of assistance in the late 1980s attracted support from both the left and right, as countering social exclusion and promoting work incentives. As various attempts were made to strengthen the rules of entitlement and to advance make work pay policies, the support of the left and particularly of trade unions became more divided. A crucial factor was the commitment of the pragmatic socialist union, CFDT, to modernising policies, expressed in support for negative income-tax and the extension of targeted benefits.

The logic that governs national solidarity benefits may, in the long run, become more one of targeting and budgetary efficacy than of social progress. As long as the benefits were financed by social contributions, insured persons have been ready to see their contributions increase to preserve their level of social protection, and social security benefits have been preserved from a completely financial logic. Because they are entirely tax-financed, national solidarity expenses are more likely to be submitted to the budgetary constraints. Indeed, the current development is not budgetary expansion but rather restriction, because of the fragile economic conjuncture and of an economic orthodoxy that wishes to reduce the level of the public spending in the name of economic competition.

Targeting the benefits on the poorest leads most often to the introduction of mechanisms of redistribution where those who pay are not those who receive the benefits. British or American examples, where targeted benefits are widely used, show that they are more easily called into question than benefits or services which are open to everybody. The middle class, forced increasingly to buy its own complementary social protection from private providers, may at some stage become reluctant to pay taxes to finance social protection for poor people who are not in work.

The development of a tax-financed welfare system, managed by the state and composed of means-tested benefits, is the main political response to the emergence of these new social risks. However, there is also a second trend, which developed recently: the introduction of activation measures to reverse inactivity traps or early exit from work. Although the main goal of the 'old' benefits was to maintain generous income replacement to maintain the living standards and status of the beneficiary, without impos-ing incentives to return to work, some new benefits have been introduced in the late 1990s with the explicit goal of reversing the 'passive' measures of social treatment of the unemployed, and replacing them by 'active' measures, encouraging unemployed people to return to work. This new orientation led to the creation of make-work-pay strategies and incentives, especially for the low-paid jobs (reduction in social contributions, PPE). Similarly, early exit schemes are being replaced by new schemes which target opportunities on those who have had hard-working conditions, to reverse the trend of early exit from work. The government is currently discussing proposals to create new work incentives for those receiving means tested RMI.

The emergence of new social risks in France revealed the inadequacy of Bismarckian institutions to cope with these problems, and facilitated the introduction of new kinds of measures, coming from another repertoire of social protection. The development of targeted measures and the appear-ance of active strategies towards work indicates that the need to introduce new measures to respond to the ineffectiveness of the Bismarckian institu-tions is now recognized. These new recipes—targeted and means-tested benefits, to encourage the return to work—are closer to the repertoire of the liberal social protection system.

References

Afsa, C. (1998) 'L'allocation Parentale d'éducation: Entre Politique Familiale Et Politique Pour l'emploi', *INSEE Première*, N° 569, Février.

Baraille, J.-P. (1993) *L'âge De La Retraite* , *Données Sociales*.

Bonoli, G. and Palier, B. (1996) 'Reclaiming Welfare. The Politics Of Social Protection Reform In France', *Southern European Society And Politics*, 1(3)(Winter): 240–59.

Commaille, J., Strobel, P., and Villac, M. (2002) *La Politique De La Famille*, La Découverte, Collection Repères, Paris.

Concialdi, P. and Ponthieux, S. (1997) 'Bas salaires et travailleurs pauvres', *Revue de l'IRES*, 5–31.

Conseil d'orientation Des Retraites (2001) *Age Et Travail*, La Documentation Française, Paris.

—— (2002) *Retraites : Renouveler Le Contrat Social Entre Les Générations*, Premier Rapport Du COR, La Documentation Française, Paris.

Credoc (1995) 'Conditions De Vie Et Aspirations Des Français : Les Personnes Agées Dépendantes, Les Dépenses De Santé', *Collection Des Rapports*, N° 166.

Daguerre, A. and Palier, B. (2001) 'Welfare Systems and the Management of the Economic Risk of Unemployment, the French Case', Roneo.

Dares, Frederic Lerais (2001) 'Une Croissance Plus Riche En Emplois', N° 7, February.

Drees (2000*a*) *Les Modes De Garde Et d'accueil Des Jeunes Enfants*, Document De Travail, N° 1, Juin.

—— (2000*b*) 'Le Nombre De Personnes Agées Dépendantes', in *Etudes Et Résultats*, N° 94, Décembre.

—— (2001*a*) 'La Prestation Spécifique Dépendance A Domicile: L'évaluation Des Besoins Par Le Plan d'aide', in *Etudes Et Résultats*, N° 136, Septembre.

—— (2001*b*) 'Les Personnes Agées En Institution En 1998: Catégories Sociales Et Revenus', in *Etudes Et Résultats*, N° 108, Mars.

—— (2001*c*) 'Les Aides Et Les Aidants Des Personnes Agées', in *Etudes Et Résultats*, N° 142, Novembre.

—— (2001*d*) *Les Comptes De La Protection Sociale* 2000, *Document De Travail, Série Statistiques,* N° 24, Septembre.

—— (2002*a*) 'La Prestation Spécifique Dépendance Au 30 Septembre 2001', in *Etudes Et Résultats*, N° 159, Février.

—— (2002*b*) 'Quel Temps Pour Les Activités Parentales ?', in Etudes Et Résultats, N° 162, March.

—— (2002*c*) 'Personnes Agées Dépendantes Et Aidants Potentiels: Une Projection A L'horizon 2040', *Etudes Et Résultats*, N° 160, Février.

—— (2003) 'L'allocation Personnalisée d'autonomie Au 31 Décembre 2002', N° 226, March.

Esping-Andersen, G. (1990) *The Three Worlds of Welfare Capitalism*, Cambridge Polity Press, Cambridge.

—— (1996*a*) 'Welfare States Without Work: The Impasse of Labour Shedding and Familialism in Continental European Social Policy', in Esping-Andersen (ed.), *Welfare States in Transition: National Adaptations in Global Economies*, Sage, London, 66–87.

—— (1996*b*) *Welfare States in Transition: National Adaptations in Global Economies*, Sage, London.

—— (1999) *Social Foundations of Post Industrial Economies*, Oxford University Press, Oxford.

Gauvin A. (2001) 'Activité Féminine Et Politique Familiale : Les Compromis Français', in *La Protection Sociale En Europe, Le Temps Des Réformes'*, Christine Daniel Et Bruno Palier, (Dir.), La Documentation Française, 169–75.

Guillemard, A.-M. (2002) 'L'Europe Continentale Face À La Retraite Anticipée—Barrières Institutionnelles Et Innovations En Matière De Réforme', in Revue Française De Sociologie, Avril–Juin, 333–69.

Huteau, G. (2001) Sécurité Sociale Et Politiques Sociales, 3ème Edn., Armand Colin, Paris.

INSEE (2000) Hommes Et Femmes Face A L'emploi, Les Dossiers Thématiques (INSEE, DARES, Liaisons Sociales), Editions Liaisons, N° 17.

INSEE (2001) B. Crepon, R. Desplatz, 'Une Nouvelle Evaluation Des Effets Des Allègements De Charges Socials Sur Les Bas Salaries', Economie Et Statistique N° 348.

INSEE (2002) Enquête Emploi, 2002.

IRES (1997) Revue De l'ires, 33, 222/2, Paris.

Join-Lambert Marie-Thérèse (Dir.) (1997) Politiques Sociales, 2ème edn., Presses De Sciences Po Et Dalloz, Paris.

Jolivet, A. (2002) 'Active Strategies for Older Workers in France', in M. Jepsen, D. Foden, and M. Hutsebaut (eds.) Active Strategies For Older Workers, ETUI, Brussels, 245–75.

Lenoir, R. (1974) Les Exclus, Seuil, Paris.

L'état De La France (2000) La Découverte, Paris.

Lewis, J. (1992) 'Gender and The Development of Welfare Regimes', Journal Of European Social Policy, 2(3): 159–73.

Maruani M. (2000) Travail Et Emploi Des Femmes, Collection Repères, Paris.

Mitterrand, F. (1998) Lettre A Tous Les Français, Presidential Campaign Address.

OECD (2000) Economic Surveys, France.

Oheix Report (1981) Contre la Précarité et la Pauvreté: 60 Propositions; report for the Prime Minister, Prime Minister's Office, Paris.

Palier, B. (2001) 'Reshaping the Social Policy Making Framework: France From the 1980's to 2000', P. Taylor-Gooby (ed.), Welfare States Under Pressure, Sage, London.

—— (2002) Gouverner La Sécurité Sociale, PUF, Paris, Le Lien Social.

—— (2003) La Réforme Des Retraites, PUF, Paris.

Paugam, S. (1993) La Société Francais Et Ses Pauvres, PUF, Paris.

Péquignot Report (1978) La Lutte contre la Pauvreté, report for the Prime Minister, Prime Minister's Office, Paris.

Pierson, P. (1998) 'Irresistible Forces, Immovable Objects: Post-Industrial Welfare States Confront Permanent Austerity', Journal of European Public Policy, 5(4) December, 539–60.

Pisany-Ferry, J. (2000) Plein Emploi, Conseil d'analyse Economique, N°30, La Documentation Française, Paris.

Plan National Pour l'Emploi (2001) La Documentation Française.

Scharpf, F. and Schmidt, V. (2000) Welfare And Work In The Open Economy—Volume I: From Vulnerability To Competitiveness, Oxford University Press, Oxford.

Schopflin P. (1991) Commissariat Général Du Plan, Dépendances Et Solidarités. Mieux Aider Les Personnes Agées, Rapport De La Commission Présidée Par P. Schopflin, La Documentation Française, Paris.

Storelu T. L. (1974) Vaincre La Pauvreté Dans Les Pays Riches, Flammarion, Paris.

Sueur, Report (2000) L'aide Personnalisée A l'autonomie—Un Nouveau Droit Fondé Sur Le Principe d'Égalité report for the Minister of Home Affairs, Paris.

6

Spain's Transition to New Risks: A Farewell to 'Superwomen'

Luis Moreno

Introduction

The Spanish welfare state belongs to the Mediterranean regime. As in other Southern European countries, Spain's single most characteristic trait is the crucial role played by the family as an institution of welfare production and distribution of income and services.

A strong household micro-solidarity, manifested in intra-familial pooling of resources and mutual support and care between family members, has allowed high levels of citizens' well-being.[1] The self-reliance of families has traditionally been taken for granted by governments in matters of social care and material support. Family transformations—and within these the changing roles of women—are the main topics of this chapter and serve as the basis for assessing the impact of old and new social risks on Spanish welfare policy.

After a period of international isolation during the rule of dictator Franco (1939–75), the country's full participation in the process of Europeanisation

Background information has been provided by the various reports prepared by Ana Arriba, Zyab Ibáñnez, Samuel Gil Martín, Vicente Marbán, Carmen Mitxelena, Olga Salido, and Gregorio Rodríguez-Cabrero for the WRAMSOC European Project (see bibliography). I am grateful to the assistance provided by Teresa Buil in additional data collection. I also thank the Spanish Secretary of State for Education and Universities (PR2002–0200) for financial support.

[1] This is reflected in the lower rates of absolute poverty as compared to other EU countries. In Spain, severe poverty rates (established as having less than a quarter of the mean equivalent household income per head) are lower due to the role of the family as a 'clearing house' in the distribution of material resources. Thus 36% of individuals but only 5% of households were categorised as severely poor in 1993 (Carabaña and Salido, 1999).

has brought about profound social transformations.[2] Since 1986 Spain's welfare has converged on the European average. Social spending has grown at a quicker and higher pace as compared to other European countries, but still remains lower than the EU mean figure.[3]

In the context of globalisation and deregulation, and with the expressed aim of favouring higher economic growth, Popular Party (PP) governments between 1996 and 2004 have actively promoted fiscal 'orthodoxy' and the achievement of 'zero deficit' budget. As a result, governmental programmes have aimed at containing the expansion of public and social programmes, which have increased at a slower pace than GDP.

From an endogenous perspective, decentralisation and consensus between the main social actors can be regarded as the two most important elements shaping Spain's welfare development. Constitutional decentralisation of powers and a latent process of federalisation have allowed substantial autonomy to the regions, which have expanded social policies and services at both regional and local level. Regional initiatives have shown how sub-national government can play a leading role in welfare policy innovation. Nevertheless, fears have been expressed that decentralisation may increase regional differences in social spending and policy inequality.

Consensual politics have shaped Spain's main political developments since the death of Franco in 1975. During the 1980s and 1990s, the two main governmental parties (PSOE, left-to-centre socialist party, in power during 1982–96, and PP, right-to-centre popular party, in office from 1996), and their parliamentary allies (mainly the Basque and Catalan nationalists and, since 1993, also the nationalists from the Canary Islands), have followed similar patterns of *diálogo social* in the development of welfare programmes. This general climate of consensus, which was highly successful in the process of post-Franco democratisation, has had effects on the low level of political discussion of welfare reform. Welfare stakeholders tend to be very fragmented and corporatist and have not established stable

---

[2] Membership in the EEC/EU has also brought increasing incentives for Spain to achieve economic 'real' convergence. Figures of economic growth are significant in this respect: in 1959 the Spanish GDP per head was 58.3% of the EU average; in 1985, 70.6%; and, in 2000, 86.6%. Spain would match the EU mean by the year 2020 if the annual 'catching-up' rate of 0.7% were maintained.

[3] According to Eurostat figures, between 1980 and 1993 social spending in Spain grew from 18.2 to 24.0% as percentage of GDP. However, it fell to 20.1% in 2000, compared with the mean figure of 27.3 for the EU-15. The relative decrease in spending was due, among other things, to higher GDP growth and the lower costs of unemployment benefits as a result of falling unemployment. Expenditure on unemployment benefits fell from 2.8% of GDP in 1993 to 1.3% in 2000 (González Temprano, 2003: 57).

channels to voice citizens' demands and needs. The level of debate between social partners in Spain is, therefore, low by European standards.

Discussions on welfare reform tend to focus on the economic dimension of social policy, particularly on efficiency and control of welfare expenditure. The main actors often concentrate on requests for funding rather than promoting open debate. At the level of service provision, NGOs have developed an active role within the *welfare* mix, and are now taken into account by public authorities as co-responsible in agenda setting and management. But in many cases they are not involved in policy-making and lack an appropriate associative infrastructure.

Population ageing and economic immigration have had far-reaching repercussions for social policy. However, it is the growth in women's participation in paid work that has had the greatest impact on developments in Spanish welfare (see Table 6.1).

Family, Work, and the Emergence of NSR

The interrelation between family and work is visible in the emergence of new social risks (NSR) in a variety of welfare areas. NSR tend to affect social groups at various stages of their life courses along non-lineal trajectories and to crosscut social divisions. Young workers, families with small children, and working women are groups mostly affected by NSR. More generally, pressing issues concern care for children and the frail elderly, household gender equality, active labour market policies, 'safety net' programmes, changes in welfare state financing, and pension reform.

The growing involvement of women in the formal labour market has important implications for issues of balancing work and family responsibilities and also for the support that families are able to provide to their members. In particular, it affects the traditional help given to those members who lack the skills necessary to find an adequately paid job, in a situation where unemployment among young people remains very high. Reforms designed to improve the flexibility of the labour market further exacerbate these new risks, because they increase insecurity and uncertainty. We will examine the development of these risks.

'Superwomen' and Households: Balancing Work and Family Life

The older cohort of women, now aged between forty and sixty-four, who could only undertake demanding professional activities in the labour market if they were prepared to combine them with traditional unpaid caring work in households, typifies the Spanish 'superwomen'. Not surprisingly, younger Spanish citizens have continued to identify the family as the most important institutional resource for vital satisfaction. Within families, 'superwomen' have contributed to maintain social cohesion in a country in the process of democratic consolidation and with the highest persistent unemployment rate in the European Union. 'Superwomen' have been evident across all Spanish social groups, classes, and geographical areas (Moreno, 2002a). Now, however, Spanish younger generations of women seem more reluctant to take on both family care and full-time paid work, resulting in lower fertility and a need for more social provision.

Sustained personal sacrifices made by 'superwomen' in the 1980s and 1990s allowed Spain to cope better with welfare retrenchment compared with Central and Northern Europe. Unpaid care within the households also reduced the exposure of Spanish welfare to public expend-iture cuts. Governments could then increase spending on welfare programmes not directly related to household and personal services, since the latter were provided by superwomen 'free of charge'. Spain still continues to be the country with the lowest expenditure devoted to families and infancy in the EU-15 (2.7 per cent of the total social spending as compared to the mean European figure of 8.2 per cent in 2000).

Mediterranean families have historically functioned as an effective (though informal) 'shock absorber' across a whole range of policy areas such as social care, unemployment assistance, housing, or social assistance. In contrast with developments in other European countries, there is evidence that internal family support intensified during the 1990s.[4] Within families the role of women has traditionally been pivotal, as they have often cared particularly for children or older relatives at the expense of erratic careers or full withdrawal from the labour market. Such commitment to unpaid domestic activities has usually translated into low rates of female employment as compared to the EU mean. However, the situation is changing if we consider the correlation between a higher level of women's formal education, a growing prioritisation for professional careers and, consequently, a greater female participation in paid work (Alberdi, 1999).

---

[4] This is reflected in the Mediterranean rites of passage and social reproduction. In 1986, for instance, more than two thirds of young people aged 20–29 were still living with their family of origin in Greece, Italy, and Spain (72% in the latter). By 1994, the proportion had increased: 71% in Greece, 78.5% in Italy, and 79% in Spain. These latter figures compared to 44% in Germany, 41% in France and 36% in the United Kingdom (Fernández Cordón, 1997).

As a result of the reforms implemented mostly in the 1980s, the universalisation of the educational system has meant that 100 per cent of the population in the 4–15 years age group has access to nursery, primary, and secondary schooling. In 2001, relatively and absolutely, more women than men were under education in all primary, secondary, and university stages (INE, 2003). These educational shifts massively increase women's chances to compete in the labour market, but impose additional pressures on 'superwomen' who traditionally bore a heavy domestic burden.

Low Fertility and Women's Labour Participation

'Superwomen' are not only found among skilled, middle-class, and highly-educated social groups. There are also examples of unskilled and low-educated 'superwomen' who chose to keep both household and professional commitments. They wanted to avoid low income or to maintain their more 'expensive' lifestyles and, after getting married,[5] a second salary in the household was welcomed. 'Dual earner' families have proliferated across the Spanish social ladder, and now account for more than half of Spanish couples of working age (see Table 1.2).

Cultural changes in peoples' value systems are key elements influencing the relationship between paid work and family life, and ought to be considered as the main explanatory variables relevant to the latest demographic transition in Mediterranean countries. Individualisation of lifestyles and prioritisation of professional concerns by both men and women have resulted in a sharp decline in fertility rates. The Spanish birth rate halved between 1976 and 1998. In 2001, 75 per cent of all persons in the age group of 25–29 years were singles, whereas in 1977 they were 35 per cent. An increasing refusal by young men and women in their twenties to commit themselves to family formation has been noticeable in the last decades.[6]

Postponement of motherhood and the decreasing number of children can be identified as the reason why the fertility rate in Catholic Spain was the lowest in the European Union in 1998 with 1.07 children per woman.[7]

---

[5] Marriage continues to be the preferred way for Mediterranean men and women to create a family. In 1997, only 14% of the Spanish population considered 'living together without being married' as the preferred option (CIS, 1997). In 1999, nine out of ten married women in Spain were mothers whereas only 5% of unmarried women had children (INE 1999).

[6] The mean age for marriage for women had risen from 23.4 in 1980 to 26.9 in 1995 (Castro Martín, 1999).

[7] This was a figure provided by a macro-survey carried out by the Spanish *Instituto Nacional de Estadística* (National Institute for Statistics) and which referred to an ill-defined 'structural fertility rate' (INE, 1999). The rate calculated in the 2002 Census was slightly higher at

Spanish couples seem to have opted more for the 'quality' than the 'quantity' of the family. Large numbers of women with higher levels of formal education who can have access to better, but also more competitive and demanding jobs simply choose not to have a second child.

In Spain around half of all births are first children. Low fertility rates in Spain should not be understood, however, as evidence of a declining interest among younger Spanish women in maternity. Younger generations of women continue to express a great desire to become mothers (nine out of ten, in the age group of 15-24 years, and eight out of ten in the 25-29). Half of all the women of childbearing age surveyed (excluding those with physical impediments) stated that they wished to have children (INE, 1999).[8]

Increased women's participation in the formal paid labour market is an important factor in explaining not only low fertility rates but also changes in welfare arrangements. Large numbers of younger women are expected to enter the labour market in the near future. Although the activity rate for women aged between twenty-five and fifty-four was only 29.1 per cent in 1976, by 2003 it had jumped to 66.0 per cent (see Table 6.1). As a whole, Spanish female activity rate was still lower (46 per cent) than the EU mean (56 per cent).[9] Spain's rate, however, increased more rapidly than that of any other EU country between 1993 and 2003 (Eurostat, 2004). In contrast to other EU countries, a negative correlation between female participation in the labour market and fertility rates persists.

Where 'superwomen' took on both paid employment and domestic responsibilities, they often managed to accomplish two-working days in one throughout a good deal of their lives. The absence of shared domestic work by other family members also meant sacrifices and long hours of commitments both inside and outside the home. Indeed, the position of Mediterranean women worsened with an increasing burden of responsibilities *tout court* and also because their limited involvement in policy-making usually translated into discriminatory outcomes (Trifiletti, 1999; León, 2001). In the case of Spain, an emphasis on women's individual civic and

1.26 children per fertile woman, but remained the lowest—together with that of Italy—in the whole of the European Union (INE, 2003).

[8] However, the 'child gap' (ratio of actual over desired number of children) was 0.5, or half the 'ideal' figure of offspring, in Mediterranean Greece, Italy, and Spain (Esping-Andersen, 2002: table 2.10).

[9] The female activity rate in the public sector in 1997 was 39.4% as compared to the mean figure of 47.0% in the European Union. Note, however, that in 1986 there was a difference of 12.8 points, which has been reduced to 7.6 points. The proportion of female civil servants within the 25-29 age group was already 105 for every 100 male public employees by 1990 (Salido, 2000).

Table 6.1 Female activity rates in Spain (1976–2003)

Age groups	1976	1980	1985	1990	1995	2000	2003
16–19	48.57	39.97	31.97	30.25	21.77	20.78	18.4
20–24	53.49	54.71	54.53	61.20	57.95	57.27	56.36
25–54	29.07	30.40	35.62	47.87	56.47	63.50	66.01
+55	13.84	11.24	10.05	8.99	8.46	8.80	9.68
Total	28.53	27.77	28.96	34.56	37.86	41.73	43.15

Note: Data collected annually on every 4th term, except for 2003 (2nd term)

Source: Spanish Active Population Survey (EPA)

political rights has often left aside the interconnection between domestic and out-of-the-household dimensions, something which is to be put into perspective against the political background of Francoism (Salido, 2002).

The current generation of working-age mothers is the first one with a majority of its members in paid work. They cannot simply reproduce past behaviour and, therefore, they have displayed innovative ways and means to deal with the 'reconciliation' of households and jobs. A brief examination of the family strategies deployed to sort out this 'impossible situation' (Nicole-Drancourt, 1989) is illustrative of the transitional phase households are facing concerning NSR.

Family Strategies, Household Gender Equality, and 'de-familisation'

For Spanish 'puzzled fathers' the preservation of their professional careers is no longer the sole, paramount objective around which the family is mobilised. Women's labour concerns have become as important, if not more decisive, than men's occupations.

The main family strategy of Spanish couples is to count on 'substitute mothers', usually a family or kin member living nearby. Three-quarters of the working mothers have a close relative living in the same town; in more than half of the cases it is their own mother (Tobío, 2001). Help provided by 'granny-mothers' has become indispensable for Spanish working mothers, who can rely on them without reservations. Moreover, 'granny-mothers', as surrogate mothers, eliminate any feeling of 'guilt' working mothers might have as they engage in paid employment.

The transfer of caring responsibilities from young parents to grandparents or relatives has traditionally reinforced the cultural bases of the model of 'family and kin solidarity' in Southern Europe (Naldini, 2003). However, such family micro-solidarity perversely permits a limited and usually passive state intervention, in many cases 'unfriendly', towards working mothers.

Two interrelated issues have emerged in debates about advancing gender equality and mobilising women into paid work: (*a*) the lack of external support for family life (child care facilities, personal social services and parental leaves); and (*b*) the unequal sharing by family members of domestic responsibilities within the household. Since 1995, maternity leave in Spain covers up to sixteen weeks with full salary for employees who are members of the contributory social security system (social insurance). Fathers may take up to four of the sixteen weeks of maternal leave. Both working parents may have their respective leaves at the same time or successively, but in practice these last options were taken up by only 1.3 per cent of those entitled in 2001 (Salido, 2002).

Debate is gradually gaining political momentum in Spain on policies of what some authors regard as a process of 'de-familisation'.[10] It has been argued that women must previously be 'commodified' as a first step to 'de-familisation' (Orloff, 1996). These processes should be mainly accomplished by state intervention. In Spain there is an ambivalent and uneasy relationship with top-down statistic policy-making. In political terms, *dirigiste* state intervention in family matters often recalls the authoritarian policies of Franco's dictatorship (Valiente, 1995).

In cultural terms, debates on 'de-familisation' in a country where mothers typically taught their daughters to assume domestic activities as a female responsibility—in the belief that household management would effectively provide women with power to become the real 'bosses' within families—are sensitive (Guillén, 1997). Discussions of 'women-friendly' policies necessarily involve the redefinition of household roles in the sharing of domestic work. In 1996 women worked on average 4 hours and 30 minutes more than men did in household activities. In 2001 the difference had been reduced by 17 min. At this rate, it would take eighty years for the time spent by women and men in housework to become equal (MTAS, 2003: 46).

Some analyses sustain that there is no 'revolution' in the private field of couple's relations, and that the traditional model might persist despite unstable and gradual changes (Gutiérrez Sastre, 2002). The promotion of choice whether to engage in unpaid or in paid work continues to be a dilemma of far-reaching consequences in Spain. It influences

---

[10] The expression 'de-familisation' is subject to no little critique. It is generally meant as externalisation of household domestic work and is regarded as a 'win-win'—or 'positive sum'—strategy for the development of national 'sheltered sectors' of personal social services (Esping-Andersen, 1999).

not only women's family and working lives but also a good deal of NSR policy-making.

In recent years, new legislation has aimed at reconciling paid work and family life through 'positive discrimination' targeted on female employees (*Ley de Conciliación de la Vida Familiar y Laboral, 39/1999*).[11] Following the approval of the Law 39/1999, two other related pieces of legislation regulated maternity leave and introduced a new risk benefit during the time of pregnancy, as well as maternity/paternity leaves concerning premature births, or post-birth hospitalisation. Since 2003, an annual tax break amounting to 1,200 euros per child under the age of three years has been made available to all working mothers affiliated to the social security system. Beneficiaries can cash monthly the corresponding amount as an anticipated payment, which is adjusted in the annual tax return.

All these public interventions may be regarded as 'modest' measures in facilitating a degree of conciliation between work and family for female employees. They indicate, nevertheless, a growing concern by society as a whole, and the political parties in particular, about the issues raised by the NSR. Concerning services of day care provision it is unreasonable to foresee that 'granny mothers' will continue to be central actors in the main family strategy of Spanish working mothers. Such arrangements will not disappear overnight.[12] However gradual the transition, considerable public effort must be addressed for the provision of care for children of working mothers but also for the frail elderly (see below).

Youth Unemployment

Unemployment has long been identified as the leading social problem in Spain, the country with the highest level of joblessness population in the EU. Some observers continue to be puzzled by the stable social situation in the country, particularly concerning groups like younger people, despite the fact that unemployment rates for those aged 20–24 are 40 per cent for

[11] Among these: (*a*) the consideration of women as a priority group for labour hiring on permanent bases, and allowing an increase of this kind of contracts from 36.6% of total contracts in 1997 to 44% in 2001; (*b*) the 'cost zero program', which establishes an exemption in the payment of social contributions for new job contracts of substitution for maternity leaves; (*c*) insertion programmes for unemployed women; (*d*) the promotion of female entrepreneurs; or (*e*) the transformation of the sixteen-week parental leave into a family right rather than a disability entitlement (Salido, 2002).

[12] According to some simulations, Italy and Spain would need to produce annual growth rates for day coverage three times higher than Denmark (standing at 57% after three decades of sustained development), if they were to comply with the EU goal of reaching 60% of female employment by the year 2010 (Esping-Andersen, 2002: 62–3).

men and 45 per cent for women. Two main factors are relevant: high spending on unemployment benefits (12.5 per cent of social spending in 1999, over twice the EU average (EU 2002: 56)); and the support of family and household networks of micro-solidarity.

The Spanish labour market is characterised by formal rigidities, costly redundancy, and high hiring costs. Historical factors must also be taken into account (Gil Martín, 2002). The 'emergence' of informal tax-free employment remains one of the main challenges in bringing employment conditions in Spain into line with those of its European counterparts. According to a much-criticised memorandum elaborated by the European Commission in March 1998, the 'underground' economy of Spain was estimated between 10 and 23 per cent of its GDP against a European average of between 7 and 16 per cent (Moreno, 2001*b*).

Within this general context, families continue to provide stability and security for the young unemployed. These can often maintain lifestyles and have family emotional support without the pressing need to take up jobs. However, one problem that is bound to 'mature' in the future is the inability for these young unemployed people to complete working biographies so that they can have later access to 'old risk' entitlements of income maintenance and contributory pensions. On the other hand, the implicit intergenerational family pact by which older members usually transfer resources and material support to younger members is becoming increasingly 'untimely', as life expectancy rises continuously, and younger families increasingly face material difficulties in 'standing on their own two feet'. Family formation is postponed and the trend to low fertility is reinforced.

Activation and Job Insecurity

Social actors, particularly trade unions, continue to press for activation policies that would enable NSR groups (especially first job-seekers) to have access to 'good quality' jobs, while employers' associations maintain their well-known complaints about the rigidities of the formal labour market and the high labour costs which damage competitiveness. The former seem to be more concerned with the preservation of passive policies for the adult working population, but they also request public policies for 'more, new and permanent' jobs. Employers and corporations have usually adopted a cautious stance of 'wait-and-see' to assess how new legal frameworks for activation policies could be consolidated.

Spanish Governments have tackled the activation of labour mainly by promoting new forms of employment contract in an attempt to help companies to create new jobs. This approach fails to understand that regulations do not always constitute 'the' compelling variable for the creation or destruction of employment in Spain (e.g. half a million jobs were created in 1987 and 400,000 were destroyed in 1993, under identical labour legislation). Certainly, governmental actions do influence the kind of jobs created, and in particular the security or otherwise of the workers who have access to them. Such an area of government intervention is important for the expansion of NSR, as developments in the Spanish formal labour market plainly show.

Training and workforce activation—introducing and modifying different sorts of job contracts so as to cut down labour costs and to improve incentives for hiring workers—have been strengthened in recent decades. However, most new jobs have been created on a temporary basis and many are of a precarious type, as they do not generate stable working biographies for the achievement of contributory entitlements and full social rights.

In fact, the immediate effect of deregulatory policies in recent years has been an exponential rise in the number of temporary and part-time occupations (in 2002 the proportion of temporary jobs stood at 30.6 per cent, which was highest in Europe and more than twice the EU mean). New contracts have benefited from fiscal subventions, but they have often consolidated the spurious practice of formalising *de jure* temporary contracts which replace *de facto* permanent working positions (Moreno, 2000).[13]

As in other European countries, labour market activation seeks to counteract the perverse effects produced by the weakening of job security. In this respect, reforms are designed to meet problems of the welfare state that creates further difficulties for the lower skilled and labour market entrants. In turn, the emergence of these new social risks put further pressures on the family, which is losing—in a gradual but unequivocal manner—its traditional capacity as 'shock absorber'.

Legacies and Reforms: The Development of Policy

NSR overlap with 'old' risks but do not necessarily 'replace' them. Both types of risks coexist in advanced welfare democracies. Trade-offs between them

---

[13] According to a report by the trade union UGT based on data by the INEM (National Institute for Employment), nearly 30% on all temporary contracts were for a period shorter than one month (*El Mundo*, 24 August, 2003).

allow for different welfare arrangements. In this section, a review of recent developments and future policy reforms in Spain is carried out with reference to the state/market/family triangle of welfare arrangements and, in particular, those issues related to new risks in work, households, and personal care.

The *diálogo social* has been a consensual practice among the political and social actors throughout the period of transition to democracy and democratic consolidation in Spain. These consensual practices produced a landmark agreement, known as the *Pacto de Toledo*. The main parliamentary political parties (PSOE, PP, IU, and CiU) worked out a pact which was ratified by the Spanish Parliament on 6 April 1995, and formed the basis for important reforms of the Spanish welfare state.

The Pact aimed principally at reinforcing the contributory nature of the Spanish system of social security (social insurance) and ensuring that welfare finances were stable and could extend universal programmes further. The major reforms aimed at a clear division between contributory social security (funded by both employers and employees), and universal non-contributory benefits (paid for through general taxation), provision for benefit up-rating and procedures for review of the system. Among other reforms to be put into effect later, there would be two general regimes within the social security system for paid labour and self-employed people. A reserve fund would be established from the annual surplus of the contributory system. Voluntary early retirement would be discouraged by reductions in pension entitlement, except in cases of industrial re-structuring or after expiry of entitlement to unemployment assistance benefits. Disability pensions would be brought within the general scheme. Means-tested supplements financed from general taxation would be paid to families whose contributory pensions did not reach a minimum level. Pensions would be up-rated in line with price increases, and voluntary and complementary private schemes were to be encouraged through tax incentives for occupational provision. Pension calculations were to be based on a minimum contributory period of fifteen years by 2001.

Pensions

Pension reform has practically 'monopolized' the debate on welfare reform in Spain in recent times, to the detriment of other areas of social protection. Consensus has been the constant rule with regard to the preservation of the 'pay-as-you-go' pension system. An agreement reached in July 2003 between the political parties on the future development of the Toledo Pact seemed to confirm such a consensual approach.

The pension system in Spain expanded to universal coverage during the period of democratic consolidation, economic restructuring and an acceleration of population ageing. All these factors made the problem of balancing spending and resources difficult. Pension spending is projected to increase from 9 per cent of GDP in 2000 to about 15 per cent by 2050, when the contributory social security system deficit would reach 6 per cent of GDP. France, Germany, and Italy, by contrast, are expected to reach 16 per cent much earlier, in 2030. However, due to strong job creation in recent years, and the increasing numbers of new employees affiliated to the social security system, room for financial manoeuvre seems greater, in contrast to the difficulties faced by other European countries. The ratio of contributors to pensioners rose sharply from 2.06 in 1996 to 2.41 by 2002.

According to the views of the main political parties, there are no risks in the Spanish 'pay-as-you-go' pension systems in the foreseeable future. It is regarded as solid and secure and its reform is a question of 'reinforcing' the current system of inter-generational solidarity, supplemented by private systems as an addition. For the trade unions a key issue in its eventual course of reform would be the attitude of NSR generations of young people whose work experience is insecure employment. Accordingly, they fear that the advocates of developing alternative private systems could win the ideological debate. If these younger generations confront as 'normal' a situation of precariousness at work, they might assume that welfare individualisation would be a better deal for securing their retirement pensions. Left-wing parties and trade unions argue that the development of individualised private pensions would undoubtedly generate new risks for those with inadequate contribution records, as developments in the United Kingdom are showing in some cases.

Provided that public opinion would continue to support the solidarity of the public social insurance, the current 'pay-as-you-go' system would be maintained at least until 2015, and no big policy changes are foreseen in the near future. Subsequently, and assuming that the demographic pressures are realised, most experts propose the implementation of a mixed pension system with the aim of implementing a 'three-pillar' system (basic state pension, individual private plan, and occupational scheme). While pension reform itself concerns the stabilising of an 'old risk' programme, the changes may generate NSR by toughening entitlement rules. For example, it seems 'inevitable' to many Spanish social actors that old-age contributory pensions should be calculated on the basis of the entire working life of the beneficiary instead of the period of the last fifteen years as at present. Similarly, agreement seems to be almost unanimous concerning the need to put the 'brake' on the current momentum of early retirement, as well as reintroducing seventy as the 'standard' retirement age.[14]

Welfare Financing

The response to NSR has been influenced by the system of welfare finance. Following the provisions of the Toledo Pact and the subsequent Act on the Consolidation and Rationalisation of the Social Security System (24/1997), a process of clarification was set in motion by which costs regarding health care and non-contributory social assistance and services were to be met by general taxation. The process of separating the sources of financing was not fully achieved by the deadline of 2002, although separate patterns for contributory and non-contributory spending were delimited.

Loans granted by the state or, in other words, public debt allocated to the social security system had traditionally been made for covering budgetary deficits mainly with relation to health care provision. However, in the year 2000, and as a result of these financial modifications, health care benefits of the National Health Service (INSALUD), running costs of the Institute of Social Services and Migrations (IMSERSO), and family protection services were financed entirely by state general revenue. The proportion of the INSALUD budget financed from contributions fell from 20.8 per cent in 1995 to zero by 2000 (Mitxelena, 2002).

The gradual separation of revenue sources has led to surpluses in the contributory system since 1999, which have been transferred to a Reserve Fund, earmarked to cover future financing shortfalls, and to strengthen the long-term viability of the 'pay-as-you-go' public pension system. In July 2003, the Fund's resources amounted to Euros 8 billion, or 1.3 per cent of the annual GNP (Rodríguez-Cabrero, Arriba, and Marbán, 2003).

At present, there are no major financial concerns in the social security system in view of the considerable rise in new employees affiliated to the social security. The arrival of immigrant workers in growing numbers, and the increasing participation of women in paid work account for the financial health of social insurance in Spain. Potential for employment growth in Spain in the coming years is also very considerable.

The mesogovernments of the seventeen *Comunidades Autónomas* have so far been emerging actors with a clear vocation for policy innovation, something with major financial implications. The process of decentralisation

---

[14] In fact, flexible retirement has already started to take place. Civil servants may now work until the age of seventy. At present, half the workers in the General Regime of the Social Security System who should have retired at sixty-five are already retired by the age of sixty (Rodríguez-Cabrero, Arriba, and Marbán, 2003).

Table 6.2 Territorial distribution of public expenditure in Spain (%)

	1981	1984	1987	1990	1993	1996	1999	2002
Central	87.3	75.7	72.6	66.2	58.3	58.9	56.2	48.7
Regional	3.0	12.2	14.6	20.5	25.8	26.9	28.2	35.5
Local	9.7	12.1	12.8	13.3	15.9	14.2	15.6	15.8

Notes: (*a*) The strong increases in regional spending between 1999 and 2002 resulted from decentralisation of responsibility for education and health; and (*b*) spending on social insurance pensions is excluded

Source: MAP (1997) for years 1981–90, and MAP (2002) for years 1993–2002

and the transfer of powers and services from the central state to the regional state, together with fiscal federalism arrangements, have allowed the public budgets of the *Comunidades Autónomas* to grow very considerably. The regional level increased their share from 3 per cent of the total Spanish spending in 1981 to as much as 35.5 per cent in 2002 (see Table 6.2). If public spending is a good indicator of the level of regional autonomy (Watts, 2001), then it should be concluded that the Spanish model can be compared to those European countries with a formal federal structure such as Austria, Germany, or Switzerland (Moreno, 2001*a*).

Labour Flexibility and Job Creation

The 1994 Labour Reform encouraged labour market flexibility by eliminating rigidities on part-time employment regarding maximum daily and weekly hours and the absolute ceiling of two-thirds of standard full-time hours. The social actors were involved, in consultations on the Spanish National Action Plans of 1998 and 1999, which followed European guidelines in putting the emphasis on a higher degree of labour market flexibility. In parallel, the mesogovernments of the *Comunidades Autónomas* have been promoting their own employment plans and implementing policies to allow for arrangements for working-time flexibility agreed at the regional level.

On November 1998, the central government and the main trade unions signed an agreement on promoting stable part-time employment, following the consensual practices of *diálogo social*. This agreement established regulations to facilitate, for example, permanent intermittent employment and replacement contracts combined with early retirement. A combination of flexibility with protection of part-time workers, the voluntary election of part-timers, and equal treatment in relation to full-time work was sought. However, the employers' association (CEOE) refused to sign the agreement, a fact that helps explain why the numbers working part time have remained stagnant since 1995, around 8 per cent of the labour force (Gil Martín, 2002).

Labour reform in 2001 modified the regulation of part-time work in line with employers' preferences, for example, eliminating the ceiling on part-time hours (previously set at 77 per cent of a standard full-time contract) and allowing a more flexible distribution of working hours. Trade unions and the left-wing political parties were convinced that the new rules would damage employment conditions for the more vulnerable social groups instead of promoting non-discriminating forms of stable part-time contracts, and vigorously opposed them.

The European Employment report stressed the precariousness of employment in Spain, particularly the high percentages of low paid/productivity and 'dead-end' jobs (European Commission, 2001). The proportion of 'dead-end' jobs in the Spanish labour market were the highest in Europe and well above 20 per cent of all jobs. 'Dead-end' jobs and low paid/productivity jobs together were close to 40 per cent of the workforce. For workers in these jobs it was difficult to find transitions into better quality jobs, and to avoid risks of social exclusion, since they were not entitled to social benefits due to inadequate contributory records. The main problem persisted as most low-paid work was regulated by vulnerable fixed-term contracts.

A dual labour market has developed between permanent and fixed-term contracts. Such a duality does not necessarily mean social segmentation if there were enough transitions between sectors, and it were a response to the different labour demands of the economy. However, in the Spanish case the duality is demand-based and, as pointed out earlier, relatively independent of regulatory changes. The political implications relate, thus, to how the costs and benefits of flexibility are distributed between different groups of employees and what the criteria and institutional arrangements are that affect the transitions between sectors (Arriba and Ibáñez, 2002). In this context, the existence of public 'safety nets' which enhance social cohesion and could eventually function as a 'trampoline' for those jobless citizens in periods of job transition or permanent unemployment is essential for both labour activation and social citizenship.

Low-Income and Public 'Safety Nets'

With an expressed aim of activation and social insertion, means-tested 'safety net' benefits for low-income groups have been implemented as responses to the increasing insecurity of the 'new poor' population and for groups which lack the traditional family support. Despite its fragmented nature and the overlapping of contributory and non-contributory systems, near-universal coverage in social assistance has been consolidated in a dual system of welfare provision, financed by social insurance and general taxation respectively (Arriba and Moreno, 2003).

Some low-income benefits are paid to people already receiving contributory pensions (Social Security Minimum Pension Supplements), or to unemployed people who have exhausted their contributory unemployment benefit period (Social Assistance Benefits for the Unemployed); other benefits in cases of the Non-contributory Social Security Pensions, Family Benefits of the Social Security and Regional Minimum Income (see below) subsidies can be claimed with no previous contribution to the social security system. Most of these cash benefits take into account the aggregate level of household income in determining eligibility. Further to this, some subsidies are differential benefits that increase existing income to an established minimum, whereas others are provided as final amounts.

All these benefits provide cash amounts which are lower than the legally established minimum wage. In other words, they provide a lower protection to beneficiaries than they could get were they to be active and employed in the formal labour market (the minimum wage, or *Salario Mínimo Interprofesional*, amounted to 516 euros per month in 2002).[15] The contributory principle is the main criterion around which the different subsystems are organised, and thus a relationship with the formal labour market background of the beneficiaries is established. All of those applicants to low-income benefits who have secured a sufficient contribution to the social security system can have better contributory benefits (retirement pensions, disability and survivors', as well as unemployment benefits). When the contributory record of the claimant has come to an end (unemployment), or is insufficient (pensions), which is the case of many NSR groups, means-tested benefits are supplemented so that a legally established minimum can be reached.

The 'unilateral' reform intended by the Aznar *Decretazo* (super-decree) in May 2002 was based upon the idea that public benefits should be only available for unemployed people who are actively seeking jobs. Beneficiaries were not permitted to refuse a job offer within broad criteria, designed to encourage social and geographical mobility. After the fierce opposition of

---

[15] The third lowest in Europe. However, the number of workers with a minimum wage was very small compared with other European countries: around 2% or 165,000 employees.

the trade unions, and the 'success' of the general strike in June 2002, the PP Government retreated from the most controversial aspects of the decree although the workfare philosophy remained.

Within the Employers' Confederation there is no monolithic position as regards social benefits for low-income citizens. Some affiliated organisations in densely industrial areas have expressed their support for the implementation of both occupational training programmes and 'decent' minimum income schemes for socially excluded groups.[16] Accordingly, public authorities should increase spending on social welfare and develop services for groups who find social integration and particularly access to the labour market difficult. Trade unions and NGOs tend to put the emphasis on the 'unsuitability' of Anglo-Saxon assumptions that individuals should be solely responsible for their poverty or exclusion. They insist that such an approach is inappropriate in the case of the labour markets in Southern Europe (Rodríguez-Cabrero, Arriba, and Marbán, 2003).

Regional Autonomy and Policy Innovation

During the 1980s and 1990s, the Spanish regions, or *Comunidades Autónomas*, became main protagonists in developing social services and programmes of social assistance. The process of deep decentralisation and latent federalisation has allowed for a great number of competencies and powers in the area of welfare provision to be transferred to the regions. The *Comunidades Autónomas* have been particularly dynamic in the development of new welfare programmes such as the minimum income programmes for insertion (RMIs).[17]

Decentralisation has made interplay between political and social actors at the regional level possible. Different actors shaped the design of the RMI programmes, although the mesogovernments were the main protagonists from the beginning of the implementation process. In fact, no explicit

---

[16] This is the case of the CEIM (*Confederación Empresarial de Madrid*) in the Madrid Region (5.2 million inhabitants), which has great influence over other employers nationally since a high number of large-scale industrial and financial enterprises are concentrated in the metropolitan area around Madrid (Rodríguez-Cabrero, Arriba, and Marbán, 2003).

[17] Between 1988 (Basque Country) and 1995 (Balearic Islands), the Autonomous Communities elaborated and implemented their regional programmes of minimum income guaranteed (RMIs) for low-income families, designed to facilitate the social insertion of recipients. Such benefits were intended to provide monetary resources to those citizens potentially active in the labour market confronting situations of need. In 2000, nearly 80,000 families with around 200,000 members, or 0.5% of the Spanish population received these benefits (Arriba and Moreno, 2004).

popular demand had been expressed in any of the *Comunidades Autónomas* for the implementation of the RMIs, before approval by regional parliaments. The institutional factor making relevant the issue of the minimum income guaranteed was precisely the constitutional entitlement for the regions to exercise their political autonomy.

The main trade unions supported these programmes. They pursued a different course of action from the traditional pathway of negotiation and eventual agreement at the national level. Confrontation between the central government and the trade unions led to negotiation at the regional level. All the pacts subscribed between the mesogovernments and the trade unions (CCOO and UGT) between autumn 1989 and spring 1990 included the establishment of programmes of minimum income. In parallel, a number of NGOs and civil society associations committed themselves to support the RMI programmes. Such a mobilisation reflects the interaction between welfare and territorial politics which is a cornerstone for the future shaping of social policy in Spain.

Care for the Dependent Elderly

The passing and implementation of a long-term care law for the dependent elderly has been acknowledged to be necessary by the majority of political parties, trade unions, and social organisations (NGOs). However, no agreement has been reached to incorporate it into the political agenda once and for all. Dependency of the frail elderly is bound to be aggravated because of the current transformations in the family informal care system.[18] Women continue to be the overwhelming majority of informal carers (83 per cent), and institutional care only is provided to around 3 per cent of the dependent population (half in nursing homes). Care provided by friends, neighbours and private caregivers is simply residual. Private care provided by economic immigrants, mainly Latin Americans, is increasing as a main support to many middle-class and professional women primarily in urban areas.

The pressing need to confront long-term care problems has led to an overall response on the part of the *Comunidades Autónomas* with the implementation of a variety of schemes (health, social, mixed). Once again the

---

[18] Although the majority of elderly people live independently, those who are dependent live with a main caregiver permanently (59%) or temporarily (16%). In terms of care, 76% of dependent elderly people get all the help they need, 8% receive some care and 16% do not demand any personal care. Most families (87%) supply informal care unassisted, and only 20% of caregivers receive any payment (Rodríguez-Cabrero, 2002*b*).

mesogovernments have proved to be very dynamic and responsive but concerns have been expressed about further regional fragmentation and inequalities in service provision. One option for the future is legislation by the central Parliament, establishing a new entitlement within the social security system. Alternatively, 'fine-tuning' among regional social services could be promoted through a general law that would guarantee central state funding, but which would not 'invade' the exclusive jurisdiction of regional governments in social assistance.

In the meantime, the growing burden put on women as informal carers for both elderly and young family members has made political parties advance initiatives and proposals mainly for electoral reasons. Other than some legislation passed in order to facilitate the conciliation of paid work and family life analysed above, central government policies have mostly been targeted on tax relief for carer households. In parallel, private companies have become increasingly 'aggressive' in order to capture services for the care of the elderly which have traditionally been within the public domain or, in some cases, have been provided by non profit-making NGOs. The shortfall in social services for the family remains significant.

Political debate on long-term care may be gaining momentum since it is regarded as the single area with widest financial implications for welfare development in the future. In a country like Spain, where caring activities have been mostly met by women's dedication within households, implications will be high in political terms. The question remains whether to opt for a 'minimal' assistance model with a growing role for the profit-making private providers or for a comprehensive model of social protection with external public support for family members.

Conclusion: From Private Affair to Public Concern

In all the areas analysed in this chapter, family changes are the main thrust for welfare renewal and constitute major challenges for NSR categories and groups. In the last decades sacrifices made by the Spanish 'superwomen' have kept functional the state/market/family triangle of welfare production and distribution. However, younger women do not appear to be willing to take on the role of informal and 'free-of-charge' household carers which confronted members of the previous generation. These combined full-time paid work and demanding domestic duties. What was considered to be a 'women's issue' can no longer be coped with 'behind-closed-doors'. Such a development would imply a substantial reorientation in citizens' attitudes, perceptions, and expectations: care and well-being would be viewed as a general concern of society as a whole and not solely as a 'family responsibility'.

Extra sacrifices made by Spanish 'superwomen' in the last decades have allowed not only a greater degree of gender equality for future generations and a general climate of social cohesion and economic prosperity, but they have indirectly challenged the political agenda on how Spanish welfare should be structured. New social risks, most of which cross-cut family life (care for children and elderly, young unemployed, or young working parents) are most affected. There is a serious vacuum in provision emerging as the hyperactivity of 'superwomen' gradually vanishes. Private providers and, to a lesser extent, consortiums of non-profit NGOs are prepared to fill in the gaps of these NSR areas.

The traditional non-participation of women as relevant actors in political debates and policy-making is changing: 36 per cent of the MPs in the Congress of Deputies, for example, are now women. After the socialist victory in 2004 General Election, gender parity was established in government. However, controversy on NSR policies mainly concern political parties and has been generally focused on economic aspects rather than social concerns (cohesion or solidarity). Other social actors and welfare stakeholders, such as trade unions, employers' associations, or NGOs, have followed a general pattern of consensual agreements and have avoided open confrontation on matters which imply radical change in welfare settlements.

The greater stress on labour market flexibility is leading to a job market model where insecurity is 'part-and-parcel' of expectations, particularly among young people. In this way social exclusion derives not only from unemployment (highest in EU-15) but also from increasing uncertainty in work. Debates on NSR affecting younger family members, for instance, remain in the fringes of public debate as there is a public perception of economic euphoria which somewhat conceals the risks faced by these 'minority' groups and their implications for the future. If anything, debates on these issues are considered to be in many cases matters of 'expert' concern.

An important institutional factor conditioning NSR developments in Spain is the proactive role for welfare development assumed by the meso-governments of the *Comunidades Autónomas*. It is expected that the regions will continue to have a crucial input in reforms related to long-term care and personal social services, as many of these matters fall within their constitutional competencies and policy-making. However, it remains to be seen whether the Spanish regions can sustain high levels of autonomous social expenditure. Budgetary decentralisation could give rise to strained relations between central government and mesogovernments, or could confirm allegations of increasing inequalities in services provided by the regions.

Potentialities for policy innovation by the regions ought not to be regarded as leading inevitably to a growth in territorial disparities.[19] So far the 'demonstration effect' between the regions has proved to be a great 'equaliser' in terms of welfare policy output. In this respect, Spain's new welfare seems to validate the thesis that countries with fragmented political institutions and a decentralised state organisation may move faster and be more responsive in the development of NSR policies. Spain's experience also shows how the emergence of gender and family issues into the political arena generates pressure for major changes in the Mediterranean social welfare settlement.

References

Alberdi, I. (1999) *La nueva familia española*, Taurus, Madrid.

Arriba, A. and Ibáñez, Z. (2002) *Minimum income guarantee and social assistance: benefits for low income people and increasing low wages*, WRAMSOC Report, UPC 02–12, Madrid, www.iesam.csic.es/doctrab.htm.

—— and Moreno, L. (2004) 'Spain: Poverty, Social Exclusion and Safety Nets', in M. Ferrera (ed.), *Fighting Poverty and Social Exclusion in Southern Europe*, Routledge, London.

Carabaña, J. and Salido, O. (1999) 'Fuentes de renta, desigualdad y pobreza de individuos y hogares (España, 1993)', in L. Moreno (ed.), *Pobreza y exclusión. La 'malla de seguridad' en España*, CSIC, Madrid, 107–52.

Castro Martín, T. (1999) 'Pautas recientes en la formación de pareja', *Revista Internacional de Sociología*, 23: 61–94.

—— (1997) *Estudio 2248*, Madrid.

Esping-Andersen, G. (1999) *Social Foundations of Postindustrial Economies*, Oxford University Press, Oxford.

——(2002) 'A Child-Centred Social Investment Strategy', in Esping-Andersen, G. et al. (eds.), *Why We Need a New Welfare State*, Oxford University Press, Oxford, 26–67.

European Commission (2001) *Employment in Europe*, Office for Official Publications of the European Communities, Luxembourg.

Eurostat (2004) *Structural Indicators,* Brussels, www.europe.eu.int.

EU (2002) *Social Protection in Europe, 2001*, European Commission, Brussels.

Fernández Cordón, J. A. (1997) 'Youth Residential Independence and Autonomy. A Comparative Study', *Journal of Family Issues*, 6: 576–607.

---

[19] Territorial imbalances account for only around 10% of the personal inequalities and this proportion has tended to decrease during the 1980s and 1990s. Personal redistribution produced by the impact of direct taxation, social contributions, and monetary transfers has greatly reduced regional disparities in Spain by between 25% and 34% (Moreno, 2002*b*).

Gil Martín, S. (2002) *An Overview of Spanish Labour Market Reforms, 1985–2002,* WRAMSOC Report, UPC 02–17, Madrid, www.iesam.csic.es/doctrab.htm.

González Temprano, A. (Dir.) (2003) *La consolidación del Estado del Bienestar en España, 1993–2000,* Consejo Económico y Social, Madrid.

Guillén, A. M. (1997) 'Regímenes de bienestar y roles familiares: un análisis del caso español', *Papers,* 53: 45–63.

Gutiérrez Sastre, M. (2002) 'Triangular público, doméstico y privado, o ¿cómo negociar en pareja?' *Revista Española de Investigaciones Sociológicas,* 99: 61–85.

INE (Instituto Nacional de Estadística) (1999) *Encuesta de Fecundidad,* Madrid.

—— (2003) *Censos de Población y Viviendas,* Madrid.

León, M. (2001) 'Reconciling Work and Family. A New Welfare Paradigm?', Paper presented at the Cost Action 15, WG2 meeting, April, Berlin.

MAP (1997) *Estudio sobre reparto del gasto público en 1997 entre los distintos niveles de la administración,* Ministerio de Administraciones Públicas, Madrid.

—— (2002) *Estimación del reparto del gasto público entre los subsectores de administraciones públicas (1982–2002),* Ministerio de Administraciones Públicas, Madrid.

Mitxelena, C. (2002) *The Financing of the Welfare System in Spain,* WRAMSOC Report, UPC 02–16, Madrid, www.iesam.csic.es/doctrab.htm.

Moreno, L. (2000) 'The Spanish development of Southern European welfare', in S. Kuhnle (ed.), *Survival of the European Welfare State,* Routledge, London, 146–65.

—— (2001*a*) *The Federalization of Spain,* Frank Cass, London.

—— (2001*b*) 'Spain, a via media of welfare development', in P. Taylor-Gooby (ed.), *Welfare States Under Pressure,* Sage, London, 100–22.

—— (2002*a*) *Mediterranean Welfare and 'Superwomen',* Working Paper, UPC 02–02, Madrid, www.iesam.csic.es/doctrab.htm.

—— (2002*b*) 'Decentralization in Spain', *Regional Studies,* 36(4): 399–408.

MTAS (2003) *Plan de Igualdad de Oportunidades entre Mujeres y Hombres, 2003–2006,* Ministerio de Trabajo y Asuntos Sociales, Madrid.

Naldini, M. (2003) *The Family in the Mediterranean Welfare States,* Frank Cass, London.

Nicole-Drancourt, C. (1989) 'Stratégies professionnelles et organisation des familles', *Revue Française de Sociologie,* 40(1): 57–79.

Orloff, A. S. (1996) 'Gender in the Welfare State', *Annual Review of Sociology,* 22: 51–78.

Rodríguez-Cabrero, G. (2002*a*) *The Reform of the Public System in Spain,* WRAMSOC Report, UPC 02–13, Madrid, www.iesam.csic.es/doctrab.htm.

—— (2002*b*) *Long-Term Care: Context, Debates, Policies and Prospects,* WRAMSOC Report, UPC 02–14, Madrid, www.iesam.csic.es/doctrab.htm.

—— Arriba, A., and Marbán, V. (2003) *Policy Maps of Welfare Reform in Spain,* WRAMSOC Report, UPC, Madrid, www.iesam.csic.es/doctrab.htm.

Salido, O. (2000) *La movilidad ocupacional de la mujeres en España. Por una sociología de la movilidad femenina,* Centro de Investigaciones Sociológicas, Madrid.

—— (2002) *Women's Labour Force Participation in Spain,* WRAMSOC Report, UPC 02–15, Madrid, www.iesam.csic.es/doctrab.htm.

Tobío, C. (2001) 'Working and Mothering. Women's Strategies in Spain', *European Societies,* 3(3): 339–71.

Trifiletti, R. (1999) 'Southern European Welfare Regimes and the Worsening Position of Women', *Journal of European Social Policy*, 9(1): 49–64.

Valiente, C. (1995) 'Rejecting the Past: Central Government and Family Policy in Post-Authoritarian Spain (1975–94)', in L. Hantrais and M. T. Letablier (eds.), *The Family in Social Policy and Family Policy*, University of Loughborough, Cross-National Research Papers, 80–96, Loughborough.

Watts, R. (2001) 'Models of Federal Power-Sharing', *International Social Science Journal*, 167: 23–32.

7

Switzerland: Negotiating a New Welfare State in a Fragmented Political System

Giuliano Bonoli

Introduction

The current structure of the Swiss welfare state is the result of a developmental process that stretches across five decades. Because of federalism and a constitutional structure that results in substantial power fragmentation, the process of welfare state building has taken longer and has progressed more slowly than in most other European countries. Switzerland had its first national pension scheme in 1948, but for a full social security system the country had to wait until the mid-1980s. In some areas, Swiss welfare remains underdeveloped by European standards, most notably with regard to provision for women and families.

Recent social changes, most notably the massive entry of women in the labour market, have made these weaknesses more visible and the demands for provision in these areas stronger. These demands are being taken up by policy-makers, but progress towards improved coverage against NSR is slow. The main reason for this is the degree of power fragmentation that results from Swiss political institutions. Federalism, referendums, a weak government and a weak state are all factors that make the adoption of new policies difficult.

This chapter reviews five instances of policy-making aimed at improving new social risks coverage which occurred in the late 1990s early 2000s. It shows the political difficulties involved in adapting social protection schemes to new needs, but it also highlights paths that lead to successful policy-making. Typically, these entail cross-class compromises, quid pro quos between different actors, or the opening of rare windows of opportunity. In general, policy-making for the provision of new risk coverage is not easy. Several conditions need to be fulfilled in order for change to be adopted.

The chapter starts with an assessment of the position of the Swiss welfare state in relation to the coverage of new risks. It then moves on to present the key features of its political system and policy-making procedures. The core of the chapter consists of narrative accounts of five instances of reform that improve NSR coverage, not all of them successful. It concludes by identifying the conditions under which adaptation seems possible, by focusing on the position of the different actors and their interaction.

Old Welfare, New Risks

The welfare state that contemporary Switzerland has inherited from the post-war years can be characterised as one with a strong old risk orientation. It is one of the biggest spenders among OECD countries in areas like old age pensions, disability benefits, or health care, but then ranks at the bottom of the league as far as family services are concerned (see Table 7.1). The only notable exception is active labour market policy, where Switzerland's effort is comparable to those of other OECD countries, largely as a result of a single reform adopted in the mid-1990s which is discussed below. Otherwise, Swiss social policy remains geared toward the protection of the income of the (male) breadwinner.

Table 7.1 Swiss social expenditure as a proportion of GDP, 1998

	Expenditure as a per cent of GDP	
	Absolute figure	OECD average = 100
Old age cash benefits	11.16	155
Disability cash benefits	2.16	132
Services for old and disabled people	0.7	74
Family cash benefits	1.2	86
Family services	0.13	19
Active labour market policies	0.77	98
Unemployment cash benefits	1.00	80
Health care	7.64	126
Total social expenditure	28.28	124

Source: OECD SOCX

Over the last fifteen years social expenditure in Switzerland has increased dramatically (Kriesi, 1999; Lane, 1999), but this has not done much to change the old risk orientation of the Swiss welfare state. Social expenditure as a proportion of GDP in 1980 equalled 82 per cent of the OECD average. By 1998 (latest year for which Swiss figures are available) it had skyrocketed to 124 per cent of the OECD average.[1] What explains this tremendous increase in Swiss social spending relative to other countries? The single most powerful explanation is economic growth differentials. Between 1980 and 1997 Swiss GDP grew at an average annual rate of 1.46 per cent against 2.50 per cent for the OECD as a whole. Had Swiss GDP grown in line with the average, social spending now would also be in the average. The second explanation refers to the increase in unemployment that took place in the 1990s and resulted in additional spending on unemployment compensation and active labour market policies. Population ageing has also contributed to increases in pension and health care expenditure. Taken together, demographic ageing, lower economic growth, and increased spending on unemployment insurance explain nearly all the change in Swiss social expenditure relative to the OECD average.

Higher spending on social protection in the 1990s was thus not the result of expansion, adaptation or modernisation. The costly welfare state that Switzerland has today provides essentially the same coverage as in the early 1980s. It is an old welfare state, in the sense that even if a big spender, Switzerland focuses its efforts on characteristic old risks, above all old age. The position of Switzerland as a high welfare spender among OECD countries is essentially due to old age and disability pensions and health care. In all other areas of welfare Switzerland remains a laggard, in particular so far as services are concerned and in the field of family policy. The country's performance in family services, for instance, is dismal, with spending equal to a fifth of other OECD countries. Switzerland has an expansive but old welfare state.

Several reasons can be invoked to account for the uneven development of the Swiss welfare state. First, Switzerland has been largely spared by many of the side-effects of post-industrialisation. Unemployment was virtually non-existent until the early 1990s, and even afterwards remained low by European standards. Job creation in the service sector was possible without the sort of sharp increases in income inequalities seen in the English-speaking countries (Bonoli and Mach, 2001). Women, if they are abandoning the traditional role of unpaid care-providers, tend to be employed on

---

[1] Excluding the Czech Republic, Korea, Mexico, Slovakia, and Turkey.

a part-time basis and continue to carry out the bulk of domestic work. Thanks to part-time employment and to a low degree of geographical mobility, families tend to rely on informal care for their children, provided mostly by grandparents. According to a recent survey, 51 per cent of households with young children who need child care rely on the grandparents (Buhmann, 2001).

Second, the scope for new risk policies has been limited by the principle of subsidiarity, which is applied forcefully in the field of family policy. There is a relatively widespread view, especially in the German-speaking part of the country, according to which the state should not intervene in family affairs. If it has to, then family policy is preferably dealt with by the municipalities and by the cantons, but certainly not by the federal government. This perception of the relationship between the state and the family has resulted in referendum votes that have literally split the country into two parts along the language divide, with French and Italian speakers favouring a stronger family policy and German speakers opposing it.

Third, policy-making in Switzerland is slow. Political institutions like federalism and referendums have delayed the adoption of social legislation by several decades in the past (Obinger, 1998). Since these institutions have not changed, we can expect the current adaptation process to take just as long.

In the meanwhile, demands for improved protection against new risks are strong and growing, and concern above all the reconciliation of work and family life, protection against the risk of being a low-paid worker and access to full social security coverage for part-time workers, most of whom are women.

With regard to *reconciling work and family life* one can identify two areas where demands are particularly strong: the introduction of paid maternity leave and improvement in the supply of child care services. Current federal legislation includes a right for all women in employment to unpaid maternity leave of eight weeks. Depending on the duration of employment, employers may be expected to continue paying the salary for part or all of the period (or to insure their employees privately). In addition, many collective agreements include more generous maternity leave provision. A few cantons offer means-tested maternity benefits (tested against household income and assets) and one, Geneva, has a fully fledged maternity insurance scheme in place since 2000. Given the existence of very fragmented provision in the field, it is extremely difficult to assess the extent of real demand in this respect. However, it is fair to say that the best protected women are those who enjoyed stable working conditions prior to maternity, those working in economic sectors with encompassing collective agreements, and those working in the public sector, where such provision is generally the most generous. In contrast, women who have been in casual employment or who have changed jobs frequently and work in sectors where collective agreements are not widespread (which is often the case in the low skill service sector) are unlikely to be protected against the risk of maternity.

Demands are probably stronger in relation to child care, as the shortage of supply affects virtually all social groups. Although there is no available data on the current number of child care places, there is widespread agreement on the fact that these are insufficient. Some estimates have put the gap in the number of child care places at 200,000 for the whole country (Ballestri, 2002: 14). Survey data have shown that lack of child care facilities is a major obstacle to employment for mothers of young children. Some 30 per cent of non-employed mothers of children aged less than fifteen say they would take up work if a solution to their child care problem could be found (Buhmann, 2001). Judging from the extent to which the issue of child care is taken up by the press and in public debates in general, one can argue that expectations and demands in this field are substantial. However, this is a relatively recent phenomenon.

The issue of *working poverty* has also been on the social policy agenda for a few years. This was largely the result of several studies which in the late 1990s showed that the number of households with at least one person employed and a disposable income lower than the social assistance benefit had increased (Caritas, 1998; Flückiger, 2001; Knöpfel, 2001; Streuli and Bauer, 2001). In 1999, some 250,000 households (7.5 per cent of the total) belonged to this category. The prevalence of the working poor is particularly strong among single parents (29 per cent), families with three children or more (18 per cent), and households where the main income comes from a part-time job (29 per cent) (Streuli and Bauer, 2001).

Changes in the labour market have also affected the ability of current workers to build up *adequate pension security rights* by the time they reach retirement age. Under current legislation, occupational pension coverage is compulsory only for employees earning more than approximately 40 per cent of average earnings per annum, a threshold that is generally exceeded by full-time workers, but not so often by part-timers. The exact number of workers that are not covered by occupational pensions is not known. In fact, those who are not compulsorily insured may still be included in pension funds on a voluntary basis. Yves Flückiger, a leading labour economist, estimates at 270,000 (or 7.1 per cent of the employed population) the number of workers who may not be covered by an occupational pension because of earnings below the lower earnings limits. Of these, 82 per cent are women (Flückiger, 1999, data for 1996).

Since pension rights are built up over the entire working life of a person, the situation at any one time is not so important. What matters instead is the duration of periods in which pension rights are not acquired. A simulation study of current typical career profiles has shown that if the Swiss pension system is likely to continue to secure good retirement conditions for the majority of current workers, individuals hit by more than one risk are unlikely to obtain pension benefits higher than the means-tested pension. Divorced women and self-employed people with low lifetime earnings are especially affected (Bonoli and Gay-des-Combes, 2003). While it is difficult to assess the true extent of the problem, the available evidence seem to have been sufficient to generate enough public concern over the issue of pension rights for part-time workers for it to be taken up in a recent reform (see below).

Strikingly, the problem of dependency in old age seems absent from political debates. According to one senior civil servant interviewed in the context of the WRAMSOC project, the absence of debate simply means that the system 'works well'. A closer analysis, however, suggests that a more likely explanation is the high degree of fragmentation in this field of social policy, where responsibility is shared between the federal government, the cantons, private health insurers and care providers. Extreme fragmentation makes it impossible to identify actors accountable for situations that may be seen as problematic. For instance, health insurance funds must now finance a considerable proportion of expenditure on long-term care (in theory all the medical aspects). This function of health insurance funds has contributed to the recent dramatic and unpopular increases in health insurance premiums, but in public debate the two developments remain unconnected. In the public domain, old age dependency seems to be subsumed under the wider theme of spiralling health care costs.

These trends in the fields of reconciling work and family life, working poverty and pension rights for atypical worker are relatively new developments that have been picked up in mainstream political debates only very recently. They have not yet resulted in any significant change in the overall orientation of the Swiss welfare state, which, as argued above, remains a predominantly old risk welfare state. However, as will be shown below, some of these emerging new pressures and demands have made it into the social policy-making arena, and have been translated into actual policy proposal. Before turning to the policy impact of social change, however, the key features of the policy-making process in Switzerland, which in international comparisons is unusual in many respects, must be taken into account.

Policy-Making in a Fragmented Political System

In order to understand policy-making in Switzerland, one needs to be aware of the peculiar set of political institutions and the established procedures and routines that are generally followed in the process. Most important is the fact that the Swiss political system is structured by a set of institutions that reduce the potential for power concentration and encourage the formation of large coalitions. The constitutional order is geared towards limiting the power of the federal government, and includes a number of points at which its authority can be challenged and its decisions overruled. The result is a political system in which the extent of agreement needed to legislate is particularly large. The federal government is unable to impose policy, but must negotiate with the parties that are represented in parliament but also with external interests. Often, policy decisions taken by parliament are very different from the government's initial plans. Rather than the ultimate holder of political power, the Swiss federal government is best seen as one actor among the many that intervene in policy-making.

There are at least three institutional features in the Swiss political system that contribute to reduce the level of power concentration available to the government: de facto separation of powers between the executive and the legislative branches of government; federalism with minority representation at the parliamentary level and a referendum system.

The relationship between the Swiss government (Federal Council) and parliament has been described as a hybrid between European parliamentarism and US separation-of-powers (Lijphart, 1984). As in parliamentary regimes, the Federal Council is elected by parliament, however, as in a separation-of-powers system, it cannot be brought down by the legislature during its four-year term. Parliamentarians are not under the same pressure to support government sponsored legislation as is the case in parliamentary systems. Conversely the Federal Council cannot dissolve parliament. The result is a system in which the government has relatively little control over parliament. As in the United States, it must negotiate policy with the legislature, since it cannot impose its will.

The second element of power fragmentation is federalism, and the representation of the member states (Cantons) in the upper chamber of parliament. Swiss bicameralism, designed after the US model, is symmetric, and while in the lower chamber (National Council) territorial representation is proportional to the size of the population, in the upper chamber (Council of States) each Canton is entitled to two representatives. The power of the numerous, but small, rural cantons is thus magnified. In addition, the upper chamber has a party composition that is much more favourable to conservative parties. As a result, it is not unusual that the two chambers vote differently on the same issue. Under such circumstances, a compromise that is supported by a majority of each chamber needs to be found.

Third, and perhaps most notably, Switzerland has a referendum system which allows voters to bring various issues to the polls.[2] In particular, every piece of legislation voted by parliament can be subjected to a national referendum. As a result, successful policy-making requires a large consensus, otherwise decisions taken by parliament can be disowned by voters. In fact, the government, in order to reduce the vulnerability of its bills to challenges from referendums, has adopted an inclusive policy-making strategy. By allowing the relevant actors to co-draft legislation, policy-makers have been able to defuse the threat-potential of referendums, and build what has become known as one of the most paradigmatic cases of consensus or consociational democracy (Lijphart, 1984; Lehmbruch, 1993).

One of the most significant features of Swiss consociational democracy is an oversized coalition government. The Federal Council, which has had the same party composition since 1959, consists of a four-party coalition that includes the Christian-Democrats, the Social Democrats, the Free Democrats, and the Swiss People's Party (ex-farmers' party). Together, these parties account for some 80 per cent of the seats of the lower chamber of parliament, and a government could rule with the support of any three of these four parties. Because Federal Councillors are elected individually, they need the votes of other parties, and in this respect they tend to be selected among the more moderate individuals in each camp. This facilitates the consensual character of the government's operations, but reduces its control over parliament and over the electorate in referendums.

---

[2] The Swiss constitution makes provision for various types of referendums. Constitutional change as well as accession to a supranational organisation is automatically subjected to a referendum. Constitutional change can also be put forward by voters by means of a 'popular initiative', if they are able to back their proposal with 100,000 signatures. For these referendums to succeed, the double majority of voters and Cantons is required. Voters can also challenge at the polls any act passed by parliament, if they are able to produce 50,000 signatures to that effect. In this case, a simple majority of voters is sufficient for the referendum to succeed (see Kobach, 1993 for a comprehensive account).

Overall, its influence on policy-making is not comparable to that of governments in parliamentary systems.

A second important consociational practice is a policy-making process in which interest groups play a substantial role in the definition of policy (Papadopoulos, 1997). Typically, legislative change is preceded by a lengthy and highly structured consultation procedure, which can be more or less encompassing depending on the potential for controversy of the relevant policy. Legislation is often drafted by 'expert commissions' which typically include representatives of all the relevant interest groups. The outcome of expert commissions is usually a compromise which is acceptable to all parties concerned, as each group has a de facto veto power which it can exert by threatening to use the referendum challenge. During the golden age of the consensus model (1950s and 1960s) the agreements reached in this way were generally accepted by parliament with very little change, thanks also to the existence of an informal core of policy-makers where most decisions were made (Kriesi, 1982, 1995). In more recent years, as will be seen below, parliament has become increasingly reluctant to ratify agreements reached by interest groups and, on various occasions, has imposed changes in a majoritarian way.

Providing Coverage Against New Risks

This section provides narrative accounts of reform in five policy fields that are related to new social risks: the adaptation of the basic pension to women's career profiles, the inclusion of part-time workers in occupational pension schemes, the strengthening of ALMP, maternity insurance, and subsidised child care. In all these fields attempts to introduce new legislation have been made, but they have not always been successful. The analysis of policy-making in these instances highlights the mechanisms and the strategies that are conducive to successful adaptation. The other major areas identified as relevant to the emergence of new social risks, like the problem of the working poor, dependency in old age or the fact of being covered by inadequate private provision, have not (yet?) resulted in policy-making. The debate on the working poor problem is quite prominent and several proposals have been floated by the relevant actors. The unions, for example, campaign for a national minimum wage, Caritas for more generous family benefits, but none of these has been picked up in the official channels of policy-making. As highlighted above, dependency in old age and even more so the inadequacy of private provision for some groups do not occupy significant space in public debates.

Adapting Pensions to New Career Profiles

If generous, the Swiss pension system until the late 1980s was clearly targeted on standard employment patterns. The target replacement rate of 60 per cent of gross earnings was easily achieved by core workers who had spent the totality of their working age in employment, but was out of reach for those whose careers had been punctuated by unpaid activities or characterised by long spells of part-time employment. The most disadvantaged were of course women, who were (and still are) much more likely to follow these 'atypical' career patterns.

The adaptation of the pension system to the new career profiles has been pursued in two distinct reforms: the 1995 reform of the basic pension scheme, which successfully passed into law and greatly enhances pension coverage for low income parents and most married women; and the reform of the law on occupational pensions, which provision that extends compulsory occupational pension coverage to more part-time and low income workers.

Adapting the Basic Pension to Women's Career Profiles (1995 Reform)

The origins of the 1995 pension reform go back to 1979, when, as a result of the adoption of a constitutional article on gender equality, it was decided that gender based provision in the basic pension, for example, with reference to how couple pensions are calculated, needed to be done away with (Bonoli, 2000). Progress with this reform, however, was slow, and it was not before 1990 that a bill was produced by the government. The key element of the bill was the introduction of gender equality, but without abandoning couple pensions. The bill made provision for the removal of any reference to gender in the pension formula, but did not take any proactive action in favour of women (such as contribution credits or sharing between spouses) as was advocated by various actors.

Because it kept couple pensions in place, the 1990 pension reform bill was seen by many with disappointment, especially by women's organisations and by women MPs in the Social Democratic and Free Democratic parties. Within the Social Security Commission of the lower house of parliament, a consensus emerged on a radical modification of the bill, so as to adopt a more progressive stance in taking into account the position of women in the labour market. By 1993 the bill had been significantly modified by parliament. It now envisaged the introduction of a contribution-sharing system between spouses and contribution credits for informal carers. Together with these measures on which there was a relatively strong consensus, the new version of the bill included also the more controversial measure of raising retirement age for women from sixty-two to sixty-four. For men retirement age is set at sixty-five. This was imposed by the right-of-centre parliamentary majority, against the Social Democrats, allegedly in order to comply with the constitutional requirement of gender equality[3] but also to achieve some savings in view of the predicted worsening of the ratio between pension scheme contributors and beneficiaries over the next few decades.

Outside parliament, the trade unions and some women's organisations attacked the bill by collecting the 50,000 signatures needed in order to call a referendum. Even though they strongly supported contribution sharing and contribution credits for carers, they could not accept the increase in retirement age for women. The move was successful and the referendum on the pension bill was held in June 1995. The bill was accepted by 60.7 per cent of voters and as a result it became law.

Survey data suggest that the success of the bill at the polls was to a large extent due to the fact that it combined expansion measures (contribution credits) with an element of retrenchment (the increase in retirement age for women). Each measure was able to attract the support of different political camps, which dramatically increased the proportion of the electorate likely to vote in favour. It is fair to say that each one of the two measures, if adopted independently from the other one, would have been at a considerably higher risk of defeat at the polls. On this occasion, the improved coverage against a new social risk, that of being insufficiently covered by post-war welfare arrangement, was made possible but at the expense of an important concession: the acceptance of the increase in retirement age for women. Seemingly, the parliamentary coalition that supported the move, and in particular the Social Democratic party, cared more about younger women, who are the winners of the reform and can be seen as new risk bearers, than about older women in employment (who now have to wait two extra years before reaching retirement age). In contrast, the unions, assessed the same situation in opposite terms.

---

[3] Even though Switzerland does have a written Constitution, there is no Constitutional court which has the task to interpret or enforce it. In practice, the Constitution is interpreted by the government's own legal services. On the issue of women's retirement age, the government view was that the constitutional gender equality requirement was not to be applied until labour market equality would be achieved.

Extending Occupational Pension Coverage to Low Paid Part-Time Workers

The reform of the occupational pension law, started in the late 1990s, had initially several objectives. Above all, it intended to adapt occupational pensions to demographic change. Even though occupational pensions in Switzerland are generally fully funded, an increase in life expectancy means that more funds need to be accumulated to pay the same benefit. The law prescribes minimum contribution levels, a minimum interest rate and a minimum conversion rate that must be applied when, at age sixty-five, the accumulated capital is converted into a pension. Because of increases in life expectancy, the parameters that had been set in the early 1980s needed to be changed. The government's intention was to reduce the conversion rate to reflect the impact of longer lives on pension costs, and to compensate this through an increase in contribution rates, so that the overall impact of the reform would be neutral for pensioners, the current target rate of a 60 per cent replacement rate being maintained (Bonoli, 2001; Hausermann, 2002).

In the initial stages of the reform, the government intended also to improve coverage for low wage (mostly part-time) workers, as anyone whose earnings are below about 40 per cent of the average wage are not compulsorily affiliated to a pension fund. At the time, the Social Democrats and the trade unions were supporting the abolition or the reduction of the lower limit for the compulsory affiliation to a pension fund. Unsurprisingly, this measure was strongly opposed by employers, on the grounds that it would generate unreasonable administrative costs, especially in relation to casual, temporary employment, and inhibit job creation for low-skilled workers. Faced with such lack of agreement the government decided not to take up the issue in the occupational pension law reform bill, that was presented in parliament in early 2000.

Because it failed to address the issue of occupational pension coverage for low paid and part-time workers, the reform was criticised by the left and the unions. The bill was initially discussed in the Social Security Commission of the lower house of parliament. It is a commission that has become known for having a pro-welfare orientation, and does not really reflect the balance of power that one finds in parliament on social policy issues. Its right-of-centre members tend to come from the 'social' wings of the respective parties, and are not always representative of them (Hausermann, 2002: 28). The result was that the commission transformed the bill presented by the government, halving the access threshold to occupational pension coverage. The bill was discussed in the lower house of parliament in Spring 2002. Even though the commission's proposal was unable to obtain the support of a majority, an agreement was found on a compromise: instead of halving the threshold, this was reduced by a quarter (to approx. CHF18,000 per annum). The measure was accepted narrowly and the main employers' associations publicly condemned the decision (*Le Temps* 16 April 2002).

The bill was then transferred to the upper chamber, which because of a different election method has a more conservative orientation, and is more responsive to employers' demands. In November 2002 a majority of the chamber's members voted against the compromise that had been put together in the National Council, and went back to the initial proposal contained in the 2000 government bill. In the end, an agreement was found thanks to a conciliation committee comprising members of both the Council of States and of the National Council, which introduced a lower access threshold at CHF18,000 per annum. For higher income workers, however, earnings will be insured only above about CHF21,000 per annum. This solution was facilitated by the fact that some influential actors in the pension industry (such as the powerful Association of Pension Funds) made clear that the extra cost due to a reduction in the access threshold were likely to be minimal. This reform is unlikely to be challenged by a referendum.

From Security to Activation in Labour Market Policy

Until the early 1990s Switzerland had been spared by one of the most serious consequences of de-industrialisation: mass unemployment. Unemployment rose rapidly from 0.6 per cent in 1990 to 5.2 per cent by 1997. Although moderate by European standards, this new social and economic problem produced much concern among policy-makers. Against the background of much soul searching and debates about the end of the successful Swiss employment model, the most pressing issue that needed to be dealt with was the adaptation of the unemployment insurance scheme, which had been thought of as a cover against frictional unemployment.

The most immediate problem was scheme finances. As a consequence of rising claimant numbers, the scheme was unable to meet its liabilities and had to borrow funds from the general government budget. In addition, both the left and the right were concerned with features of the legislation in force at the time: the former felt that the funds available for active labour market policy where wholly inadequate, given the change in the labour market conditions; the latter disliked the fact that the law allowed claimants to remain indefinitely in the system as long as they regularly took part in some form of activation measure. These divergent preferences provided the basis for a compromise that came to constitute the core of the 1995 unemployment insurance reform.

The new law was drafted by a joint group of representatives of employers and trade unionists, and accepted by parliament without major changes. As a clear compromise between different conceptions, it included measures going in diverging directions. On the one hand the financial base of the scheme was strengthened and more funds were made available for labour-market programmes, such as vocational training and job creation schemes. On the other hand, a maximum entitlement period of two years was introduced in the law. The contribution rate was raised to 3 per cent (1.5 per cent each for employers and employees), payable on earnings of up to 160 per cent of average salary. An additional, temporary, contribution at one per cent is charged on earnings between 160 per cent and 400 per cent of average salary.

As far as benefits were concerned the entitlement period was fixed at two years. During this period unemployed persons are required to undertake retraining, to take part in a job creation scheme or take up temporary work. Failure to do so can result in sanctions which can lead to a sixty-day benefit suspension period. Cantons are required to set up and run active labour market policies, but 85 per cent of the costs are met by the unemployment insurance scheme. Altogether, the new law was expected to result in the creation of approximately 25,000, new places in active labour market policies. The new law also strengthened work test requirements for claimants. Unemployed persons must agree to take up an 'adequate job offer', which is defined in terms of salary (at least equal to benefit level), of distance (2 h travel time per day is regarded as acceptable) and of compatibility with the skills of the recipient. What is more, during the two-year entitlement period, an unemployed person may be required to take up a job with a salary lower than his or her benefit, the difference being compensated by the unemployment insurance scheme (Giriens and Stauffer, 1999).

The compromise reached in the 1995 unemployment insurance reform achieved three goals. First it solved the financial problems of the scheme. Second, as requested by the left, it made substantially more funds for active labour market policies. Third, in compliance with employer's demands, it introduced a two-year limit on the entitlement period. This was not challenged by referendum, which is extremely unusual for an important social policy reform. Its strength stemmed from the fact that it resulted from a political deal struck between employers and the unions, which was found to be acceptable by parliament and government. The unions clearly traded their support for the law against the inclusion of funds earmarked for ALMP. They also had to renounce the security that is guaranteed by a system that allows unemployed people to receive a relatively generous unemployment benefit indefinitely. The impression here is that the unions regarded the need of young, low-skilled unemployed people (those who can benefit most from ALMP), as more important than those of older unemployed workers for whom the security guaranteed by an unlimited entitlement period was certainly more important than access to ALMP.

Helping Parents Reconcile Work and Family Life

Maternity Insurance

The most significant event in this field in the 1990s has certainly been the failed attempt by the government to introduce a maternity insurance scheme. The federal constitution gave the federal government the power to introduce a maternity insurance scheme in 1945, but so far the scheme has not been implemented. After a series of failed referendum initiatives in the 1980s, most of which were sponsored by the left, the government finally put forward a proposal consisting of an insurance benefit replacing 100 per cent of earnings for sixteen weeks, with a ceiling of three times the maximum AVS-AHV benefit (then CHF70,560 per annum) in 1994. Financing was to come from a new contribution, equal to 0.4 per cent of total earnings, calculated according to the same rule used for the AHV-AVS pension scheme (i.e. equally split between employer and employee). Expenditure was estimated at CHF660 million per year (Jaggi, 1994: 181–2).

The proposal was subjected to a consultation procedure, as is usual for complex and potentially controversial legislation, like a new social insurance scheme. From a very early stage, the proposal was criticised because it provided benefits only to employed women and not to those who spend their entire time caring for their children. This point was made most forcefully by the Christian-Democrats (PDC-CVP). As a result of the view expressed in the consultation procedure, the proposal was slightly modified, and turned into a bill, which was presented to parliament on 25 June 1997. The Maternity Insurance bill included the following provisions:

–A 14-week paid leave, at 80 per cent of previous earnings, with a ceiling at
  97,200 CHF per annum (it is the same ceiling used for the 'accidents

insurance' scheme, and slightly higher than the ceiling adopted in the previous proposal).

–A basic benefit (*prestation de base*), consisting of a one-off payment for all women whether in paid work or not. The benefit was to be means-tested, with the base amount equivalent to four times the existing minimum monthly AVS-AHV (at the time, CHF3,980). Entitlement expired at six times the minimum level.

–Financing was to come from an increase in social contributions of 0.2 percentage point. It is a lower rate than the one put forward in the previous proposal. Because of the reduction in the generosity of the scheme and new calculations, it was deemed sufficient to cover costs and generate a slight surplus. Social contributions were earmarked for the financing of earnings-replacement benefits; basic benefits were to be directly financed from federal tax revenues. The total costs of the new scheme were estimated at CHF493 million (Jaggi, 1997: 182–7).

Notwithstanding extensive prior consultation, the bill was met with substantial criticism by several interest groups and political parties. The strongest opposition came from employers and the UDC-SVP party. Soon after the presentation of the bill in parliament, the director of the main employers' organisation declared that '. . . an increase in labour costs will slow down the economic recovery we so badly need. Employers will accept no compromise' (Hasler, quoted in Jaggi 1994). Criticism focused on the financing method chosen (an increase in social insurance contribution rates) rather than on the idea of a maternity insurance scheme, on which there seemed to be a general agreement. An opinion poll carried out just after the publication of the bill, revealed that a strong majority of the public was in favour of the proposal (69 per cent), though support was considerably stronger in the French speaking part of the country (83 per cent) than among German speakers (64 per cent) (*Sonntagsblick*, 29 June 1997).

The bill was discussed in parliament in 1998, and an amended version adopted on 18 December 1998. It consisted of all the elements included in the original bill as far as benefits were concerned, but modified the financing method. Rather than increasing social contributions, financing was to come from another compulsory insurance programme, which provides earnings replacement to those serving in the country's militia army, and which has been generating surpluses for the last few years. This programme was to become a military service and maternity insurance scheme. If funds turned out to be insufficient, then additional finance could be brought to the scheme either through an increase in the VAT rate, or by raising the contribution rate of the new military/maternity scheme, currently at 0.3 per cent of earnings, up to 0.5 per cent (Jaggi, 1999: 34).

The version of the bill adopted by parliament seemed to have taken into account the sharper criticism made in relation to the financing method that had been chosen by the government. If employers could not agree on an increase in social contribution, there was now the possibility to make use of VAT.

In spite of the changes made, soon after the adoption, a committee against the scheme is founded. It consisted of German speaking representatives of the FDP-PRD and SVP-UDC parties, and of employers. Most politicians directly involved in the committee were women (*NZZ*, 7 January 1999). The main argument put forward by opponents was the extra cost for the public purse, in spite of the revised financing method (*NZZ*, 18 January 1999). In a few months, the committee was able to organise the collection of the 50,000 signatures needed to call a referendum against the proposal, and the vote took place on 13 June 1999.

At the polls the proposal was clearly rejected, by 61 per cent of voters. The vote was split according to three main cleavages: the left-right axis (left-wing voters being considerably more likely to accept the proposal); age, those aged 40+ being more likely to reject the proposal, and language, French and Italian speakers being more likely to vote 'yes'. Among the reasons given by voters who rejected the proposal as to why they chose to do so, a majority (71 per cent) argued that the scheme was not needed because provision in this field existed already; 60 per cent thought that the country could not afford the new scheme, and 20 per cent based their decision on the claim that the new scheme was going to benefit mostly foreigners (Kriesi et al., 1999).

After the negative referendum vote, the government started working on a new project for paid maternity leave, this time in the shape of maternity pay imposed upon employers for a period of 8–12 weeks. This proposal was floated in a consultation procedure to receive strong opposition from employers, especially small ones who would have had to bear the full cost of maternity leave. A counter-proposal came precisely from the leader of the Swiss small business peak organisation (USAM-SGV), Pierre Triponez, who is also a member of the National Council for the Free Democrats, in the shape of a private member's bill (*initiative parlementaire*). His suggestion was to go back to the idea of a maternity insurance scheme, providing only earnings replacement to working women, but no coverage for those who are not involved in paid employment, and introduce a fourteen-week paid leave, the benefit replacing 80 per cent of earnings (Martin, 2002). The proposal was accepted by a majority of his fellow parliamentarians with very little change in June 2003. Shortly afterwards the right-wing populist party SVP-UDC made known its intention to challenge the law in a referendum. It collected the required 50,000 signatures and a national vote will take place in 2004 or 2005.

Federal Subsidies for Day Care Centres[4]

Like the Triponez model for maternity insurance, this initiative did not originate from the government, but from an MP, the Social Democrat Jacqueline Fehr, in the shape of a private member's bill. Such initiatives rarely lead to legislation, but on this occasion a rather unusual set of circumstances provided an extremely favourable context for the proposal. About a year after the private member's bill was presented in parliament, the main employers' association, *Union Patronale Suisse*, published a report which claimed that bottlenecks due to labour shortage were to be expected in future years, as a result of demographic and economic trends.

The report went on to argue that women constituted the ideal labour reservoir to solve this problem. This, however, required considerably more widespread availability of child care facilities. Crucially, the report also said that even though the increase in child care places had to come about as a result of private initiatives, the state had a role to play as well (Ballestri, 2002: 38–40).

During the past few years, Swiss employers had consistently opposed every proposal for welfare expansion, publicly declaring that the country needed a social moratorium. The change of direction, if moderate and very limited in its scope, was nonetheless significant. Ms Fehr's private member's bill was discussed in parliament shortly after the publication of the employers' association report, and fully benefited from its support. The bill which made available CHF100 million subsidies per year for new or expanding day care centres over a four-year period, was voted by the lower chamber in Spring 2001, with the full support of the Social Democrats and the Christian Democrats, and with a significant number of votes of the Free Democrats. Only the right-wing populist Swiss Peoples Party opposed the bill. The support that the bill obtained from the right-of-centre parties can be explained with reference to the employers' association reports, which had de facto turned a family policy and gender equality issue into a problem for the national economy.

---

[4] This account of the policy-making process that led to the adoption of the law on subsidies to child care centres is largely based on the work of Ballestri (2002).

The bill was then transferred to the upper chamber of parliament, where it was also put to the vote, but in a less generous version: subsidies were to total CHF50 million. The bill returned to the lower chamber which voted in its new, less generous version. The bill was not challenged by referendum and is now law. The political significance of this decision goes beyond the mere sums involved. It was supported by the centre-right parties (except the right-wing populist UDC-SVP) and by employers: two actors that in the past had been at the forefront of opposing state intervention (and spending) on matters relating to the family. The early years of the twenty-first century seem to coincide with a change in employers' orientation to family policy. Presumably because of a tight labour market, and of the political problems in getting the authorities and a significant group in the population to accept a higher level of immigration, employers are clearly turning to women as a growing source of skilled labour during the next decades.

Discussion

The preceding sections provide an overview of policy-making in the provision of coverage against new social risks in five fields: adaptation of the basic pension to women's career profiles, inclusion of part-time workers in occupational pensions, the provision of active labour market policies to the unemployed, the introduction of a maternity insurance scheme and the provision of subsidies to day care centres. These five reforms share a striking feature: none of them has been adopted following the standard policy-making procedure that is described in political science textbooks, based on structured consultation procedures, expert commissions, and the like. Some of these reforms have been initiated with these standard measures, but the inclusion of measures that provide coverage against new risks has generally happened in parliament. The only exception is the 1997 maternity insurance bill, which, however, was rejected in a referendum.

All instances of successful or partially successful new risk coverage reforms have been initiated by parliament. In the 1995 pension reform and in the occupational pensions law reform, this came as a result of an initiative taken within the Social Security Commission of the national council. The same happened in the case of the 1995 unemployment insurance reform. Even though it was based on a deal between employers and the unions, the agreement was not reached in one of the standard loci of consensus building (such as an expert commission), but in a meeting instigated by the relevant parliamentary committee (Giriens and Stauffer, 1999: 117). Even more unusual are the two most recent measures in the field of reconciling work and family life. Both the 'Triponnez' initiative for a maternity insurance scheme and the introduction of federal subsidies for day care centres originated from private members' bills. According to the standard textbook view, private members' bills 'play only a marginal role. They can be used as tools of self-regulation by parliament, but have just an ancillary function, even though in theory they could play a bigger role' (Kriesi, 1995: 175).

The question is thus why is parliament playing such an important role in policy-making in the provision of new social risks? Standard policy-making procedures based on traditional consensus-building practices seem unable to put forward the kind of measures that would improve the lives of new social risks bearers. These measures remain highly contested, they refer to fundamental social changes that are taking place at different speeds among different social groups. They may be regarded as essential by some, but as superfluous and wasteful by others. The contested character of these measures reflect differences in terms of life experiences in relation to new social risks, and are naturally translated into politics. Traditional consensus-based policy-making procedures are unable to cope with highly contested issues.

The pattern of policy success and failure presented above can be explained with reference to the position taken by key political actors on individual instances of policy-making. On all five occasions, the Social Democratic party has consistently and fully supported new risks coverage measures. If there is an actor in the Swiss political system that seems to represent the interests of new social risks bearers it is the Social Democratic party, even distancing itself from the unions in case of conflicts of priorities. This was well illustrated in the 1995 basic pension reform, opposed by the unions and supported by the Social Democrats. Equally consistent, but in the opposite camp is the right-wing populist Swiss People's Party. With the exception of the 1995 pension reform, it has consistently opposed all the new risk coverage measures discussed in this chapter. It has a general anti-welfare and anti-state orientation, but most of its voters tend to be in the older age groups, so that exceptions to this line are visible in pension policy, but not in policies for younger people. The Swiss People's Party has been the most vociferous critic of new risks coverage policies, attacking them also on grounds that they would mostly benefit foreigners, an argument that does have some weight among its constituents (see the section on maternity insurance above).

The two centre-right parties, the Christian-Democrats and the Free Democrats, have adopted a less consistent attitude towards new risks coverage policies. Often, their decisions have made the difference between success and failure of given policy measures. The Christian-Democrats were initially somewhat unsettled by the life choices that led to the emergence of new social risks, especially those related to the family. In the 1995 basic pension reform, they initially expressed concern for a reform that seemed to disadvantage traditional one-earner couples in favour of those with two incomes. In the end this was not the case, and the party supported the reform. The adaptation measures, however, were adopted at the instigation of Social Democratic and Free Democratic members of parliament. In the 1997 maternity insurance bill, the Christian-Democrats demanded the inclusion of a benefit for mothers that are not involved in paid employment for essentially ideological reasons. More recently, however, possibly also as part of an attempt to stop a decade-long process of electoral decline, the party has decided to put the family at the centre of its policy (Ballestri, 2002). As a result, in the more recent instances of policy-making, it has sided with the Social Democrats in supporting new risk coverage policies (as in the introduction of federal subsidies to day care centres).

The Free Democrats have also had a changing position and have often been divided on specific issues. The party contains a dominant pro-business wing, but there are a few 'social modernisers' within it, mostly women, who have sometimes played a very active role in defending the new social pol-icies. When, as in the case of subsidies for day care centres, the measures were also endorsed by employers, the majority of the party supported them. Otherwise, it has tended to be split.

The unions have a less clear-cut position on new risks. They supported most of the measures discussed here, but when policy conflicted with the protection of people exposed to old social risks, they tended to defend the latter. The exception here is the unemployment insurance 1995 reform where the political deal involved losses for older workers (most likely to be long-term unemployed) and gains for younger unemployed (most likely to benefit from ALMP). In the 1995 pension reform, the interest of older women in employment, many of whom probably live in low income households, prevailed over that of younger female workers. The unions were also virtually absent from the debate on subsidies for child care facilities. Concerns about the impact of higher women's employment on wages may have been the reason (Ballestri, 2002).

Finally, employers have had to deal with two conflicting priorities. The first, possibly most important, is to prevent further expansion of the welfare state. Employers are concerned with the increase of public expenditure that has taken place over the years, and their instinctive response to expansion initiatives is rejection. The second priority is to have a social protection system that contributes to an efficient functioning of the labour market, which can explain their support for measures like active labour market policies and child care subsidies. The fact that some leaders of employer organisations are also members of parliament may constitute an additional pressure on them to favour new risk policies that are particularly popular. If these figures represent the business community, in order to be re-elected they may also need the votes of women and younger voters.

Conclusion

The successful adaptation of welfare states to new social risks is a politically difficult process everywhere. In Switzerland, because of its fragmented political system, success seems to depend very much on the ability to strike compromises among the key actors involved in policy-making. In the absence of this level of encompassing support, policy proposals are at high risk of defeat first in parliament and then with the electorate, as it is always possible for opponents to new legislation to challenge it with a referendum. In the past, during the golden age of the Swiss consensus model of politics, referendum-proof compromises were easily achieved, thanks to various consensus-building mechanisms. Since the early 1990s, however, politics has moved in the direction of polarisation, with the two parties at the extremes of the ruling coalition gaining ground at the expense of the more centrist parties. As a result, compromises seem more difficult to achieve. In the 1990s, on several occasions, a successful policy-making strategy has been what could be described as a 'modernising compromise', a reform package containing both elements of retrenchment in relation to 'old risks' and elements of expansion in relation to 'new risks'. Such compromises are well suited to the new, polarised, political climate. Actors do not agree thanks to reciprocal moderation or convergence of interest, but because their own priorities are included (at least to some extent) in the package.

Such modernising compromises may offer the best way forward in the adaptation of the Swiss welfare state to new risk structures. They seem the only viable option given existing institutional constraints. At the same time, modernising compromises are not always possible. In some of the reforms that are currently being debated in parliament they certainly seem far away. This may be due to a tightening of economic conditions (even though unemployment is lower in the early 2000s than it was in the 1990s), but more likely to an even stronger polarisation in politics which makes it difficult to develop the sort of reform packages, internally inconsistent but capable of generating support, that had been successful in the past.

References

Ballestri, Y. (2002) *Le nuove politiche sociali in Svizzera*, dissertation, Institute of Political Science, University of Berne, Berne.

Bonoli, G. (2000) *The Politics of Pension Reform. Institutions and Policy Change in Western Europe*, Cambridge University Press, Cambridge.

—— (2001) 'Mandating Pensions: The Swiss Experience' Paper presented at the Conference 'The Political Economy of Pension Reform', Institute for Advanced Studies, Delmenhorst-Bremen, 3–5 May.

—— and Gay-des-Combes, B. (2003) *L'avenir de long terme de l'AVS : une simulation à l'horizon 2040*, Federal Office of Social Insurance, Berne, Research Report.

—— and Mach, A. (2001) 'The New Swiss Employment Puzzle', *Revue suisse de science politique*, 7(2): 81–96.

Buhmann, B. (2001) 'Faits et chiffres sur la prise en charge externe des enfants', *Questions au féminin*, 2.2001, 1–4.

Caritas (1998) *Les working poor en Suisse: ils sont pauvres, et pourtant ils travaillent*, Editions Caritas, Lucerne.

Flückiger, Y. (1999) *Inégalité, bas salaires et working poor en Suisse*, Unpublished Manuscript, University of Geneva.

—— (2001) 'Bas salaires: reconnaître le problème pour y apporter une solution', *Sécurité sociale*, 3: 118–19.

Giriens, P.-Y. and Stauffer, N. (1999) 'Deuxième révision de la loi sur l'assurance-chômage: genèse d'un compromis', in MACH, *André Globalisation, néo-libéralisme et politiques publiques dans la Suisse des années 1990, Editions Seismo, Zurich*.

Hausermann, S. (2002) *La première révision de la LPP*, Unpublished Manuscript, IDHEAP, Lausanne.

Jaggi, M. (1994) 'Un avant projet pour une assurance maternité. Enfin!', *Sécurité Sociale*, 4: 181–3.

—— (1997) 'Pas essentiel sur le long chemin menant à l'assurance maternité: le Conseil fédéral a approuvé le projet de loi et le message', *Sécurité Sociale*, 4: 182–7.

—— (1999) 'La nouvelle loi fédérale sur l'assurance maternité: une étape importante de la politique familiale suisse', *Sécurité Sociale*, 1: 32–9.

Knöpfel, C. (2001) 'Le problème des working poor en Suisse: le point de vue de Caritas', *Sécurité Sociale*, 3: 132–3.

Kobach, K. (1993) *The Referendum. Direct Democracy in Switzerland*, Aldershot, Dartmouth.

Kriesi, H. (1982) 'The structure of the Swiss political system', in G. Lehmbruch and P. Schmitter (eds.), *Patterns of Corporatist Policy Making*. Sage, London, 133–62.

Kriesi, H. (1995) *Le système politique suisse*, Economica, Paris.

—— (1999) 'Note on the Size of Public Sector in Switzerland', *Swiss Political Science Review*, 5(2): 105–7.

Kriesi, H., Dubouchet, J., Konishi, M., and Lachat, R. (1999) Analyse des votations fédérales du 13 juin 1999, Bern, Vox Anlayse No 68.

Lane, J.-E. (1999) 'The Public/private Sector Distinction in Switzerland', *Swiss Political Science Review*, 5(2): 94–104.

Lehmbruch, G. (1993) 'Consociational Democracy and Corporatism in Switzerland', *Publius: The Journal of Federalism*, 23: 43–60.

Lijphart, A. (1984) *Democracies. Patterns of Majoritarian and Consensus Government in Twenty-One Countries*, Yale University Press, New Haven.

Martin, N. (2002) *Entre efficence et protection: L'assurance maternité comme politique d'adaptation de l'Etat social suisse aux enjeux contemporains*, Paper Presented at the Annual Meeting of the Swiss Political Science Association, Fribourg, 8 November.

Obinger, H. (1998) 'Federalism, Direct Democracy, and Welfare State Development in Switzerland', *Journal of Public Policy*, 18: 241–63.

Papadopoulos, Y. (1997) *Les processus de décision fédéraux en Suisse*, L'Harmattan, Paris.

Streuli, E. and Bauer, T. (2001) Les working poor en Suisse. Etude de la problématique, de l'ampleur du phénomène et de ses causes, Info:social, No. 5 (April 2001).

8

New Risks at the EU Level; A Spillover from Open Market Policies?

Trine P. Larsen and Peter Taylor-Gooby

Introduction

The European Union has been remarkably successful in developing common economic institutions and policies that transform the context in which national policy-making takes place. It has been much less successful in creating a common framework for European social policy. Most EU social policy-making either follows immediately from EU economic integration and commitments to a fair competitive arena and equal treatment of citizens as workers, or is part of a policy coordination strategy that is much less directive. The policies that result are mainly focused on new rather than old social risks, and are intended to contribute indirectly to economic goals. An important reason for this is that member states face social issues which they are unable to manage at the national level, partly as a result of constraints imposed by EU economic policies. The success of the European Union in establishing a Single European Market spills back into pressure for social policies to deal with emerging new social risks at the European Union level. This chapter considers the development of EU social policy and examines the current focus on new risks in balancing work and family, access to the labour market, and social inclusion within it.

Papers by Anne Daguerre and Andreas Aust contributed to this chapter.
This chapter draws extensively on personal interviews with senior EU officials and representatives of CEEP, ETUC, UNICE, and Members of the European Parliament, carried out in April, May, and June of 2003.

European Union Decision-Making

As a governmental system, the EU may be characterised as multi-tiered, with limited sovereignty and, in most areas, weak legal powers (Leibfried and Pierson, 1995: ch. 2). Commentators draw attention to the 'joint decision trap'—the problem of securing agreement across member states on common policy directions when multiple veto points exist—and the 'democratic deficit' that results from detachment from the lives of most citizens and the lack of direct electoral engagement with them (Scharpf, 1988: 240; Mazcy, 2001: 42). In this context, the success in securing a binding commitment to a common economic framework is the more impressive (Wallace and Wallace, 2000: 86).

The EU policy-making has been understood as being driven by developments at a number of levels: in the external environment, economic change, globalisation, and enhanced competition are important; at the national level, progress is seen to depend on success in negotiating compromise between different national governments; and within the EU, the processes whereby advocacy coalitions and other groupings are formed to support particular policies, facilitated by normative entrepreneurs (Finnemore and Sikkink, 1998; Sabatier, 1998), and influenced by the objectives of the Commission, attract detailed attention. Economic changes pose dilemmas for social policy that are substantial and intractable, as we argued in Chapter 1. In addition, approaches to social policy at the national level vary greatly between different European countries. For these reasons, coalitions of interest in the social policy field are particularly hard to construct. Attempts to develop substantive EU-wide social policies or to harmonise national systems in the 1980s and 1990s have been largely unsuccessful. However, new social risk policies in relation to the mobilisation of the labour force, the opportunities available to women and the fight against social exclusion resulting from economic and social changes have become increasingly prominent on the EU agenda in recent years.

One underlying reason is that pressing social issues confront all EU member states, as we have shown in the preceding chapters. The most important issues concern the cost of pensions, health, and social services for older people, the costs of high levels of unemployment, and the needs occasioned by change in the family (Pierson, 2001: 99). Traditional approaches to these issues might involve higher taxes or social contributions to finance expanded social provision, the use of fiscal policies to increase employment or the use of tariffs and trade policies to protect national industries and create jobs. In a globalised market, such policies may lead to repercussions, in the form of currency instability and a weak trading position. A number of writers and politicians argue that social spending contributes to these problems by increasing labour costs and encouraging dependency (see Scharpf and Schmidt, 2000: ch. 2 for discussion). In addition, the EU's single market policies remove member states' capacity to control national currency (Mayes, 2002: 199). The Growth and Stability Pact makes provision for penalising countries which exceed a three per cent limit in relation to the budgetary deficit, so that spending increases bear directly on electorally unpopular taxes (EC No 1467/97; Scharpf, 2002: 649). The principle of free competition in an open internal market further constrains national governments. The competitive pressures on tax and spending policies and the concern that mobile firms will migrate to the areas with the lowest taxation are intensified (Scharpf, 1999: 40–1).

The EU economic integration thus creates a context in which it is increasingly difficult for member states to manage individually the social pressures that confront them through traditional neo-Keynesian methods. The dilemma is reinforced by the EU's lack of competencies to intervene in the social policy field and to use fiscal instruments, along with member states' reluctance to cede any authority to EU institutions over social policy and industrial relations (Ross, 1995: 358; Mayes, 2002: 203; Mosher and Trubek, 2003: 66). Without intervention at the EU level, member states may be tempted to restructure social policies to retain and attract domestic and foreign capital and business (Scharpf, 1999: 41). Policy actors, who share a concern to retain the European tradition of welfare provision, have turned to the EU to defend their social priorities (Begg and Bergham, 2002: 179).

The area of new social risks, compared with old social risks, offers particular opportunities in this context. New social risk policies can be broadly understood as investment, supporting economic competitiveness by expanding the workforce, rather than as an additional burden of welfare consumption. They thus fit the discourse shift from neo-Keynesian to 'pragmatic monetarist' strategies at the economic level (Chapter 1). Since national governments in most European countries are less concerned with new than old social risks and spend less on them, and the interests of social partners and other organisations are typically less heavily involved, the opportunities to develop new policies are more open. From the EU's point of view, they allow Europe-wide policy-making to engage with needs experienced by ordinary citizens and thus promote the legitimacy of the supra-national tier of government. For these reasons, new risks figure more prominently in the European Union than in national social policy activity. In this chapter we will review the development of EU social policy and the activities in the specific areas of work-life balance, employment, and social exclusion, before going on to assess progress thus far.

European Social Policy

European social policy is largely restricted to areas directly related to the construction of an open market in labour and goods: employment rights, equal opportunities, public health, free movement of labour, working conditions, social dialogue, worker participation, and employment opportunities for young and disabled people. There have also been poverty and social inclusion programmes and provision for action in relation to care for older people (Leibfried and Pierson, 2000: table 10.2; Geyer, 2000: 204–5).

The key development in European policy-making was the initiative to implement the Single European Market. The approaches of the various social actors may be located between two positions: those who understood the project as essentially de-regulatory (the construction of an integrated free market with open competition and minimal state and EU intervention), and those who saw the market as the first step in a process of institution-building at the European level (Young and Wallace, 2000: 92–105; Lintner, 2001: 325–30). The first position was supported by the UK government, parts of the Commission, and business, the second by governments especially in the more corporatist European countries, trade unions, and other groups in the Commission. These groups called for a 'social dimension' to European integration (prefigured, for example, in the Val Duchesse agreements between employers and unions in the 1980s), which would involve minimum standards in social rights to be guaranteed at the European level and the development of a European social dialogue between the social partners.

Compromise between these two positions was achieved through the creation of a charter of social rights at the 1989 Strasbourg summit and a Social Action Programme complementary to the single market, coupled with a doubling of resources for the structural funds (Geyer, 2000: 144). The justification for these policies was not so much the emergence of new social risks as the desire to limit 'social dumping', to shield the national systems from adjustment pressures and to protect the most vulnerable social groups. Most of the Social Action Programme initiatives—directives, recommendations, and action programmes—were directly related to market integration: for example, the broadening of free movement of workers provisions to include further groups, the establishment of European Works Councils or the directive to regulate posted workers. Almost all proposed directives focus on labour market issues, indicating the limits of European legal authority. Traditional welfare state policies were touched only marginally and the recommendations of the Commission on the convergence of social protection aims and the guarantee of minimum benefit levels did not have the legally binding status of the directives.

The British government under Thatcher strongly opposed social legislation at the European level, refused to sign the charter and tried to stop or dilute the directives following from the SAP (Lintner, 2001: 238). The Commission and several governments attempted to change the institutional rules of the Treaty by expanding qualified majority voting in the area of social policy and integrating the European social partners into the decision making process. Since it proved impossible to find agreement, the British government was permitted to 'opt out' of the proposed chapter on social policy, which was annexed to the Maastricht Treaty as a separate protocol applicable only to the other eleven signatories (Falkner, 1998: 78).

The aspirations of the Social Dimension were summed up in the 1993 Green Paper, which linked social policy directly to democratic citizenship (COM 1993a 551: 33–4) and stressed the goal of convergence in social policy (p. 73). However, the employment White Paper of the same year advanced a different set of priorities, promoting monetary stability and an open and decentralised labour market characterised by greater flexibility, with the United States advanced as the example of successful job-creation policies (COM 1993b 700: 12–16). The refusal of the Council in 1994 to accept the Fourth Poverty Programme (funded at more than double the level of previous programmes), instead expanding the previous Third Programme but linking it directly to employment and training, marks the limits of the ambitions for an independent social policy as a major component in the European project (Geyer, 2000: 163). The Amsterdam Treaty in 1997 finally incorporated the full Social Protocol and ended the United Kingdom opt out. In addition, the Treaty introduced the principle of gender mainstreaming which institutionalised the promotion of gender equality as a cross-cutting task for all policy areas (Art. 3II); and explicit reference was made to affirmative action programmes to combat gender discrimination (Art. 141IV); and qualified majority voting (QMV) was extended to the area of social exclusion (Art. 137II). However, there were no new spending commitments, and measures for improving the position of the elderly and of disabled people were dropped from the final text.

The Fourth Social Action Programme (1998–2000) as finally adopted reflects the labour-market orientation of EU social policy: it stresses 'jobs, skills and mobility' and 'the changing world of work', with 'an inclusive society' as the third priority. Later efforts to further expand QMV or the scope of European social policy in the Treaty of Nice in 2000 failed. The European social policy agenda gradually shifted in the 1990s from a strategy which attempted institution-building at the European level to the 'Open Method of Co-ordination' (OMC). EU social policy has followed an uneven path of development and is mainly linked to employment rights, and various related activities concerned with specific programmes on poverty, disability, youth, and women's opportunities in employment.

The 'Open Method of Coordination' as the New Framework in European Social Policy

In response to the 'post-Maastricht crisis' of the mid-1990s, the principle of subsidiarity became increasingly important in EU policy-making. The Commission changed its strategy and stressed its own role as an agent for mutual policy learning (COM 1994 333; Kleinman, 2002: 94–102). The main focus of the new thinking became the creation of employment. In order to achieve a better employment performance a reform of the welfare state and the institutions of the labour market was required (COM 1993*b* 700). In that context, competitive pressures were no longer regarded as a problem but as a tool of modernisation (Blair and Schroeder, 1999). As centre-left governments predominated in the main EU member states in the late 1990s, a new approach to social policy was sought which avoided both the traditional EU approach of European centralised state-building and an uncoordinated neoliberal agenda of competition at the level of welfare regime.

The evolving approach is visible, for example, in reports to the European Union by Ferrera and colleagues (2000) and Esping-Andersen (2002). Both argued that the crisis of the welfare state does not result from liberalisation and market integration so much as social transformations at the national level, the maturing of welfare provision, demographic shifts and changes in family structure (see also Pierson, 2001: 82; Esping-Andersen, 2002: ch. 1). Accordingly, the main task of welfare reform is to 'recalibrate' welfare states to the new risk structures of the post-industrial society. Following current 'modernized' social democratic thinking, these authors called for welfare state reforms that stressed the flexibilisation of labour markets, equal opportunities instead of redistribution of incomes, social inclusion mainly through integration into paid work, and the creation of a 'social investment state' through supportive social provision instead of compensatory transfer benefits.

In this context social policy was no only longer seen in the traditional way as a policy of 'decommodification', protecting people from the pressures of the market (Esping-Andersen, 1990; Polanyi, 1944) but as an element in a supply-side economic policy intended to raise the efficiency of the markets and the productivity and employability of the workers (COM 2003 6: 23). At the European level this approach has been largely taken up by the European Employment Strategy (EES) and the reform agenda of the Lisbon process to modernise the European Social Model from 2000 onwards (Aust, Leitner, and Lessenich, 2002).

This strategy focused on the reform of national welfare states. Accordingly, the role of the European Union was mainly to promote change at the national level. The OMC established a coordination procedure that allowed the European Union to negotiate common targets and to propose certain policies without conflicting with the primary responsibility of the member states in the area of employment and social policy (Scharpf, 2002: 652). The governments were obliged to implement the European guidelines and to report on their activities and policy efforts in the so-called 'National Action Plans'. The overall process was to be monitored and evaluated jointly by the Commission and the Council of Ministers. However, in contrast to the economic guidelines set in the Growth and Stability Pact (Official Journal, 1997), there are no sanctions for member states that fail to apply the guidelines or achieve the targets. The emphasis is on policy learning through information exchange, benchmarking, peer-review, deliberation, and, as a last resort, 'blaming and shaming'.

Using the instruments of 'soft' coordination, the European Union gradually expanded its scope into the areas of employment and general welfare policies. The 1994 Essen Council adopted short and medium-term guidelines for action and declared that reducing unemployment was a priority for the European Union. In 1997 the Treaty of Amsterdam introduced a chapter on employment policies, which prepared the ground for the EES. At the Lisbon summit, the European Union set itself the target of becoming 'the most competitive and dynamic knowledge-based economy in the world, capable of sustainable growth with more and better jobs and greater social cohesion' (Presidency Conclusions, 2000a: 3). The employment strategy is heavily focused on modernising the labour market. The Nice Council in 2000 made the link between employment strategy and social policy explicit. Social policy has a dual character, as a 'productive factor' and as a mechanism for 'social protection, the reduction of inequalities and social cohesion' (Presidency Conclusions, 2000b: annex I). The statement goes on to say that 'an approach of this kind presupposes in the first instance an increase in labour market participation, especially by groups that are under-represented or disadvantaged in it'. The Council agreed to extend the OMC from the area of employment, initially to social exclusion and poverty and later, in 2001, to pensions policies. Currently discussions are taking place regarding health and long-term care.

The EU's Policy Responses to New Social Risks

Labour Market Policies: New Ways to Promote Employment

In recent years, the EU's employment policies have moved beyond a limited legislative approach, confined to the areas of free mobility of workers and health and safety regulation, to include coordination of member states' active labour market policies. The new policies acquired legal standing in the Amsterdam Treaty's Employment Chapter and are concerned with raising employment rates through diverse means, rather than the harmonisation of social security systems (Roberts and Springer, 2001: 30; Geyer, 2001: 56).

This change of direction was a response to the rising economic pressures on member states, reflected in high unemployment rates, which were analysed in the 1993 Employment White Paper (COM 1993 700: 1; Mosher and Trubek, 2003: 66; DGESA interviews). An increasing number of states were concerned that escalating unemployment would impose severe pressures on social security budgets, and could undermine public support for the monetary union. Moreover, the political climate changed in Europe as governments of the centre-left were elected in France (1997), in the United Kingdom (1997) and in Germany (1998). Pressures from national social policy ministries and from unions to give the European Union 'a human face' also advanced social policy issues on the political agenda (DGESA MEP and EP Social Protection Committee interviews). As a result, the European Council decided on a common strategy against rising unemployment at the 1994 Essen Summit (Geyer, 2000: 55). This set new priorities relating to equality, training, working time, flexibility, non-wage labour costs, active as opposed to passive policies and priority groups. The priorities were later reconfirmed and strengthened in the employment chapter of the Amsterdam Treaty, which laid the foundations for the EES (Roberts and

Springer, 2001: 31). The strategy was further developed at the Luxembourg Summit in 1997 and specific targets were set at the 2000 Lisbon summit.

The EU employment strategy rests mainly on non-binding commitments; member states may implement the policies according to their own traditions. In addition, a number of directives have been adopted under different treaty articles to improve working conditions and employment rights (Geyer, 2001: 59, 149; Roberts and Springer, 2001: 42). The most important policy tools have been the OMC, target-setting and funding from the ESF and the EU Medium Term Action Programmes. The objectives for the OMC are organised around four pillars: improving employability; developing entrepreneurship; encouraging adaptability of business and their employees; and strengthening equal opportunities.[1] Specific guidelines and recommendations are framed in relation to the pillars. The targets set by the employment strategy are that 70 per cent of the population of working age, 60 per cent of women and 50 per cent of those between 55 and 64 should be in employment, and that child care should be available to 90 per cent of children aged between three and school entry age and 30 per cent of those aged three or below by 2010. A separate target of reducing the gender pay gap by half is under active discussion (interview with member of EP Women's Rights Committee). A new streamlined version of the employment strategy has been proposed by the Commission for adoption in Autumn, 2003 (COM(2003) 6 final: 8).

The Medium Term Action Programmes and the Social Fund have concentrated on funding national projects which promote education and training for various groups to facilitate adaptation to industrial change and

---

[1] The first pillar focuses on employability and tackling the skills gap. There is a particular emphasis on ensuring that young people and the long-term unemployed are equipped to take advantage of new employment opportunities in the fast-changing labour market. The second pillar explicitly refers to the implementation of active labour market policies. The benefits and training system must be reviewed and adapted to ensure that they actively support employability and provide real incentives for the unemployed to seek and take up work or training opportunities. It also stresses the importance of life-long learning. The third pillar derives from the recognition that the creation of more and better jobs requires a dynamic enterprising climate. This aim is to be achieved through deregulation and simplification of market access by small firms. The fourth pillar acknowledges the need for better adaptability for both business and the workforce. It focuses on the adaptability of enterprises and workers to changing technologies and markets and industrial restructuring through union-negotiation and work reorganisation. The concept of *flexi-security* encapsulates this strategy since '*it recognises explicitly that a balance must be struck between the need of business for flexibility, and the needs of employees for security and employability*'. This pillar refers to the need to integrate disadvantaged groups in the labour market, especially disabled workers, older workers, women, and increasingly so, ethnic minorities. Progress in terms of access to the labour market between men and women is a central concern, especially in the context of an ageing society.

labour market entry or re-entry (Hantrais, 1995). Among the most recent programmes are PETRA, for vocational training for the young, LINGUA to support language acquisition, COMETT promoting cooperation between business and universities and ERASMUS (later SOCRATES) supporting mobility among university students (Geyer, 2000: 198; Rees, 1998a: 1245).

The commitment to training, better working conditions and employment rights rather than more direct intervention in national social security systems is in keeping with the work- rather than the benefit-centred approach of the EU's 'pragmatic monetarism' described in Chapter 1. National governments have been reluctant to countenance coordination of employment or unemployment policies at the EU level. The Treaty of Rome stipulates that the Commission may only pass legislation if it can show that national frameworks prevent free movement of labour. This served as justification for the introduction of qualified majority voting in relation to worker mobility and health and safety in the 1986 Single European Act. The labour mobility argument has been deployed, along with the Social Charter and the institutional changes in the Maastricht Treaty, as a Trojan horse to advance EU legislation on working conditions and employment rights. Among the new initiatives are the Pregnant Workers' Directive (1992), the Working Time Directive (1993), the Young Workers' Directive (1994), the Posted Workers' Directive (1996), the Atypical Workers' Directive (1991) and the European Work Council Directive (1994—Geyer, 2000: 77).

The sensitivity to national concerns of employment policy may also be seen in article 30 of the Amsterdam Treaty, which lays down that the EES must not have any budgetary impact. In addition, the Open Method of Co-ordination emerged as a compromise solution (CEEP interview) and even within the OMC, objectives have been difficult to negotiate. The wording of the Lisbon Conclusions suggested that 'member states should *consider* (our italics) setting national targets', rather than requiring them to do so (EU, 2000b: para. 210). Governments naturally prefer targets they are confident they will meet. Denmark and Germany express concerns for different reasons: Denmark because it believes the OMC is unnecessary, since employment issues are already included in the broad economic guidelines, and Germany because the national government does not have the constitutional power to implement all targets within the Länder (DGESA interviews).

The tensions behind the employment strategy also include the ideological debate regarding the balance of economic and social aspects. Although the European Council has tried to integrate the two aspects by encouraging a closer coordination of the Broad Economic Guidelines and the Employment Strategy, tensions between the two groups continue. The national ministers for economic and financial affairs along with the Directorate General for Economic and Financial Affairs and the Economic Policy Committee advocate linking social policy to productivity, while the DGESA, the Employment Committee, the Social Protection Committee and the national ministers for social affairs wish to include, for example, quality of work and opportunities for advancement. However, economic concerns dominate the debate, although the social concerns have achieved more attention in recent years (DGESA, DG Internal Market, Social Protection Committee interviews).

In general, EU intervention in national employment policies has mainly been restricted to new social risks, and has not tackled old social risk tax and benefit policies. Equal opportunities policies have also been heavily coloured by economic and labour market concerns.

Equal Opportunities—Promoting Women's Access to the Labour Market

The European Union has a long-standing commitment to advance equal opportunities between men and women and promote women's equal access to paid work from the 1957 Treaty of Rome onwards. Positive actions have been promoted since the early 1980s, including training and education, access to leadership positions, availability of child care and violence against women. The 'mainstreaming' of gender from the mid-1990s required that all EU policies should integrate consideration of these issues (Pollack and Hafner-Burtonm, 2000: 2). The Treaty of Amsterdam provision that gender equality is a cross-country responsibility relevant to all policy areas and placed under qualified majority voting is the clearest expression of this (Leibfried and Pierson, 2000: 273).

The increased attention given to equal opportunities has primarily been due to developments in the late 1980s and early 1990s. The expansion of qualified majority voting, the Social Charter, and, later, the strengthening of equal opportunities in the Amsterdam Treaty, along with the 1986 Single European Act, provided the context in which the European Commission was able to promote the resolution on child care provisions (1992) and the directives on maternity leave (1992), parental leave (1996) and part-time work (1997). The newly created co-decision procedures enabled the European Parliament to pursue its long-lasting commitment to gender equality and to ensure the selection of women-friendly commissioners in 1995 and 1999 (EFCW Briefing 2, 1996; Pollack and Hafner-Burtonm, 2000: 11).

The Council of Ministers accepted the importance of incorporating equal opportunities in the 1994 Social Action Plan in order to develop the internal market. The commitment to promote women's access to the labour market has been reinforced by the Lisbon (2000), Stockholm (2001) and Barcelona (2002) summits, which also expanded the scope of equal opportunities to include the reconciliation of work and family life. Child care and parental leave and working arrangements dominated the agenda, and the issue of long-term care did not initially receive specific attention. When this area was included on the agenda at the Stockholm Summit in 2001, a commitment strengthened at the 2003 Spring Summit, the primary reasons were concerned with economic rather than equal opportunity issues (Presidency Conclusions, 2001a: part 1; Brussels (2003): part 2; DGESA interviews).

The different initiatives taken at the EU level in this area have mainly been related to labour market issues, which have spilled over into new social risks (Table 8.1). They include equal treatment directives, which are reinforced by the jurisdiction of the European Court of Justice, the gender mainstreaming approach, Medium Term Action Programmes, the Structural Funds and the Employment Strategy. The Medium Term Action Programmes have fostered pilot projects and the exchange of best practices in areas such as reconciliation of work and family life, including child care, political representation of women, retraining along with creating networks of experts and advocates in women's rights issues (Rees, 1998b: 1; Pollack and Hafner-Burtonm, 2000: 2; COM 2000 335: 1). The latest Medium Term Action Programme has a specific annual theme in relation to equal opportunities. In 2001 it was equal pay, in 2002, the reconciliation of work and family life, and in 2003 the role of women in decision-making. These themes also form the basis for co-ordination between the Commission, the European Parliament and the European Council's equal opportunities policies (DGESA interview).

Most of these policies rely on the so-called 'soft law' procedures. They represent a move away from the traditional EU social policy approach concerned with attempts to negotiate harmonisation of national laws. The OMC, the Medium Term Action Programmes funded by the EU's structural funds and the gender mainstreaming approach are also based on a voluntary approach, which tries to promote a multi-level involvement of actors through mutual exchange of best practices among the European Union, national, regional, and local levels. Moreover, these initiatives are based on activation and training measures rather than more interventionist policies, which might, for example, promote equal opportunities by eliminating discrimination over pensions matters or through financial support to enable families to provide child care). The role of the basic EU supply-side economic philosophy in this has already been mentioned. In addition, the EU's legal competence in areas other than equal treatment of workers has not been clearly defined (MEP and EU interviews; EWL, 2003). Third, EU intervention in areas such as social assistance, social protection, and financial redistribution requires unanimity in the Council, which makes action difficult.

The most recent example of the difficulties experienced by the European Union in intervening in member states' social policies is the proposed directive on equal opportunities in areas other than employment based on Article 13. With the support of the ETUC, European Women's Lobby and the 2000 Nice European Council, the DGESA drafted a directive in 2001–2 to outlaw discrimination against women in access to and supply of goods and services, social assistance, education and taxation (DGESA interview, COM 2003 657: 2). Measures to prevent the publication of material which promoted sex discrimination or incited sexual hatred were included in the first draft, but reconciliation of work and family life, violence against women, and the inclusion of women in decision-making were excluded, leading to complaints from the European Women's Lobby (EWL 2003, EP Women's Rights Committee interview). The media and the advertising industry criticised the draft on the grounds that it would curtail editorial freedom (European Publishers' Council: 1/7-03; Advertising Association; July, 2003; *Financial Times* 27/6-03). The insurance industry, parts of the Commission (especially the Commission's legal service), the DG for Education and Culture and the DG for the Internal Market were also sceptical, along with some member states (Advertising Information Group, 27/6-03; COM 2003 657: 7). The Commission postponed approval and narrowed the scope of the directive to cover only women's access to goods and services. The Commission presented the final proposal to the Council on 5 November 2003 and is awaiting the final decision according to the unanimity procedures (COM 2003 657: 11).

A similar resistance to intervention is reflected in the policy trajectory of the European Union with respect to equal opportunities. Table 8.1 shows that EU legislation applies chiefly to equal treatment in the labour market and has to some extent been subject to qualified majority voting. Gender mainstreaming and positive action in areas such as retraining, women's access to leadership positions, targets for women's employment rates, and

Table 8.1 Selected equal opportunity measures adopted by the EU

Equal treatment directives	Reconciliation of work and family life directives	Equal treatment, retraining and harassment recommendations etc.	Reconciliation of work and family life recommendations etc.	Gender mainstreaming (GMS) resolutions
1975: Equal pay for work of equal value	1992: Health and safety, pregnant workers	1982: Retirement age	1974: Social action programme	1995: UN Beijing Conference: EU introduces GMS
1976: Employment, training, promotion	1993: Working time	1984: Positive action for women	1989: Social charter	1996: EU GMS commitment
1978: Statutory social security	1996: Parental leave	1984: Combating women's unemployment	1992: Childcare and parental leave	1996: Structural funds include GMS
1986: Occupational social security		1987: Vocational training for women	1998: Employment strategy guidelines	1997: Treaty of Amsterdam includes GMS
1986: Self-employed		1990: Dignity of women and men at work	2000: Balanced participation women and men, family and work	1999: Employment strategy includes GMS
1995: Gender and development co-operation		1992: Sexual harassment	2000: initiatives for specific measures	

1997: Part-time directive	**1994**: Equal opportunities via structural funds	**2002**: Barcelona child care targets: 3 to school age: 90%; 0–3 33% childcare by 2010.	**2001**: Action programme, GMS in community development
1997: Sex discrimination—burden of proof	**1994**: Equal participation in EU employment intensive economic strategy		
	1995/1996: Balanced participation in decision-making		
	1998: Employment strategy/positive action guidelines		
	1999: Women and science		
2002: Amendment 1976 equal treatment directive	**2000**: Lisbon employment targets: 70%; women 60%; older workers 50%. by 2010		
	2001: Stockholm targets: overall 67%; women 57% by 2005		

Source: Rees, 1998*a*, DGESA equal opportunity web page: http://europa.eu.int/comm/employment_social/equ_opp/index_en.htm.

support for the reconciliation of work and family life have mainly been subject to recommendations, the OMC and soft laws which are not legally binding.

Poverty and Social Exclusion—a New Entrant to the EU's Social Agenda

Poverty and social exclusion issues appear in EU legislation but have had a relatively low political profile. The Treaty of Rome speaks of promoting 'a high level of . . . economic and social cohesion and solidarity among member states' and, more recently, the Social Protocol states that combating social exclusion is 'a major objective' and that the European Union should be concerned with 'the integration of persons excluded from the labour market' but few policy measures have been implemented (Treaty of Rome, 2 and 3; Social Protocol, 2). The issue was also included on the agenda at the Lisbon and Nice Summits, where the European Council promoted coordination of national social inclusion policies (Presidency Conclusions, 2000a: 11, 2000b: annex 1). The most recent development is the Commission's proposals for intensifying and streamlining the current cooperative exchanges on social protection to create a more coherent framework of the OMC for social inclusion, pensions, health, and long-term care policies, which also complies with the existing treaty-based provisions for economic and employment policy coordination (COM 2003: 3).

Social exclusion became increasingly important in EU policy debate following the recession of the mid-1990s, both directly and as a result of the contribution of rising social spending to the problems faced by the euro in establishing itself. In 1997, 18 per cent of the EU population (or more than 60 million people) were living in households where the income was below 60 per cent of the national median income. Half of this population had been living at this level for three successive years (EU 2001: 7). The incorporation of the Social Protocol into the Treaty of Amsterdam in 1997 gave the European Union the official right to intervene. Articles 136 and 137 enable the Community to take action in relation to the integration of people excluded from the labour market and to adopt measures to fight social exclusion. The decision-making procedure allows qualified majority voting and co-decision with the European Parliament. However, the articles do not clarify the meaning of social exclusion nor do they specify which actions may be pursued (Schoukens and Carmichael, 2001: 86). With the support of various NGOs and ETUC, the Commission (in collaboration with the Portuguese Presidency) drafted a proposal which was adopted at the 2000 Lisbon Summit and strengthened subsequently (DGESA interview).

The policy instruments used to implement the new strategy were similar to those employed in the employment strategy: the newly adopted OMC for social inclusion, the European Social Fund and the National Action Plans (NAPs), rather than legally binding directives. The DGESA discussed the feasibility of a directive on minimum income in 2001–2, but did not take the idea further, chiefly because there is no scope for qualified majority voting in the field of social protection. A senior official concluded: 'the OMC is the only way to achieve convergence between the member states' social inclusion policies' (DGESA interview, April 2003).

The procedure for the submission of NAPs for the OMC for social inclusion, involving the European Council, the Commission, the Council, the Social Partners, and groups at regional and local levels, is broadly similar to that for the European Employment Strategy. However, the OMC for social inclusion is not based in any EU treaty, so that developments in this area depend on continuing mandates at the various summits. Sceptical countries can delay progress through control of the agenda when they hold the Presidency (DGESA interviews). Second, the strategy is not based on specific guidelines, but consists instead of four broad objectives: facilitating participation in employment and common access to resources, rights, goods, and services; preventative work against the risk of exclusion; help for the most vulnerable; and the mobilisation of all relevant bodies (Presidency Conclusions, 2000b: annex 1). The eighteen indicators for assessing the impact of member states' NAPs along with the first joint report on social exclusion were adopted by the European Council at the Laeken Summit (Atkinson, 2003: 263).

Medium Term Action Plans and the ESF are also relevant to social exclusion, but neither were originally established to help specific excluded groups. The ESF seeks to improve employment opportunities and living standards and to mitigate regional inequalities via employment, training and mobility schemes (Hantrais, 1995: 146). The different Social Action Programmes include general measures to tackle poverty, in almost all cases employment-centred (Geyer, 2000: 161–4). Some of them are aimed at specific groups with particular labour market needs such as young people (YOUTHSTART), women (NOW), disabled people (HORISON) and those affected by industrial restructuring (ADAPT-BIS—Rees, 1998a: 180). The most recent Community Action Programme (2002–06) focuses on information exchange, supporting best practice and improving knowledge rather than new substantive policies (*Official Journal*, 12.1.02: annex).

The EU initiatives to eliminate social exclusion and poverty have been dominated by the view that paid work is the best route out of poverty, mainly because member states have been unwilling to commit themselves to more interventionist policies. The Fourth Social Action Programme was vetoed by the Council of Ministers in 1994 as described earlier. Some countries doubted the need for doubling the funding of the programme, while others demanded more control by the Council in deciding the different elements of the budget. However, it was the German challenge on the grounds that the programme threatened the subsidiarity principle that finally blocked the Commission's proposal (Geyer, 2000: 162; Pochet et al., 1994: 235–6). Similarly, the 1993 Green Paper on European Social Policy, which proposed action to combat social exclusion, was also unsuccessful. France and Italy claimed that the social policy agenda should instead follow the direction of the 1993 Employment White Paper, Germany referred to the subsidiarity principle and the UK criticised the lack of an agreed definition of poverty (Geyer, 2000: 162).

Some member states, most notably the Southern European countries (but also Germany) have disputed targets for social inclusion. German resistance has mainly been at the level of the Länder, who fear a recentralisation of national social policy when defining common EU targets. The Southern European countries and UNICE have opposed common unemployment targets, in contrast to the Nordic countries (CEEP and DGESA interviews). Most member states also opposed the poverty target of halving the poverty rate by 2010 at the Lisbon Summit and again resisted the Commission's proposal for social inclusion targets based on the poverty line of 60 per cent of median income at the 2002 Barcelona Summit (Atkinson, 2003: 266).

Controversy surrounds the definition of poverty. Although the Amsterdam Treaty gave new competencies to combat social exclusion, the term remained vague, leaving room for alternative definitions. One division is between approaches based on target groups (such as young people, older people, or ethnic minorities—favoured by the United Kingdom); another focuses on access to paid work (France); a third, shared by the Nordic countries, refers to a broader conception of social citizenship. The Commission has side-stepped this debate by proposing eight areas where work on social inclusion should be focused: the right to work, adequate income, adequate education, capacity to support the family, the promotion of children's rights, the delivery of services and regeneration for disadvantaged urban and rural areas (Social Agenda, 2002). Work on appropriate indicators is under way (Atkinson, 2003: 270).

An Assessment of EU New Risk Policies

It is hard to establish how far EU policies have made a difference in the field of new social risks, for two reasons: first, evidence is necessarily limited, since the policies are in the process of development. Secondly, the authority of the European Union is also limited. As we have seen, policies in most areas are implemented through soft law rather than directives, so that it is difficult to attribute outcomes directly to particular reforms. We review the statistical evidence of progress towards the targets set in OMC policy for employment, women's participation in paid work and child care, and in relation to social inclusion.

The Statistical Picture

In relation to employment, the EU's major evaluation of the EES in 2002 claims a substantial impact: 'there have been significant changes in national employment policies, with a clear convergence towards the common EU objectives set out in the EES policy guidelines' (COM 2002 621 final: 2). The overall EU employment rate rose from 62.2 per cent of the working-age population in 1999 to 64.2 per cent in 2002, bringing the European Union somewhat closer to the Stockholm target of 67 per cent by 2005 and the Lisbon target of 70 per cent by 2010. By contrast, unemployment fell from 8.7 per cent in 1999 to 7.7 per cent in 2003 (Eurostat, 12/11-2003a). However, the candidate countries do not follow this trend. Their overall employment rate declined from 58.4 per cent in 2000 to 56.1 per cent in 2002 while their unemployment rate rose from 13.6 to 14.8 per cent in the same period—implying future difficulties in reaching the employment targets following enlargement (Eurostat, 29/8-2002, 14/7-2003). Despite the relative success of the EES, the EU's evaluation report also stated that unemployment (especially long-term unemployment), low productivity and regional differences were areas of weakness and expressed concern that the targets are unlikely to be achieved by the dates set (Commission, 2002: 5f.).

Enlargement presents further challenges. A recent EU analysis concludes that 'labour markets in the candidate countries are challenged by decreasing employment rates and by high and persistent unemployment. Moreover accession countries will be affected . . . by a future drop in fertility, becoming 'ageing societies' like the current member states' (EU, 2003: 31). It is at present unclear how these issues will be incorporated in the EES targets.

There is some evidence of a shift from passive to active measures in labour market policy as recommended by the EES, but the pattern is heavily influenced by national circumstances. In all cases, spending on passive benefits and early retirement policies fell (except in Greece and Portugal where it rose) between 1997/8 and 2000/1, a period when unemployment across Europe was either levelled or falling. Spending on active policies rose in Austria, Belgium, the Netherlands, Greece, and Spain, and then fell, but more slowly than spending on passive benefits elsewhere, with the exceptions of Sweden and Portugal. This implies that a shift from passive to active spending is taking place at different speeds in different national contexts. Where active spending is rising, the shifts are relatively small, so that the most important causal factor is a decline in passive spending. The changes are based on policy shifts that date back to the early 1990s in most cases (as discussion in Chapters 2–7 shows), and it is difficult to judge how far they can be attributed to the EU strategy.

Progress in the area of women's participation in the EU labour market remains slow, increasing from 52.7 per cent in 1999 to 55.5 per cent in 2002, while falling in the candidate countries from 52.8 to 50.3 per cent. This cast doubts on the likelihood of reaching the intermediate target of 57 per cent by 2005 and the 60 per cent target by 2010 (Eurostat, 14/7-2003). Of particular concern is the persistent gender pay gap (women earning 16 percentage points less than men's average gross hourly earnings in 2000—Eurostat, 12/11-2003f) and the low participation rate of older and younger workers. Only 15.5 per cent of younger and 39.8 per cent of older workers were in employment—making it even harder to reach the employment target of 50 per cent for those aged 55–64 (Eurostat 14/7-2003, 20/3-03, 12/11-03).

In the area of equal opportunities, the statistics on women's participation in paid work and on the gender pay gap given above indicate that progress is limited. In addition, the large number of women working part-time (33.5 per cent compared to 6.6 per cent of men) and on contracts of limited duration (14.3 per cent compared to 12.1 per cent of men) shows that equal opportunities still are far from being achieved (Franco and Jouhette, 2003: 6). However, the number of part-time female workers is much lower in the candidate countries (12 per cent) and only 8 per cent of the workforce is employed on short-term contracts (Eurostat, 29/8-2002).

The availability of child care has a major impact on mothers' employment. As the preceding chapters showed, in member states with more limited child care coverage, such as Germany, Greece and Spain, mothers tend to be workless or part-time workers (Franco and Winqvist, 2002: 3). Family care is particularly important in the Mediterranean countries. This makes it even more important that the European Union attains its child care targets by 2010. However, only Belgium, Denmark, France, Italy, and the Netherlands have reached the 90 per cent target for children between three and mandatory school age by 2010. Greece (46 per cent), Ireland (56 per cent), Finland (66 per cent), and the United Kingdom (60 per cent) still have considerable ground to make up. Similarly, the 30 per cent target for children from zero to three years remains a distant goal. Child care facilities are particularly limited in Greece (3 per cent), Austria (4 per cent), Italy (6 per cent), Spain (5 per cent), Germany (10 per cent), Portugal (12 per cent), and the Netherlands (6 per cent), making it difficult for mothers to reconcile work and family life (OECD, 2001: 144).

In relation to social exclusion, evidence is necessarily limited, due to the recent implementation of the policy and the development of indicators including measures to assess income inequality, persistent unemployment and workless households among vulnerable groups. The most recent statistics indicate that poverty has fallen in the European Union from 17 per cent in 1995 to 15 per cent in 1999, while the average poverty rate in accession and candidate countries is 14.3 per cent (Eurostat, 2002). However, the risk of poverty varies widely between individual states, ranging from 23 per cent in Turkey, 21 per cent in Portugal and Greece and 18 per cent in Estonia to 11 per cent in Slovenia, 9 per cent in Sweden and 8 per cent in the Czech Republic. Of those EU citizens at risk of poverty, more than 9 per cent (around 33 million) were subject to persistent poverty in 1999 (Eurostat, 7/4-2003; Dennis and Guio, 2003: 2). People with low educational attainment are particularly exposed to the risk of poverty. Only 7 per cent of highly educated men and women, but 12 per cent of men and 21 per cent of women with low educational skills lived in poverty in 1996 (Mejer and Siermann, 2000). The EU study of the candidate countries explicitly linked to the labour market stresses poverty risks and argues that 'poverty and social exclusion . . . probably represent the most serious challenge presented by future EU enlargement' (EU, 2003: 246).

Social transfers (excluding pensions) reduce the poverty rate from 24 to 15 per cent overall. The impact is most evident in Sweden (a drop of 19 per cent), but is less significant in Mediterranean countries (only one per cent in Greece—Eurostat, 7/4-2003). Employment is also a crucial factor for social inclusion not only with respect to incomes, but also as means of social participation and personal development (Eurostat, 7/4-2003). The long-term unemployment rate declined from 3.5 per cent in 2000 to 3.1 per cent in 2001, while increasing in the candidate countries from 6.6 to 7.6 per cent (Eurostat, 12/11-2003e). Despite the relatively low number of long-term unemployed in the EU-15, the proportion of people living in workless households remains high (12.2 per cent in 2001, Eurostat, 7/4-2003). The limitations of the EES recognised in the evaluation report mentioned earlier are likely to have implications for the success in EU's social inclusion policy.

The risk of poverty for vulnerable groups remains substantial. Relatively more women than men are exposed to the risk of poverty (16 against 15 per cent of men in 2001, Eurostat, 12/11-03c, 12/11-03d). The proportion living in workless households ranging from over 50 per cent in Spain, Portugal, Italy, Belgium, and Luxembourg to just above 20 per cent in British single households in 2000, with a particularly high proportion of lone mothers (Franco and Winqvist, 2002: 2, 4). The 1996 European Community Household Survey showed that single women were more at risk than single men (25 against 19 per cent) and that 21 per cent of children lived in poverty. Particularly children of lone parents and children living in large households (defined as those with more than three dependent children) ran a poverty risk markedly above the EU average (Mejer and Siermann, 2000: 2, 4). In addition, disabled people are at roughly twice the risk of unemployment and three times the risk of worklessness than those without disabilities (Dupré and Karjalainen, 2003: 6).

The Legal Framework and Policy Reform

We now move beyond statistics on outcomes to examine the effect of EU policies on development at the national level. EU legislation has a mixed impact on national policies. For example, a study of the impact of the Parental Leave directive indicated that it resulted in a real policy innovation in Ireland, Luxembourg, Belgium, and the United Kingdom. None of these countries except for Belgium had any general binding legal provisions on parental leave (and in the Belgian case only in the public sector—Falkner and Treib, 2003: 9). However directives are not always fully implemented. Women and men do not receive equal pay for equal work despite the EU Equal Pay directive of 1975. The provisions of the Parental Leave Directive for time off work for care responsibilities are not always implemented in practice (Larsen, Baldock, and Hadlow, 2003: 60, 99). Similarly, although the Working Time Directive stipulates a 48-hour working limit, 8.3 per cent of European employees work more than a 48-hour per week (Eurostat, 2001: 35). The limited success of EU legislation implies that soft laws, particularly the voluntary OMC, might have even less impact.

In relation to the provisions of the EES, many member states (including the Scandinavian countries and the Netherlands) declared in their national reports that appropriate employment policies were already in place at the time of the 1997 Luxembourg Summit. France and Greece and to a lesser extent Belgium and Germany stated that the EES had exerted a positive influence on national employment policy (Commission, 2002: 3). Evaluations of the impact of other OMC policies are not yet available.

The EU policies may challenge member states' traditional ways of governing, leading to greater long-term impact. For example, the Social Charter allows the use of collective agreement to implement EU labour market directives, but the Commission has challenged this approach. Denmark has been forced by the Commission's lawyers under threat of legal actions to implement the working time directive through legislation rather than the traditional national system of collective agreement (Larsen, 2002: 8; Kommission, 26/9-2001). Similarly the setting of OMC targets for employment has implications for practices in Germany, where regional rather than federal government has the role of setting such targets according to the national constitution.

The different employment, social inclusion and economic strategies may also come into conflict due to their different legal base. The economic policies designed to ensure the stability of the Euro, including the European Central Bank's responsibility for regulating the inflation, but not the unemployment rate, are clearly specified in European treaties. By contrast, the EES is contained in treaties, but only has voluntary status. The design and direction of social policies (especially the EU's social inclusion, pensions and health and long-term care policies) depend on mandates given by the European Council at the various summits. Consequently, the European Central Bank's rulings for the Euro may cause problems in periods of economic recession, as neither the member states nor the Commission are empowered to intervene to secure the employment targets or social inclusion, equal opportunities and pensions policies. Currently, the public deficit limit contained in the Growth and Stability Pact effectively constrains member states' capacity to invest in areas like public daycare or labour market interventions, severely limiting the range of options available to meet child care or employment targets. The concessions granted to France and Germany at the November 2003 Council meeting regarding their public sector deficits in an area subject to treaty-based law (Politiken, 23/11-2003) call into question the capacity of the European Union to develop coordination through rather weaker instruments in the area of social policy.

Conclusion

Social issues concerning both old and new risks confront European welfare states. The single market economic policies of the European Union have intensified social pressures and constrained the range of measures available to meet them at the national level. Many member states turn to the European Union as the best place to defend their social commitments (Mosher and Trubek, 2003: 66). Thus, EU involvement in policy-making at the social level follows from its success at the economic level. The European Union has developed more active welfare policies and a range of instruments based on regulation rather than redistribution, which allow room for national traditions, as well as more flexible and inclusive approaches to combat new social risks. These policies have been founded on the underlying ideology of an active society. They go beyond measures to prevent social dumping, and include an element of supply-side economic policy intended to support economic integration, growth and the employability of workers (COM 1993, 551). This strategy has been pursued mainly through resolutions, recommendations, targets, positive action programmes funded by EU finances, gender mainstreaming and the OMC rather than mandatory legislative measures (Roberts and Springer, 2001: 32f).

The application of the different policy instruments and the development of EU involvement vary widely across the spectrum of European social policy areas depending on formal competencies. Traditional welfare state taxation, redistribution, and spending remain largely outside the EU's domain, even when it comes to dealing with new social risks. The EU's increasing role within new risk areas has resulted from the willingness of member states to give the European Union the competencies to promote coordination within new social risk fields. The Social Charter, the Maastricht treaty, the Amsterdam Treaty and, most recently, the Treaty of Nice have extended the EU's legal base to permit common actions within the fields of employment, equal opportunities and social exclusion. Long-term care and health are the only policy areas not included, but recent developments indicate that they are likely to be incorporated in future treaties.

The various European Council summits have gradually permitted greater EU regulation within new social risk areas. As a result, new social risk policies may offer a solution to the dilemma that currently faces the European Union, between the limits that European economic and monetary policies impose on the capacity for member states to deal with both new and old risks, and member states' resistance to further EU intervention in domestic affairs. The new social risk policies currently being pursued are compatible with the market-centred approach fundamental to the EU's principal objective of economic integration. They limit the risk of uncoordinated competition between national welfare regimes which might lead to a 'race to the bottom'. However, they also offer an opportunity to avoid the European state-building through the statutory harmonisation of social policies which had previously proved unacceptable to member states. In addition, enlargement, and the recent concessions regarding the French and German public sector deficits, indicate real challenges for the EU's ability to sustain support for common economic and social policies. Enlargement also implies a need to strengthen the social provisions to prevent social dumping and secure EU citizens' social rights, creating an open 'policy window' for the European Union to legitimise its supra-national tier of government. Under these circumstances, new social risk policies present the best opportunity available for the European Union to advance its social dimension. The real question is whether it will be possible to promote policy convergence under the voluntaristic regime of the OMC.

References

Advertising Association, July (2003) *Proposal for a Directive Implementing the Principle of Equality Between Women and Men*, AA Position Paper.

Advertising Information Group (27/6-03) Notices, no. 171.

Atkinson, A. B. (2003) Social Europe and Social Science, *Social Policy and Society*, volume 2 number 4, Cambridge University Press.

Aust, A., Leitner, S., and Lessenich, S. (2002) 'Konjunktur und Krise des Europäischen Sozialmodells: ein Beitrag zur politischen Präexplantationsdignostik', *Politische Vierteljahresschrift*, 43 (2): 270–99.

Begg, I. and Berghman, J. (2002) 'EU social (exclusion) Policy Revisited?', *Journal of European Social Policy*, 12 (3): 179–94.

Blair, T. and Schroeder, G. (1999) *Europe: a Third Way*, Labour Party, London.

COM (1993*a*) 551, Green Paper *European Social Policy: Options for the Union:* European Committees, Brussels.

COM (1993*b*) 700 final, *White Paper on Growth Competitiveness, and Employment*, European Communities, Brussels.

—— (1994) 333 final, *White Paper—European Social Policy—A Way Forward* European Committees, Brussels.

—— (2000) 335 final, *Towards a Community Framework Strategy on Gender Equality* (2002–05), Communication from the Commission, Brussels.

—— (2002) 621 final, *Draft Joint Employment Report* 2002, Commission of the European Communities, Brussels.

COM (2003) 657 final, *Proposal for a Council Directive-Implementing the Principle of Equal Treatment Between Women and Men in the Access to and Supply of Goods and Services*, Commission of the European Communities, Brussels.

—— (2003) 6 final, '*A Strategy for Full Employment and Better Jobs for All*, Communication from the Commission, Brussels.

Commission (2002) Impact Evaluation of the EES: Background paper—Employment Policy Mix and Policy Making, EMCO/30/060602/EN_REW 1.

COM (2003) final *Strengthening the Social Dimensions of the Lisbon Strategy*, Commission of the European Communities, Brussels.

Dennis, I. and Guio, A. C. (2003) M*onetary Poverty in EU Acceding and Candidate Countries*, Statistics in Focus, Population and Social Conditions, Theme 3, number 21. EC No 1467/97, (1997) *Council Regulation on Spending Up and Clarifying the Implementation of the Excessive Deficit Procedure* European Communities, Brussels.

Dupré, D. and Karjalainen, A. (2003) *Employment of Disabled People in Europe in 2002*, Population and Social Conditions, Theme 3-26/2003, Eurostat, Brussels.

EWL (2003) '*The Draft Directive "Implementing the Principle of Equality Between Women and Men"* ', EWL Briefing no. 1, 7/7-03, Brussels.

EFCW Briefing 2 (1996) *Childcare* European Forum for Child Welfare, Brussels.

Esping-Andersen, G. (1990) *The Three Worlds of Welfare Capitalism*, Polity Press, Cambridge.

—— (ed. 2002) *Why We Need a New Welfare State*, Oxford University Press, Oxford.

EU (2000*a*) *Presidency Conclusions, Nice Council*, EU, Brussels.

—— (2000*b*) *Presidency Conclusions, Lisbon Council*, EU, Brussels.

—— (2001) *Draft Joint Report on Social Inclusion*, Council of the European Commission, Brussels.

—— (2003) 'Social Protection in the 13 Candidate Countries', DGESA, Brussels.

Euroline (2000) Progress on the EU Charter of Fundamental Rights.

Eurostat (2001) *Social Situation 2001*, European Communities, Brussels.

—— (2002) *Co-Operation with Candidate Countries: Statistics on Income, Poverty and Social Exclusion*, Brussels.

—— (2003) European Social Statistics; *Labour Market Policy—Expenditure and Participants*, Eurostat Free Data Series, Brussels.

—— (12/11-03*d*) *At-Risk-of-Poverty Rate—After Social Transfers—Males Social Cohesion*, Eurostat Free Data Series, Brussels.

—— (12/11-2003) *Gender Pay Gap in Unadjusted Form: Difference Between Men's and Women's Average Gross Hourly Earnings as a Percentage of Men's Average Gross Hourly Earnings—Employment.*

—— (12/11-2003*a*) *Total Unemployment Rate-Unemployed Persons as Share of the Total Active Population—Employment* Eurostat, Free Data Series, Brussels.

—— (12/11-2003*b*) *At Risk of Poverty Rate after Social Transfers*, Social Cohesion, Eurostat Free Data Series, Brussels.

—— (12/11*e*) *Total Long-Term Unemployment*, Social Cohesion, Eurostat Free Data Series, Brussels.

—— (14/7-2003) *Labour Force Survey-Spring 2002—Employment Rate in the EU up from 63.9% in 2001 to 64.2%* in *2002*, Eurostat news Release, 80/2003, Brussels.

—— (20/3-03) *Young Europeans, 21 March 2003: Spring Day in Europe*, Eurostat News Release, 35/2003, Brussels.

—— (29/8-2002) *Labour Force Survey*, Eurostat News Release, no 101/202, Brussels

—— (7/4-2003) *Poverty and Social Exclusion*, Eurostat News Release n. 43, Brussels.

—— (12/11-2003c) *At-Risk-of-Poverty Rate—after Social Transfers—Females Social Cohesion*, Eurostat, Free Data Series, Brussels.

Falkner, G. (1998) 'EU's Social Policy in the 1990's—Towards a Corporatist Policy Community', Routledge, London and New York.

—— (2001) *The Treaty on European Union and its Revision*, S. Kuhnle (ed.), *Survival of the European Welfare State*, Routledge, London and New York.

—— and Treib, O. (2003) 'The EU and New Social Risks: The Case of the Parental Leave Directive', *The Politics of New Social Risks* Conference, Lugano, Switzerland, 25–27 September.

Ferrera, M. et al. (2000) 'Recasting European Welfare States', *West European Politics*, 23.2, 4, 1–10.

Finnemore, M. and Sikkink, K. (1998) 'International Norm Dynamics and Political Change', *International Organization* 52 (4): 887–917.

Franco, A. and Winqvist, K. (2002a) *More Women than Men Living in Workless Households*, Statistics in Focus, Population and Social Conditions, Theme 3 number 15, Brussels.

—— and —— (2002b) *Women and Men Reconciling Work and Family Life*, Statistics in focus, Population and Social Conditions, Theme 3 number 9, Brussels.

Franco, A. and Jouhettes (2003) *Labour Force Survey Principal Results 2002 EU and EFTA Countries,* Statistics in Focus, Eurostat, Theme 3-15/2003, Brussels.

Geyer, R. R. (2001) *Exploring European Social Policy,* Polity Press, Cambridge.

Hantrais, L. (1995) *Social Policy in the European Union*, Macmillan Press, London.

Kleinman, M. (2003) *A European Welfare State? European Union Social Policy in Context*, Palgrave, Basingstoke.

Kommission (26/9-2001) *Begrundet Udtalelse*, Kommission for De Europæiske Fælleskaber, Brussels.

Larsen, T.P. (2002) *Aftalemodellen en hellig Ko*, Speciale Opgave, Aulberg Universitet.

——, Balclock, J., and Hadlow, J. (2003) *New Kinds of Family*, Report to the European Commission, Brussels.

Leibfried, S. and Pierson, P. (1995) *European Social Policy*, Brookings, Washington.

—— (2000a) 'Social Policy—left to Courts and Markets' in (ed.), Wallace, H. and Wallace, W. Policy-making in the European Union, 4th edn., Oxford University Press, Oxford.

—— (2000b) 'Social Policy', in H. Wallace and W. Wallace (eds.), *Policy Making in the European Union*, Oxford University Press, Oxford.

Lintner, V. (2001) 'European Monetary Union', in J. Richardson (ed.), *European Union: Power and Policy-Making*, Routledge, London.

Mayes, D. G. (2002) 'Social Exclusion and Macro-Economic Policy in Europe: A Problem of Dynamic and Spatial Change', *Journal of European Social Policy*, 12 (3): 195–209.

Mazey, S. (2001) 'European Integration', in J. Richardson (ed.), *European Union: Power and Policy-Making*, Routledge, London.

Meier, L. and Siermann, C. (2000) Income Poverty in the EU, Statistics in Focus, Theme 3, no. 12, Brussels.

Mosher J. S. and Trubek, D. M. (2003) 'Alternative Approaches to Governance in the EU: EU Social Policy and the European Employment Strategy', *Journal of Common Market Studies*, 41 (1): 63–8.

OECD (2001) *OECD Employment Outlook*, OECD Report.

Official Journal (1997) *Regulation* 1466/97, L209/1, EU, Brussels.

Polanyi, K. (1944) *The Great Transformation*, Rhinehart, London.

Politiken (23/11-2003) *Tyskland og Frankrig får særbehandling i EU.*

Pollack, M. A. and Hafner-Burton, E. (2000) *Mainstreaming Gender in the European Union*, Jean Monnet Working Paper no. 2, Harvard.

Presidency Conclusions (2000*a*) *Lisbon European Council*, 23/24 March 2000, SE 100/00, EN, European Communities, Brussels.

—— (2000*b*) *Nice European Council*, 7-10 December European Communities, Brussels.

—— (2001*a*) *Stockholm European Council*, 23 and 24 March European Communities, Brussels.

—— (2001*b*) *Laeken European Council*, 14-15 December European Communities, Brussels.

Presidency Conclusions, Brussels (2003) Brussels European Council 20 and 21 March European Communities, Brussels.

Rees, T. (1998*a*) *Mainstreaming Equality in the European Union—Education, Training and Labour Market Policies*, Routledge, London.

Rees, T. (1998*b*) *Women and the Labour Market: Mainstreaming Equality in Leonardo da Vinci*, University of Bristol, European Training Village.

Roberts, I. and Springer, B. (2001) *Social Policy in the European Union—Between Harmonization and National Autonomy*, Lynne Riener Publishers, Inc.

Ross, G. (1995) 'Assessing the Delors Era and Social Policy', S. Liebfried and P. Pierson (eds.), *European Social Policy—Between Fragmentation and Integration*, The Brookings Institution, Washington, DC.

Sabatier, P. (1998) 'The Advocacy Coalition Framework', *Journal of European Public Policy*, 5(1): 98-130.

Scharpf, F. (1988) 'The Joint Decision Trap: Lessons from German Federalism and European Integration', *Public Administration*, 66(3): 239-78.

—— (1999) *Governing in Europe-Effective and Democratic?*, Oxford University Press, Oxford.

—— (2002) *'The European Social Model: Coping with the Challenges of Diversity'*, *Journal of Common Market Studies*, 40 (4): 645-70.

—— and Schmidt, V. (eds. 2000) *Welfare and Work in the Open Economy*, Vol. I. Oxford University Press, Oxford.

Schoukens, P. and Carmichael, L. (2001) 'Social Exclusion and Poverty' in D. Mayes, J. Berghman, and R. Salais (eds.), *Social Exclusion and European Policy*, Edward Elgar, Cheltenham.

Wallace, H. and Wallace, W. (eds.) (2000) *Policy Making in the European Union*, Oxford University Press, Oxford.

Young, R. and Wallace, H. (2000) 'The Single Market', in H. Wallace and W. (eds.), *Policy Making in the European Union,* Oxford University Press, Oxford.

9

New Social Risks and Welfare States: New Paradigm and New Politics?

Peter Taylor-Gooby

The social changes associated with the post-industrial transition increase the exposure of some groups to new needs. These give rise to the new social risks that we identified in Chapter 1, associated primarily with family and labour market changes and welfare state reform. This chapter reviews the development of such risks in European countries and analyses policy responses. We will consider how new social risk issues are best understood in terms of the evolution of European welfare states and in terms of the political processes that will shape future patterns of welfare state development. In the former area we will discuss issues of convergence and path dependency, of whether the instruments used to meet new social risks are qualitatively different from those used to tackle old social risks and of the goals and processes of welfare state policy-making; the key question is whether new social risks contribute to a new paradigm of policy-making, or whether new social risk policies are best understood as following the existing pattern of differentiation by welfare state regime. In Chapter 1 we suggested that the impact of new social risks tends to be reinforced or mitigated by the existing welfare settlement, and that regime framework also exerts a strong, but not determining, influence on policy response. In the latter area of political process, the focus will be on the extent to which new social risks lead to a realignment of political forces and to a 'new politics' of welfare. Our Chapter 1 hypothesis was that changes will be most marked in areas where the interests of more powerful social actors coincide with those of new social risk bearers, and will be shaped by those interests.

As in the case of the introductory chapter, I am grateful to the WRAMSOC groups for ideas and suggestions generated in debates during the course of the research project.

The Emergence of New Social Risks and Responses to Them

The accounts of experience and of policy-making at the national and EU level in Chapters 2–8 shows how institutional structures influence both the emergence of and the response to new social risks. Contemporary analysis of European welfare states typically categorises them in a framework derived from Esping-Andersen's influential work on regimes (1990, 1999), as was discussed in Chapter 1.

Regime categories offer a convenient framework for summarising old social risk policies. We show that regimes shape the emergence of new social risks, but in many cases policy responses involve new departures. These indicate possibilities for a 'new politics' of welfare. New social risk policies do not restructure the pattern of regime differences. They are insufficiently substantial in public spending terms, accounting for less than three per cent of GDP across the European Union (Table 1.1). Even in France, the evolution of the targeted 'second world of welfare' described in Chapter 5 has resulted in an increase in the proportion of social benefits administered through means-test from 10.9 to only 11.5 per cent between 1991 and 2000 (Eurostat, 2003a). The impact of reforms on citizens' lives is limited, being focused primarily on transitions into paid work or specific phases in the family life cycle. However new risk policy-making does reveal opportunities for welfare state dynamism and innovation even in those areas where immobility and austerity pressures seem strongest.

Following recent discussion of regimes (summarised in Jaeger and Kvist, 2003: 555–7) we also distinguish Mediterranean welfare states. These have developed rapidly, with universal health care systems and social insurance pensions, but are much weaker in family benefits and provision for those on low incomes (EU, 2002a: chart 15). They also tend to rely on family-based informal care, and are hampered in some areas by the slow development of administrative capacity (Matsanganis et al., 2003: 643–4).

The European Union is also included in the analysis of this book because it has taken a strong interest in the area of new social risks and is likely to become more influential in the future. Its approach to welfare does not fit neatly into the traditional regime framework and its authority is limited. As Chapter 8 shows, 'open market' policies, reinforced through legal and financial sanctions, dominate EU policy at the economic level and exert a real indirect influence on national welfare systems (Leibfried and Pierson, 2000: 269). The EU's attempts to construct a 'social dimension' on a similar scale to its economic policies through the *rapprochement* of national systems were unsuccessful. Overt engagement with social provision is now chiefly through the more circumspect 'open method of co-ordination'. The strongest element in OMC has been the employment strategy, with its commitment both to broadly market-centred goals of greater flexibility, and to a more progressive vision of expanding opportunity through investment in human capital. This is paralleled in the social inclusion and education strategies and the mainstreaming of equal opportunity policies for women which bear in practice on work, education, and training (Leibfried and Pierson, 2000: 271; Geyer, 2001: chs. 5 and 7). As an embryonic welfare system, the EU's approach appears to reflect some feature of the market-oriented liberal regime, but also to include commitments to intervention intended to promote more universal access to the benefits of market-led growth.

The regime approach groups welfare states on the basis of the policy frameworks developed to meet old social risks. How well do the emergence of new social risks and the policy responses fit within these categories? The experience of the representative countries included in this book indicates that both processes correspond loosely to regime categories (in other words, old social risk regimes condition the emergence of new social risk regimes), but that there are also substantial areas where the traditional regime categorisation is less helpful. Continuing conflicts over new social risk issues indicate possible future directions for reform in labour market activation and in child and elder care policies. These conflicts are most marked in corporatist and Mediterranean countries, where new risk innovations imply the strongest challenges to the old social risks regime and where policy-making typically requires the lengthy negotiation of compromise.

Nordic Countries

Nordic countries have established traditions of social service support to enable women to function as citizen–workers, and the two case-studies included—Finland and Sweden—provide good examples. Both spend more than twice the EU average on services for women with children and about three times the average on services for older and disabled people (Table 1.1). The commitment to support for all 'citizen-workers' is reflected in the narrowness of the gap between men's and women's participation in paid work (along with Denmark, the narrowest in the European Union) and the fact that, along with other Nordic countries, they comfortably exceed the EU's Stockholm targets (Table 9.1). Both countries also have well-developed

Table 9.1 Employment 2001

	Overall employment rate	Men's employment rate	Women's employment rate	Women's full-time employment rate	Long-term unemployment
Denmark	76	80	71	56	2.3
Finland	68	70	65	56	2.4
Sweden	75	77	74	53	1.1
Austria	68	76	60	44	0.8
Belgium	60	69	51	34	3.4
France	62	69	55	42	3.2
Germany	66	73	59	39	4.1
Netherlands	74	83	65	27	1.0
Switzerland	79	88	70	39	0.8
Greece	56	71	41	37	4.0
Italy	55	69	41	32	6.0
Portugal	69	77	61	52	1.6
Spain	59	74	44	37	5.8
Ireland	65	76	54	36	2.0
UK	71	78	65	32	1.4
EU-15	64	73	55	41	3.3
2010 Target	70		60		

Note: Full-time means at least 30 hours a week; long-term means more than twelve months
Sources: Calculated from OECD (2003*a*: tables B, D, E, G)

schemes for ensuring that those without jobs have access to programmes to enable them to develop new skills and lead the European Union in Active Labour Market Programmes throughout the 1990s. However, recent cutbacks on spending in these areas (particularly on job subsidies in Sweden) as employment improves, coupled with a greater emphasis on activation policies in corporatist countries, lead to a situation in which activation spending in the latter group parallels or exceeds that in the former (Table 9.2).

The long-standing tradition of provision to address the issues which have emerged more recently as new risks in other countries generates a rather different structure of new social risks in Nordic countries from that elsewhere in Europe, as Chapter 4 shows. Groups such as immigrants, lone

Table 9.2 Spending on active and passive labour market measures (% GDP, 1997–2001)

	1997–98		2000–01	
	Active measures	Passive measures	Active measures	Passive measures
Denmark	1.66	3.83	1.56	3.00
Finland	1.40	2.56	0.95	2.02
Sweden	1.96	1.93	1.09	1.19
Austria	0.44	1.27	0.53	1.07
Belgium	1.22	2.64	1.30	2.18
France	1.35	1.84	1.31	1.65
Germany	1.27	2.28	1.20	1.92
Netherlands	1.58	2.52	1.58	1.86
Switzerland	0.77[a]	1.10	n.a.	0.48
Greece	0.44	0.44	0.46	0.47
Italy	n.a.	0.86	n.a.	0.63
Portugal	0.77	0.83	0.61	0.90
Spain	0.70	1.40	0.73	1.33
Ireland	n.a.	n.a.	n.a.	n.a.
UK	0.38	0.78	0.36	0.56

Notes:
[a] 1999 figure

Source: Calculated from OECD (2003a: table H)

parents, and large families have had to face increasing pressures during the last decade and are less well served. In addition, recent welfare state reforms that curtailed the main pay-as-you-go financed state pension scheme and established compulsory private funded pensions alongside it, give rise to future possibilities for the emergence of new social risks among those whose private pension component performs badly.

Nordic social welfare systems have been broadly successful in maintaining incomes among those most affected by the recessions of the 1980s and early 1990s, and the consequent rise in unemployment and spending constraint, so that poverty levels remain the lowest in the European Union and inequalities the least marked (Table 9.3). New risks in these countries are thus potential rather than actual. As a number of commentators have pointed out (Kuhnle, 2000; Esping-Andersen, 2002: 17) the main issue

Table 9.3 Poverty and inequality (ECHP, 1999)

	% Population at risk of poverty, 1999	Inequality ratio
Denmark	11	4.2
Finland	11	3.4
Sweden	9	3.2
Austria	12	3.7
Belgium	13	4.2
France	15	4.4
Germany	11	3.6
Netherlands	11	3.7
Switzerland	—	—
Greece	21	6.2
Italy	18	4.9
Portugal	21	6.4
Spain	19	5.7
Ireland	18	4.9
UK	19	5.2
EU-15	15	4.6

Notes: The poverty line is 60% of median equivalised disposable income for the country; the inequality ratio is measured as the ratio of the total equivalised income of the top quintile to that of the bottom quintile

Source: ECHP: EU (2003*b*)

confronting the Nordic welfare system is whether it will be possible to maintain the tax and employment rates necessary to sustain it in the face of growing international competition from countries with greater degrees of social inequality and lower spending. This issue also emerges powerfully in internal debates, with some influential private sector figures leading the case for greater flexibility in employment, see pp. 98, 109. Thus the emergence of new social risks in this context is shaped by the existing high level of universal and wide-ranging provision which caters effectively for the needs experienced elsewhere in Europe as new risks. Existing policies impose particular pressures on welfare provision and these seem likely to influence the extent to which reforms in the future may lead to the emergence of further areas of new social risks.

Corporatist Countries

The study includes the two most important European examples of corporatist welfare states—France and Germany—and also Switzerland, where welfare reflects key features of corporatism, but in some areas achieves provision closely related to employment status through compulsory occupationally related private insurance, rather than social insurance (Adema, 2000). In these countries old social risks policies have developed around the needs of a male breadwinner industrial working class, and new social risks present substantial challenges. There is one key difference: in relation to the risks surrounding women's access to paid work, France stands out among corporatist countries in terms of the extent to which it has developed extensive pre-schooling and child-care support policies which enable women to maintain a higher degree of commitment to paid work when responsible for young children (Table 1.2). Women's overall participation in the labour market is in fact close to the EU average and lower than that in most corporatist countries, but women who do work are more likely to be able to do so full time (Table 9.1). One development in the 1980s has been the APE benefit, which pays cash benefits to support women who stay at home to care for their children, leading to what is effectively a dual system. This may be responsible for a decline in recent labour market participation by mothers (pp. 130–1). The further extension of child-care provision is a major topic of debate. A national scheme of support for elder care has emerged only in the late 1990s.

In general, new social risks in these countries have emerged in ways that are shaped by the existing structure of old risks welfare: the Bismarckian model resulted in relatively weak provision for child care in Germany and Switzerland, and provision has expanded only recently. Christian Democrats in Germany have tended to stress the equal worth of paid work in the formal labour market and care work in the home. In 1986 the Kohl government implemented a major reform of parental leave and of other policies which had the effect of promoting part-time working for women (p. 39). More recently, Social Democratic/Green Party Federal governments have pursued policies which encourage state governments to extend the primary school day and increase provision of child care, through specific subsidies and more indirect support. The political conflict over mothers-at-home benefits against day care provision has some similarities to that in France in the 1990s. In Switzerland much provision is cantonal, but very recently federal subsidies have been provided to promote day care (pp. 178–9).

In all three countries, in line with an approach to welfare that focuses primarily on the needs of male industrial workers, care for older people tends to be provided informally and supported through local assistance schemes. Both France and Germany enacted national schemes to provide benefits to older people to enable them to pay for care (from relatives or others) in the 1990s—the German scheme was a new pillar of social insurance, the French scheme was tax-financed. Both schemes do not provide sufficient resources to cover full care costs and have been subject to continual debate and reform. Thus the existing policy model shapes the way new social risks have emerged in relation to child and elder care. Recent policy responses have involved substantial change to the system, and are a focus of political conflict.

For labour market policy, the old social risks regime was designed in the context of broadly neo-Keynesian labour market management. Social insurance is shaped round the interests of established industrial workers. There is little opportunity for those who are weakly unionised, who work part time or are on short-term contracts to present their interests. The response to the pressures on employment in Germany and France through the 1970s and 1980s was to expand early retirement schemes—'welfare without work'—which defended the interests of labour market insiders by reducing the supply of workers who might compete for their jobs and providing adequate pensions for those no longer needed. This restricted the access of other groups to stable employment and increased the numbers competing for the newly developing areas of work. Those without relevant skills were at high risk of social exclusion. By 1992 over a third of unemployed people in both countries had been without work for more than a year (OECD, 2003*b*: p.20).

During the 1990s there has been a tendency to cut back such schemes, to promote more limited and flexible work contracts that do not carry the expensive social insurance contribution obligations of established jobs and to develop extensive activation programmes, particularly through training and subsidised employment (OECD, 2003*a*: table H). Concern about social insurance contributions in France centred on the issue of how far employment costs damaged the competitiveness of national industry. French social insurance contributions raise 15.2 per cent of state revenue and are the highest in Europe (Table 9.4). They bear particularly heavily on employers, fuelling anxiety among business groups.

In France, the reforms have been part of the process whereby a 'second world of welfare' has developed alongside the social insurance system to meet the needs of groups weakly attached to paid work (p. 132) . This world

Table 9.4 Social security contributions

	Employees' contributions, 2000 (% GDP)	Employers' contributions, 2000 (% GDP)	Social security contributions as % of total tax revenue	
			1992	2000
Denmark	1.9	0.3	4	5
Finland	2.2	8.9	22	24
Sweden	1.9	11.9	28	28
Austria	6.1	7.2	32	30
Belgium	4.4	8.5	36	28
France	4.0	11.2	44	34
Germany	6.5	7.3	38	36
Netherlands	8.1	4.7	38	31
Switzerland	3.9	3.9	36	23
Greece	6.2	5.2	31	30
Italy	2.3	8.3	20	25
Portugal	3.3	5.1	24	24
Spain	1.9	8.6	35	30
Ireland	1.3	2.7	13	13
UK	2.5	3.5	17	16
EU-15	4.0	6.5	27.3[a]	25.3[a]

Note:
[a] EU-14 figures

Source: Calculated from OECD (2003*b*); OECD (1994)

consists of means-tested support, typically linked to requirements to engage in activities likely to increase employment opportunities. Thus social inclusion spending, almost all of it means-tested, has increased at just over one and a half times the growth rate of state spending as a whole between 1991 and 2000 (Eurostat, 2003*a*). A negative income tax (*Prime pour l'Emploi*) has been introduced to enhance work incentives. Insurance unemployment benefits have been reformed to increase pressure to pursue work.

In Germany, the fact that economic growth was the slowest in Europe throughout the 1990s (at 1.3 per cent, roughly two-thirds the European average—OECD, 2003*b*: 14) dominated political debate on labour market reform. Debates about insurance contributions were also coloured by concern about electoral punishment as the gap between gross incomes and take-home pay grew wider. Employee contributions are roughly equivalent to employer contributions and raise 6.5 per cent of total tax revenue, the second highest proportion in Europe (Table 9.4). Reforms have emphasised job subsidies (especially in the context of the dislocations to the labour market resulting from the reunification with the East) and on the promotion of 'mini' and 'midi' jobs to enhance labour market flexibility (pp. 35–7). A particular concern was long-term unemployment—highest in Europe after Italy and Spain (Table 9.1), and continuing to rise to 48 per cent of all unemployed by 2002 (OECD, 2003*b*: 20). The 1998 Red/Green government initially reacted against the more liberal measures of the previous government, but by 2002 was implementing tougher entitlement criteria, stricter activation measures and introducing a new more directive means-tested benefit for the long-term unemployed.

While unemployment in Switzerland has remained relatively low by European standards, the levels reached in the mid-1990s (5.7 per cent by 1997) were sufficiently high to generate intense policy debate. Social contributions are much lower than in other corporatist countries, since so much of pensions and health care is financed through occupational insurance (p. 223). However, increased claims jeopardised the finances of the schemes. The legislative response in 1995 incorporated both increased contributions and time limits on entitlement (to restore financial stability) and subsidies for cantonal activation programmes. This enabled a compromise between the programmes of right and left parties and the interests of employers and unions to be achieved, in keeping with the consociational basis of Swiss policy-making.

The impact of welfare reforms in creating further risks has applied mainly to pension restructuring in France and Germany and to those whose access to unemployment benefits is curtailed and who are required to enter negative activation programmes. In both France and Germany, changes to the well-established, expensive, and potentially costly pension systems have involved a number of legislative measures and protracted political conflicts in a policy area previously marked by consensus. Both countries have enacted reforms which change entitlement formulae and contribution requirements to contain future costs. In Germany, a small optional private funded pension has been established alongside the state scheme, but this has attracted relatively few savers. In France the expansion of private saving through life insurance and similar vehicles indicates a declining confidence in the capacity of state provision to maintain former standards. The German scheme is highly regulated and there is considerable debate about the extent to which the restrictions limit returns deter investors.

Old social risks policies clearly play an important role in regulating the emergence of new social risks in corporatist countries in two ways, passively by ensuring that resources are directed to the particular needs of a life-course structured by the traditional industrial labour market (so that policy-makers have been slow to recognise the new needs of mothers and carers seeking to enter paid work and those unable to access employment); and actively by reinforcing labour market structures and systems of family life which compound the exclusion of such groups. Policy-making has been delayed by struggles between reformers and the entrenched interests surrounding old social risks policies, who typically have access to a range of veto-points in corporatist systems, and is in most places incomplete.

In general, new risk policies in these countries have involved departures from the pattern of old risk policy-making, although there are national differences. Most reforms have been based on tax-financed provision (the exception being the new German long-term care insurance benefit). Most have involved provision directed at particular groups, and the policy departure involved in the construction of a system of targeted support outside the social insurance regime has been particularly significant in France. There have been new departures in policy-making concerning the de-regulation of some aspects of paid work and the re-regulation of private sector care services and pensions. The responses to new social risks do not sit comfortably within the established structure of the corporatist regime.

New social risk policy-making has led to political conflict over welfare and has contributed to the breakdown of the inter-party consensus on social policy in Germany during the 1990s. Conflict continues in both France and Germany, centred on labour market and pension reform but also involving provision for long-term care.

Liberal Countries

The United Kingdom is the foremost example of the liberal regime in Europe. Here new social risks needs were largely neglected by the self-consciously monetarist Conservative governments in the 1980s and 1990s on the assumption that a freer and more flexible labour market would absorb those at high risk of unemployment, and that child care could also be managed primarily through the market. However, policies to meet such needs formed a major part of the New Labour programme from 1997 onwards (pp. 66–7). The New Labour approach followed the central theme of the liberal model: highly targeted provision, directed at the enhancement of market success. It involved new departures in the UK context (substantial extension of policy intervention in areas which had previously been treated as largely private concerns and enhanced regulation of the private sector) and was linked to a modernised social democratic agenda of the promotion of citizen interest through equal opportunities and supportive provision.

New social risks in the United Kingdom have emerged in ways influenced by the existing welfare system and particularly by the weaknesses in provision that result from reliance on the market. Child-care provision had been limited and largely privately provided, so that, while female employment is relatively high (Table 9.1), mothers are much less likely to engage in paid work than elsewhere, or to move from full-time to part-time employment (Table 1.2). The shift away from traditional industrial breadwinner employment was more rapid than in most other European countries. The proportion of the labour force employed in the industrial sector in the United Kingdom fell from fourth highest in the European Union after Germany, Spain, and Italy in 1991 to fifth from the bottom (exceeded by France, Sweden, the Netherlands, and Greece in 2001—OECD 2003b: 16). Privatisation in areas such as pensions opened up potential new social risks among those with low or uncertain incomes. The relatively deregulated labour market combined with weak provision for more vulnerable groups had produced high levels of poverty and inequality (Table 9.3).

The policy response by New Labour was to establish targeted schemes directed at specific need-groups, to promote vigorously a 'make work pay' strategy and to seek to extend the regulation of private provision. The national child-care strategy relies principally on the expansion of private provision, and payments for care are subsidised through targeted tax credits. Direct provision of extra places through Sure Start and similar schemes is focused on areas of high deprivation. Long-term care is also chiefly financed privately with some means-tested state support and provided mainly through regulated private agencies. The New Deal programme is designed to activate unskilled labour market entrants and other groups among the unemployed, and is targeted through means-testing. 'Make work pay' policies include a national minimum wage, set at a relatively low level, the indexation of short-term benefits to prices rather than earnings and targeted support for low-paid people through tax credits. The overall objective is to reduce poverty by mobilising those on low incomes into paid work.

The development of risks as a result of welfare state reform is most obvious in the area of pensions, where the continuing policy of shifting the majority of pension provision to the private sector led to inadequate provision for some groups. The government has found difficulty in establishing a regulatory regime which will both guarantee the security and adequacy of pensions and provide suitable incentives to the industry to supply them. One result of the recent strengthening of regulation and the increased recognition of demographic pressures is that many occupational schemes have closed or been restructured on a 'defined contribution' basis, and employers have taken the opportunity to cut their contributions. The gap between pension savings committed and those necessary to ensure adequate provision is estimated at £27 billion and continues to increase (ABI, 2002: p 2). Incentive policies have failed to encourage employers or individuals to prioritise saving, and government has strengthened targeted provision for the poorest pensioners through a substantial extension of tax credit to this group.

In general, the approach to new social risks of the liberal regime reflects the key features of the liberal model—targeting of state help and a reliance on market forces. The New Labour version seeks to use these techniques to achieve ends closer to those of social democratic states, so that its interventions are on a greater scale than is customary in the United Kingdom and extends to new areas. Commitment to welfare goals through private market means also highlights issues of control which emerge in the areas of child and elder care and pensions, where it is necessary to regulate private suppliers, and in labour markets where a minimum wage regime has been established. In all these areas conflicts between providers and government have developed. In relation to long-term care, government has been forced to abandon a proposed regulatory standard in order to ensure continuity of provision from the private sector. In pensions, government has been unable to address the problem of introducing compulsion for occupational providers or for individuals in relation to pension savings because this would conflict with the market principle of autonomy, and is thus unable to deal with a substantial and growing pension savings gap.

Mediterranean Countries

Spanish experience with new social risks typifies many of the issues facing Mediterranean countries. New risks have emerged most powerfully in relation to high levels of unemployment, especially among young people (over 22 per cent for 15–24 year olds in Spain in 2002—OECD, 2003*b*: 20), and for the long-term unemployed where the rate is the highest in Europe after Italy, Greece and Germany (Table 9.1). They are also beginning to appear in the conflict over reconciling work and family life for women. As the table shows, women's overall employment rate in Mediterranean countries (with the exception of Portugal) is the lowest in Europe, although engagement in full-time work is closer to the European average and higher than in liberal and some corporatist countries.

Existing old social risk welfare systems are less well-developed than elsewhere in Europe, and have influenced the emergence of new risks through the weakness of provision for those without secure labour market attachment and the dominant assumption that care is provided informally by women (pp. 139–40). Family solidarity has traditionally sustained more vulnerable members, and helped to manage issues of poverty in the absence of robust state support. New social risk policies that deregulate employment have intensified the risks for some groups. Limited access to secure jobs and weak assistance benefits contribute to the highest poverty rates in Europe and highly unequal societies (Table 9.3).

The chief policy direction in relation to the labour market has been the slackening of regulation, most notably through legislation passed in 1994, resulting in the creation of a large number of short-term and part-time jobs. About a third of the Spanish labour force hold short-term contracts. There are targeted benefits for the long-term unemployed, and a regional system of means-tested support (*Rentas Minimas*) has developed through the initiatives of meso-level government.

The main new risks to emerge from reforms to old risk policies concern labour market deregulation. Policies designed to promote flexibility and competitiveness in the context of globalisation and membership of the Single European Market impose new risks on those who become vulnerable to unemployment. The welfare settlement contained in the 1995 Toledo Pact and confirmed in 2003 appears to ensure stability for the medium-term future. However, there are real concerns about the pension prospects of workers with interrupted contribution records on the part of left-wing parties and unions.

Plans to promote more equal opportunities for women have been developed. Child and elder care provision is limited, local and variable. Legislation for modest long-term care provision has been postponed repeatedly since 2000. A new system of tax relief for child-care costs has been introduced. This is of more value to higher-paid workers, and contributes mainly to support for middle-class women, who are most able to afford day care.

Mediterranean welfare states have not developed extensive new social risk policies. One result is a dramatic decline in fertility, since women are unwilling to balance the roles of informal domestic carer and paid worker and opt increasingly for the latter (Castles, 2003: 209, Moreno, 2002: 6), but this issue is only now entering policy debate.

The EU Level

The EU commitment to the principle of subsidiarity means that it is insufficiently active in social policy to influence the emergence of new social risks. However, Open Market and associated Growth and Stability Pact policies have had an indirect influence on social issues. In the former case, industrial restructuring associated with freer European competition impacts on the pressures for greater labour market flexibility and for reduced labour costs at the national level, and contributes to the reforms in the more regulated labour markets of corporatist and Mediterranean countries. The pact imposes additional pressures for spending constraint and these have contributed to policies such as the round of pension reforms that took place across Europe in the early and mid-1990s (Lintner, 2001: 330). Many of the national policies discussed above have been pursued in the shadow of EU economic policy. Enlargement, which will broaden the open market to include more diverse economies, at different stages of development, is likely to increase pressure for economic flexibility, with repercussions for social policy.

Support from member states for initiatives to harmonise welfare across Europe lost support in the early 1990s. An important set of recently developed policies attempts to influence reforms at the national level through targets set in the OMC. This influence is applied at the level of policy outcome, with the choice of measures left to the individual state. The five-year impact evaluation of the EES (the most advanced OMC policy relevant to social issues) concluded that 'there have been significant changes in national employment policies, with a clear convergence towards the common EU objectives', and highlighted activation policies, employment-friendly labour taxation, greater flexibility and improvements in child care (EU, 2002c: 1). While policies which promote activation, reform tax to reduce labour costs, advance equal opportunities, expand child care and encourage the availability of more flexible jobs can be identified in EU member countries, it is hard to establish how far these developments are the outcome of EU-level activity or of more far-reaching and simultaneous social changes. The report admits that labour market participation is still 'far below the Lisbon targets' (EU, 2002b: 16) The lack of EU-level enforce-ment mechanisms (as exist for economic and fiscal policies in the Broad Guidelines for Economic Policy, EU, Regulation 1466/97. L 209/1) and of subsidies to promote the required changes makes major departures in reform inspired at the EU level unlikely (Chalmers and Lodge, 2003: 6).

Directives in areas such as parental leave and working time have required national governments to improve the level of provision to a common standard and, perhaps more important, stimulated 'surprisingly far-reaching effects' in voluntary reforms exceeding the level required (Falkner and Treib, 2003: 20). EU 'soft law' also provides legitimatory resources to national policy actors and acts as a catalyst in the formation of coalitions—for example in relation to assistance in Spain and other Mediterranean countries (Matsaganis et al., 2003: 652) or for pension reform in France (Palier, 2003: 5) and stimulated policy-learning (O'Connor, 2003: 12).

The EU policies thus have real but weak effects on outcomes at the national level. Whether the OMC provides a setting in which more direct-ive policies will be possible in the future is at present unclear. It may be argued that the open method is a considerable threat to existing policy advance in European integration, on the grounds that the establishing of OMC practice with no enforcement mechanism institutionalises and legitimates national differences (Chalmers and Lodge, 2003: 15).

Convergence, Path-Dependency, and a 'new paradigm'

Two overall conclusions can be drawn from this review: first, existing welfare policies have shaped the emergence of new social risks in various European societies. Thus regime differences, determined in large part by responses to old social risks, are powerful factors in influencing the pattern of new risks that different European countries now recognise. The second conclusion, however, is that the new social risk policies now being devel-oped do not invariably reflect the characteristics of the existing old social risk regime. In Nordic countries, to be sure, where new risk regimes were established earlier, the risks are in general catered for within the existing settlement. Further new social risks for groups such as migrants may be tackled through extension of those policies. In the corporatist countries, which make up the majority of European welfare states, new social risk responses indicate new directions in welfare, but reforms are currently incomplete, so that the scale of the changes is uncertain.

In cases such as France this may be understood as the emergence of a parallel 'second world of welfare', means-tested and tax-financed, alongside the social insurance system; in Germany it represents a drift away from the Bismarckian basis of state welfare in the face of pressing labour market issues. In liberal countries the pattern of previous provision (targeted responses and a reliance on the market) may be identified in new social risk policies, although there is a simultaneous contrary shift to greater regulation. Development of new social risk policy appears limited in Mediterranean countries, in part because strong family systems have so far provided informal child care and cushioned the high levels of youth unemployment. There are indications that younger women may not be willing to both participate full time in paid work and act as traditional informal household carers. The moves to deregulate employment are a new direction in the context of the Mediterranean regime.

New social risk reforms are shaped overall by path-dependency, but involve in some contexts new departures. The instruments used to tackle the needs vary. A decline in the contribution of social insurance contributions to the finance of state spending may be noted among the corporatist countries (particularly in France, which has the greatest reliance on this system of finance in Europe) leading to some convergence, and reflecting the growth of tax-financed welfare among this group (Table 9.4). Labour market controls have been loosened in corporatist countries to assist the creation of jobs with low social contributions, although in the liberal UK the implementation of a minimum wage implies somewhat stronger regulation for the most vulnerable groups. There are, thus, weak tendencies to convergence in some policy areas evident in the data.

New social risk policies in general apply to fewer citizens for shorter periods in their lives than old social risk policies. They also absorb a much smaller proportion of welfare state spending. They do not amount to a restructuring of the welfare settlement. However they may indicate fresh directions within countries which were seen as immobilised in a 'frozen welfare landscape' (Esping-Andersen, 1996: 2; Pierson, 1998). The ways in which new social risks have emerged and been recognised have been extensively shaped by the existing policy regimes. Protection of the interests of 'insider' workers in corporatist systems has hampered labour market changes to provide for new and low-skilled entrants; assumptions about family roles limit the expansion of social care facilities; existing liberal commitments to market solutions influence the extension of those solutions in the area of new social risks. However, the emergence and expansion of tax-financed targeted provision within the corporatist model with assumptions about entitlement that stress obligations to prepare for employment rather than contribution record, and the encroachment of social care on family divisions of labour indicate the possibility of a gradual shift towards a different approach to the newly emerging welfare needs.

In Chapter 1 we described the shift from a neo-Keynesian interventionist paradigm in economic policy towards a 'pragmatic monetarism' that placed much greater reliance on the support of market freedoms. The strong emphasis on the mobilisation of the citizen worker in a more flexible and competitive labour-market and the tendency to develop welfare that erodes the traditional gender division of formal and informal labour indicate that policies for new social risks are adapting to this new approach.

New Social Risks—New Politics?

The Institutional Context

New social risks policy is influenced, but not governed, by old risk regimes. We move on to consider the political processes and factors that have influenced the development of the new social risks policies discussed above. These include institutional frameworks and the interactions of key policy actors. Institutions are conveniently thought of in terms of the extent to which constitutional structure (in the broadest sense, including informal frameworks of interaction with social partners and the role of religion and political culture as well as the legislature, executive, and judiciary) promotes consensus or majoritarian decision-making, and the extent to which different groups are able to promote their own interests at the policy level (Lijphart, 1999: ch.1). Relevant policy actors, in addition to political parties and local and national governments are the social partners (with their interests in national economic competitiveness, in labour costs and business regulation and in the working conditions of union members), the groups representing those most affected by new social risks and new social risks-bearers themselves as a political force.

Neither employers nor unions present a united front in relation to new social risks. Some industries are in greater need of skilled employees than others, and unions may represent groups in different industries or with a different balance of older employees (for whom the old social risks concerned with health, retirement, and pensions predominate) and younger employees (closer to new social risks). Some employers' groups in Germany, Spain, and the United Kingdom have campaigned for more child care provision. 'Modernising' unions such as CFDT in France or Unison in the United Kingdom have assented to activation reforms such as PARE,

PPE, and RMA or the New Deal and the Single Gateway, while others, such as FO or the TGWU, have been more concerned to defend existing entitlements and work contracts.

New risk bearers themselves lack social and political influence. An indication of weak authority is that women are roughly half as likely to be managers, a third as likely to be members of national or the EU parliament, and about a quarter as likely to be senior civil servants or judges, compared to men in European countries, with rather higher levels of participation in Nordic countries (Eurostat, 2002: charts 87, 91, 92, table 8; see Bonoli, 2003). Their ability to exert electoral influence is limited by the fact that, for most people, exposure to new social risks is a transitory phase of the family life cycle, concerned with child rearing, elder care, or labour market entry, and the scope for political activity is further hampered by traditional assumptions about gender roles and informal care.

The polities we examine include the most majoritarian constitutional framework, the United Kingdom (where first-past-the-post voting, a weak second chamber, lack of an effective constitutional court, or an independent regional tier of government and a closely controlled executive branch, confer exceptional authority on a highly centralised government), and Switzerland, where the highly fragmented governmental system with a Federal council elected by but not subject to recall by a parliament which it cannot dissolve, bicameralism, strong federalism, and opportunities for voters to challenge legislation through referenda, lead to coalition and policy-making through the evolution of consensus. Between these extremes the institutions of other countries give different degrees of influence to social partners and other actors in relation to social policy.

Much welfare in Nordic countries is under central control and there is a high degree of public commitment to high quality social provision. Although the Social Democratic party has retained power for almost all the post-war period in Sweden, the conflict between the need to manage the pressures on social welfare and the obvious electoral punishment of governments that seek overt cuts has led to the lengthy negotiation of reform. In Finland, the recent coalitions have supported a similar tendency. In the corporatist countries, social partners have been influential in welfare policy-making and (in some cases) in the management of policy, so that even in France, with its high degree of centralisation and its presidential system, welfare policy solutions require extensive negotiations with employers and unions and are at present incomplete. In Germany the federal 'semi-sovereign' (Katzenstein, 1987) state has been forced to manage change gradually. In relation to labour market and pension policy the severe tensions of high unemployment and rising contributory costs, exacerbated by the pressures of reunification on public spending and of globalisation on the German economic model, led to a breakdown of the inter-party consensus over the direction of social policy during the 1990s. The search for a solution which will command adequate support is thus even more time-consuming. Proposed unemployment benefit and pension reforms are under active debate at the time of writing.

In Mediterranean Spain, the reform process has been shaped by the commitment to democratic conciliatory solutions resulting from the recent experience of authoritarian rule. The existing settlement is contained in the 1995 Toledo Pact between the main political parties and the social partners. The important role of regional government in spending and service provision has required further compromise in this area. At the EU level, policy-making is dependent on a slow process of negotiation between the various national actors. Once a policy is agreed, however, it is available as a resource for policy actors at the national level seeking to promote change or to develop new coalitions, as Chapter 8 shows.

The constitutional frameworks of the European countries, apart from the United Kingdom, all contain multiple veto-points, so that reform processes tend to be slow and directed to the areas where change is easiest to achieve. The fact that a number of actors have interests in relation to new social risks opens up the possibility of alliances between different groups that render reforms possible, despite the weakness of the new risk bearers themselves.

Political Actors: Women and Paid Work

Social democratic parties have been at the forefront of support for policies which enable women to participate in paid work. In Nordic countries 'interaction between social democratic governments and strong women's movements, in the context of strong unions and favourable policy legacies . . . has produced the strongest new risk policies in Europe' (Huber and Stephens, 2003: 18). The Swedish Social Democratic Party has been committed to the view that gender equality can only be secured through equal opportunities in paid work, since Olaf Palme made this the basis of his speech to the 1972 conference (Hirdman, 1998: 41). In France, Germany and the United Kingdom the most vigorous expansion of child care has taken place under social democratic governments, and in Switzerland social democrats consistently supported adaptation of the basic pension to women's career patterns, the introduction of maternity insurance and subsidised day care. Other actors have adopted more complex positions. Christian-Democrat parties in the corporatist countries have tended to favour policies which subsidise mothers who care for their children themselves, on the grounds that this supports greater choice in employment, with the result that the labour market participation of younger women (particularly those unable to command high incomes) is inhibited.

One crucial factor has been the response of employers. While employers' organisations tend to argue for constraint in state spending, their support for child care has been significant in Switzerland and Germany. The employers' association that represents business and industry rather than finance capital in the United Kingdom (the CBI) has promoted greater state commitment to child care under both Conservative and Labour governments. The slower emergence of the issue in policy debate in Spain may be due to a lack of employer interest occasioned by an overfull labour market.

Policies for long-term care have tended to develop according to a rather different logic, and one that did not focus so strongly on the labour market role of women. The policy debate emphasised generalised concern about the failure of the existing disability scheme to meet the needs of frail elderly people and at the provisions for recouping care costs from the inheritance of their children in France, the problem of resolving the increasing pressures on local finance from the local social assistance-based scheme in Germany, and the issue of bed-blocking in the NHS and popular concern about the costs of private care responsibilities in the United Kingdom. Since the debates have not centred so strongly on the availability of women for paid work, the issue has been less salient in debate, for example, enabling the French government to ignore the calls of some unions for a social insurance scheme in 1997, and the UK government to disregard the 1999 Royal Commission recommendation for a national tax-financed scheme. In Spain, the complexities of negotiation between central, regional, and local government have delayed reform, in the absence of articulated and effective pressure for change.

One explanation for the slower development of policy in this area is that the impact on women's capacity to take paid work and therefore the potential for gaining support from employers' groups and from women engaged in the labour market is less marked. Fewer women of prime working age are likely to be engaged in substantial elder care than in meeting child-care needs, as we argued in Chapter 1 (p. 10). Only 36 per cent of women aged between twenty and forty-nine who care for a child are in full-time work as against 57 per cent of non-carers in Europe. Corresponding figures for 50–64 year-old women caring for a frail relative are 19 and 27 per cent, so the potential for releasing paid workers is much less (Eurostat, 2002: tables A.20, 21).

Political Actors: Labour Market Reform

In relation to labour market policies, patterns of support have been more complex. The breakdown of the neo-Keynesian paradigm in the 1980s and its replacement by a loose 'pragmatic monetarism' as described in Chapter 1, coupled with the experience of high unemployment and persistent long-term unemployment, and concerns about the position of European countries in increasingly competitive global markets, led to widespread dissatisfaction with existing affairs. Policy debates have often taken the need for change as their starting-point and centred on which reforms should be pursued. Employers' groups and centre-right parties have tended to promote the extension of negative activation, with benefit entitlement closely linked to the active pursuit of work and 'make work pay' policies which hold down benefit levels relative to wages. Social democrats have promoted more positive activation, which supports entry into the labour market and the development of skills. One policy direction has been a tendency to revise labour market regulation in order to promote greater flexibility, especially in relation to the well-established job security and wage bargaining rights of corporatist and Mediterranean countries. The Swiss activation scheme achieved a compromise between employers and unions by including time limits to unemployment insurance benefit entitlement and releasing federal funds for cantonal ALMP measures at a time when the finance of the scheme was in jeopardy as a result of rising unemployment.

In Nordic countries the strong endorsement of existing ALMP systems means that debates are about future reforms rather than current developments, but employers' associations have argued for greater labour market flexibility, accepting the likelihood that this would lead to enhanced income inequality. In France, and particularly Germany, the encouragement of jobs outside the existing pattern of regulation has been pursued. In both countries, benefit reforms following a logic of 'make work pay' rather than of replacement income have been introduced, and benefit entitlement has been linked more closely to the active pursuit of work. In the former case, the role of a modernising union (the CFDT) and the employers' association, MEDEF, has been important in enabling labour market and benefit reform to take place as a result of the campaign for a more active *refondation sociale*. In Germany, splits within the key actors (business, experts, and the major political parties) coupled with the strong opposition of trade unions, diluted and delayed reform of the less regulated 'mini-job' sector and the expansion of subsidised low-wage jobs in the 1990s. A gradual shift to *Fördern und Fordern* (carrot and stick) policies has taken place during the last decade, but all parties agree that the reform process is incomplete. Proposals for a unified benefit scheme for all long-term unemployed, which would be more directive, means-tested and tax-financed are currently before parliament.

In the United Kingdom, the New Labour government is able to impose a policy reform agenda which combines positive and negative activation, both policies highly targeted. Shifts in the position of trade unions, which initially opposed any dilution of social insurance-based unemployment benefits, but favoured the more positive activation of New Deal and the Minimum Wage, and of employers (concerned about extra spending, but reassured by government commitments on taxation, by the low level at which minimum wage was set and by upskilling policies) enabled these reforms to proceed.

In Spain, the chief direction of reform since 1994 has been towards greater labour market flexibility. An agreement on the protection of part-time workers between government and unions was rejected by employers in 1998 and the right-wing Popular Party government implemented further de-regulation of part-time work in 2001, despite opposition by the left and unions. One reason why central government has tended to focus on regulation issues may be that the regional level of government has become increasingly prominent in relation to assistance benefits. It was this tier that pioneered *Rentas Minimas* minimum income schemes between 1988 and 1995, with support from unions and in line with other EU countries and the expectations of the Maastricht Social Chapter. An attempt by central government in 2002 to introduce strong negative activation measures (including the debarring of those who did not take any job offered from the means-tested assistance benefit) failed after a general strike and opposition from unions and the left. Employers' organisations were divided on the issue and the government accepted seven out of the eight modifications proposed by the unions.

Political Actors: New Risks Resulting from Welfare State Reform

Since the reform of old risk social policy is a continuing process, the implications of such changes for the generation of new social risks and for political responses are at present uncertain. The most important area appears to be pension reform, and here the changes are potential rather than actual.

New policies, driven by concern about the costs of demographic shifts, may impose new risks, particularly on those who are most vulnerable in the labour market. Pension reform has involved government, social partners and the mass public, who hope one day to have access to adequate, secure pensions, and also important interests from the private pension industry. The issues cross-cut the traditional politics of old social risks, and the considerations of cost containment, personal responsibility and contribution to labour market flexibility that characterise debates about new social risks.

In corporatist countries, reform has been slow, and is at present unresolved, due to problems in achieving a viable compromise solution between the interests of the various actors. In France, public sector unions were able to halt a restructuring of their pensions proposed by the Juppé government in the mid-1990s, and careful negotiations have been necessary to permit the introduction of a more limited and as yet incomplete reform programme. In Germany, a series of measures designed to resolve pension issues have been implemented, in each case leading to reforms that required yet further legislation within a few years. In both countries governments of the centre-left have been able to move further in introducing spending cuts and encouragement to the private sector than those of the right. In the Swiss case, pension reform has proceeded through compromises that trade off the established interests of policy actors, most importantly business and trade unions.

The leading Scandinavian country, Sweden, achieved a settlement through lengthy negotiations between political parties, civil servants and expert advisers (see pp. 107–8). The fact that the social partners were excluded from these negotiations appears to have helped those involved to agree on a solution that balances a reform to the state scheme (which contains costs) with a modest funded private scheme, designed to provide additional retirement incomes. In Spain the pension settlement of the Toledo Pact (1995) was restated in 2003, and appears to have been achieved in a context where the pressures on pension spending were less severe than elsewhere. Nonetheless, current debates indicate that a move towards private pensions is likely, and this may lead to greater vulnerability for those without good employment records in a more flexible labour market.

The liberal bias of the New Labour government in the United Kingdom has made it difficult to resolve the conflict between commitment to market freedoms for employers and citizens, with a strong ideological emphasis on personal responsibility, and the desire to produce secure well-regulated pensions, in a context where the interests of a powerful financial sector must be safeguarded. The UK constitutional framework allows government to make and implement policies rapidly, without extensive consultation. However, despite a series of consultations and independent reports, no settlement in the area of pensions appears likely in the immediate future.

The new social risks that emerge in these contexts concern those who are less well protected, typically because their work records do not give them entitlement to good pensions. The problems of labour market flexibility appear likely to be most severe in Spain, but issues surround the development of mini-jobs in Germany and the capacity of the private sector to provide good coverage for such groups in the United Kingdom. A secondary concern is the impact of pension privatisation, and the extent to which this transfers risk directly to the individual. The politics of pension reform has mobilised a wide range of political actors but the minorities most likely to be directly affected by new risks nowhere exert influence. The entrenched interests of the more powerful actors among the social partners have delayed reform and ensure that pension restructuring remains incomplete in all of the countries studied. The Swedish solution is again the exception, in that reforms that seem least likely to generate new risks have been developed through a process in which the social partners did not have a strong role. The capacity of different welfare states to generate (with considerable labour) new policies to manage the problems of old risk provision—which is often taken to indicate resilience to the pressures discussed in Chapter 1— in fact appears likely to generate new risks for particular groups of citizens.

New Social Risks—a New Departure Alongside the Traditional Paradigm

New social risk reforms are able to make headway in European countries, despite the fact that new social risk-bearers are themselves a relatively weak political force. Reform processes depend in most cases on the programme favoured by the political actors who are able to exert an influence. The capacity to make such compromises depends on institutional structure and on the interests mobilised around the particular issue. The fact that the welfare state settlements based on old social risk interests are vulnerable to modification indicates that systems which have sometimes been seen as 'immovable objects' admit shifts in the positions of relevant social actors. It is these shifts, and sometimes splits, within the established groupings of actors that are of particular importance in the development of new social risk policies.

Realignments of Policy Actors

In the UK context, the crucial shift has been the change in position of the Labour party, from commitment to a traditional welfare state (which provided national insurance benefits, modified Keynesian support for employment and allowed child care to remain a private issue) to a 'modernised' settlement, which included both positive and negative activation policies and highly targeted support for child and elder care costs. This enabled alliances to be formed with some groups in business, particularly over child care and activation, and precipitated a shift in the position of leading unions who were otherwise excluded from political engagement within the majoritarian centralised institutional framework. The liberal context shaped reforms within a targeted and market-centred approach, but the peculiar dominance of the party of government in the UK context plays a major role in the scale and rapidity of reform in all areas except pensions.

In the corporatist countries reviewed, a shift towards the construction of new social risk welfare systems alongside the traditional social insurance structure has emerged. Institutional framework has clearly played a role. The more centralised polity of France, with its particular roles for the social partners in the social insurance system and its traditions of citizenship and of commitment to support for women workers, has developed a tax-financed arm of the welfare system based on the discourse of *national solidarité*, but has found difficulty in carrying through a coherent package of labour-market reform. In Germany, the more consensual institutions and multiplicity of veto points have slowed reform and facilitated a greater role for social insurance institutions. In both cases, realignments of social actors have been important, in the role of modernising unions and employers' representatives in France and of the failure to rebuild consensus among the key actors on the desired direction of change in Germany. Attempts to construct agreement around the 1998 tripartite 'Alliance for Jobs' did not succeed. New policies (Agenda 2010) build on the strategy of local Job Centres, more regulatory benefit reform and modest deregulation proposed by the Hartz Commission. In Switzerland, the high degree of consensus required for successful reform has led to more limited changes. The difficulty in finding a middle ground between the actors is indicated by the fact that innovations to meet new social risks have tended to originate outside the traditional pattern of government commissions.

In Spain, the relations between central and regional levels of government as well as between social partners and parties, and the opportunities for mobilisation around particular issues, have produced new opportunities for reform. Regional government has been able to carry out innovative reforms with the support of the left-wing political parties and unions (as in the case of assistance), but not independently (as in the case of long-term care). In recent years, central government allied with employers' groups has promoted deregulation, but found it more difficult to implement negative activation policies in the face of vigorous opposition by the unions. In the Nordic countries, an enduring consensus that government should enable all citizens to contribute as workers has led to extensive new social risks provision, so that attempts to cut services, curtail spending or introduce more negative activation are largely unsuccessful.

Power Resources and Policy Communities

Accounts of welfare reform are based on two broad models—'power resources', which stresses the capacity of social interests to promote policies which they believe will best serve their interests, and approaches which stress the importance of groupings of social actors as the driving force behind change. The latter tend to focus on the role of policy communities, issue networks, advocacy coalitions, discourse coalitions, and similar associations, often enabled by normative entrepreneurs, in negotiating, developing and promoting common ideas (for a brief review of literature on 'groups at the centre of policy construction', see Schmidt, 2002: 211). Analyses then consider how the ability of either interests or actors is influenced by political institutions, welfare state regimes, policy feedback, government action and so on (Heclo, 1974; Skocpol and Amenta, 1986; Esping-Andersen, 1990; Pierson, 2001).

These perspectives correspond loosely to materialist and idealist epistemologies and tend to develop in different contexts. The power resources model originated among analysts of Nordic welfare states (Korpi, 1983; Huber and Stephens, 2001: p.17), where developments have been shaped by struggles to reduce class and gender inequalities in a universal welfare citizenship. Approaches which centre on the interaction of key actors reflect the way in which policy evolves in systems with a broader range of power-holders, such as the corporatist European countries, the United States and the European Union (Richardson, 2001: 7–11). From the former perspective the chief political constraint on new social risk policy-making is the lack of specific mobilised power-resources. Unskilled would-be labour market entrants and those whose lives are dominated by care responsibilities are not well organised to exert political power. The alliances between an organised working class (to some extent in collaboration with middle-class interests) that have been seen as driving change in industrial welfare states (Baldwin, 1990) are not available. From the latter, the difficulty lies more in identifying how reforms that affect new social risks can enter the policy discourse or in tracing the process whereby support from more powerful actors is negotiated (Wallace and Wallace, 2000: ch. 3). Both approaches focus on linking new social risk-bearers to other groups.

The review above indicates that new social risk policies in relation to labour market reform, child care, and the new pension policies that impose particular risks on some groups, have developed primarily as a result of the power resources and negotiating capacity of more influential political actors than the actual risk-bearers. Political conflicts over the direction of policy continue. The outcomes so far appear to be labour market reforms that combine in different degrees commitments to negative incentive-based activation and de-regulation, chiefly supported by the right and employers, and training and opportunity policies supported by social democrats, with no dominant overall pattern. The pattern of reform is clearly influenced by the old social risk policies that compose the regime type. However, even in corporatist countries with multiple veto-points in policy-making and high levels of union influence, reforms that cut back the systems of secure income replacement benefits established in the 'golden age' of the welfare state have been implemented, alongside the expansion of activation spending documented in Table 9.2. Responses to new social risks entail new directions in specific policy areas within the old risk welfare states.

The expansion of child care and of policies designed to promote paid work shows that new social risks provide a context in which European welfare states are pursuing the mobilisation of those who encounter difficulty in gaining access to paid work alongside the provision of traditional services and benefits to meet old social risks. It is not surprising that the Nordic countries, where support for the worker–citizen is a central policy objective, lead Europe in new risk policy-making, nor that new social risks are seen by the European Union as a relatively undeveloped area, in which policy leadership can be offered and through which a transnational agency can seek to increase its contact with the lives of ordinary citizens.

New risk reforms have tended, with some exceptions, to follow the pattern of old social risks provision, and lead to the readjustment rather than the restructuring of welfare state regimes. Institutional structure makes a difference in facilitating or delaying change, and channelling it in particular directions, and in providing particular opportunities for compromise or for alliance between political actors. New social risks do not generate a new paradigm of welfare, nor do they lead to a new welfare state politics. They are rather to be seen as a modification, but one which contradicts the view that European welfare states face insuperable problems in adapting to new welfare needs. There are some indications that success in dealing with the problems that face traditional welfare states may itself generate further new risks among those who fare least well in more flexible labour markets.

The emphasis on mobilisation into paid work through activation fits with the shift away from neo-Keynesian full-employment economic management in overall policy paradigm. The greater salience of child care also reflects women's involvement in paid work. It is in employment-centred issues that new social risk policy has made the strongest headway within the constraints of the various regime types. EU pursuit of the Open Method of Co-ordination recognises and acquiesces in these differences. The real progress in policy innovation indicates that the future of European welfare states continues to surprise and can be summed up neither in terms of the bleakness of a 'retreat to austerity' nor the intransigence of a 'frozen welfare landscape'.

References

ABI, 2002 What makes people save? Research Report, Association of British Insurers, London.

Adema, W. (2000) 'Revisiting Public Expenditure Across Countries', OECD *Economic Studies*, 30(1): 191–6.

Baldwin, P. (1990) *The Politics of Social Solidarity*, Cambridge University Press, Cambridge.

Bonoli, G. (2003) *Providing Coverage Against New Social Risks in Mature Welfare States*, Paper presented at the New Social Risks conference, Lugano, September.

Castles, F. (2003) 'The world turned upside-down', *Journal of European Social Policy*, 13 (3): 209–27.

Chalmers, D. and Lodge, M. (2003) 'The Open Method of Co-ordination and the European Welfare State', CARR, LSE, Discussion Paper no 11.

Esping-Andersen, G. (1990) *Three Worlds of Welfare Capitalism*, Polity Press, Cambridge.

—— (1996) *Welfare States in Transition*, Sage, London.

—— (1999) *The Social Foundations of Post-industrial Economies*, Oxford University Press, Oxford.

—— (2002) *Why We Need a New Welfare State*, Oxford University Press, Oxford.

EU (2002a) *Social Protection in Europe*, Brussels.

—— (2002b) *Impact Evaluation of the European Employment Strategy (Technical Analysis Supporting COM 416, Employment and Social Affairs*.

—— (2002c) *Taking Stock of Five Years of the EES*, COM 2002/416 Final.

Eurostat (2002) *The Life of Women and Men in Europe, 1980–2000, Office of Official Publications of the EU, Luxembourg.*

Eurostat (2003) *Social Protection, 1991–2000.*

Geyer, V. (2001) *Exploring European Social Policy*, Polity Press, Cambridge.

Heclo, H. (1974) *Modern Social Politics in Britain and Sweden*, Yale University Press, New Haven.

Hirdman, V. (1998) 'State Policy and Gender Contracts: Sweden in E. Drew, R. Emerek, and E. Mahon (eds.) *Women, Work and the Family*, Routledge, London, 36–46.

Huber, E. and Stephens, J. (2001) *Development and Crisis of the Welfare State*, Chicago University Press, Chicago.

—— and —— (2003) *Determinants of Welfare State Approaches to Old and New Social Risks*, Paper given at the ISA RC19 Conference, Toronto, August.

Jaeger, M. and Kvist, J. (2003) ' Pressure on state welfare in post-industrial societies', *Social Policy and Administration*, 37 (6): 555–72.

Katzenstein, P. (1987) *Policy and Politics in West Germany: The Growth of a Semisovereign State*, Temple University Press, Philadelphia.

Korpi, W. (1983) *The Democratic Class Struggle*, Routledge and Kegan Paul, London.

Kuhnle, S. (ed.) (2000) *The Survival of the European Welfare State*, Routledge, London.

Leibfried, S. and Pierson, P. (2000) 'Social Policy', in H. Wallace and W. Wallace (eds.), *op cit.*

Lijphart, A. (1999) *Patterns of Democracy: Government Forms and Performance in 36 Countries*, Yale University Press, New Haven and London.

Lintner, V. (2001) 'European Monetary Union', in Richardson (ed.) *op. cit.*

Matsanganis, M., Ferrera, M., Capucha, L., and Moreno, L. (2003) 'Mending Nets in the South', *Social Policy and Administration*, vol 37 (6) 639–55.

Moreno, L. (2002) *Mediterranean Welfare and 'Superwomen'*, Madrid UPC, Working Paper 02–02.

O'Connor, J. (2003) 'Measuring Progress in the European Social Model', Paper given at the ISA RC19 Conference, Toronto, August.

OECD (1994) *Revenue Statistics for Member States, 1965–93.*

—— (2003*a*) *Employment Outlook 2002.*

—— (2003*b*) *OECD in Figures*, 2003.

Palier, B. (2003) *The Europeanisation of Welfare Reforms*, Paper presented at the Toronto Conference of the ISA RC19, August.

Pierson, P. (1998) 'Irresistible forces, immovable objects: post-industrial welfare states confront permanent austerity', *Journal of European Social Policy*, 5, (4): 539–60.

—— (2001) 'Coping with Permanent Austerity: Welfare State Restructuring in Affluent Democracies', in Pierson (ed.), *The New Politics of the Welfare State*, Oxford University Press, Oxford, 410–56.

Richardson, J. (ed.) (2001) *European Union: Power and Policy-Making*, Routledge, London.

Schmidt, V. (2002) *The Futures of European Capitalism*, Oxford University Press, Oxford.

Skocpol, T. and Amenta, E. (1986) 'States and Social Policies', *Annual Review of Sociology*, 12:

Wallace H. and Wallace, W. (2000) *Policy-Making in the European Union*, Oxford University Press, Oxford.

Index

abortion reform, Germany 40
activation policies 243
  European spending on 19, 206
  Finland 99, 217–18
  France 124–7, 133, 222
  Germany 48, 222
  and Nordic welfare states 88
  Spain 146–7, 152–4
  Sweden 100, 217–18
  Switzerland 162, 173–5
  United Kingdom 19, 69–72, 75–6
Amsterdam Treaty (1997) 189, 191, 192,
    194, 195, 202, 204, 210
apprenticeships, Germany 46, 47
austerity, and future of welfare state 7, 24–5

benefits:
  decline in average level of 7
  Germany 48
  Spain 152–4
  United Kingdom 63, 71
Blair, Tony 65
Blüm, Norbert 46
Braun, Théo 128

capital mobility 6
Carers and Disabled Children Act
    (UK, 2000) 68
child care:
  and European Union 193, 196, 206–7
  Finland 90, 92–3
  France 117, 129–30, 131, 221
    spending on 15–16
  Germany 33, 38–9, 40, 41–2, 51, 221
  and new risk policies 10, 243
  politics of 234–5
  Sweden 90, 92–3
  Switzerland 164, 165, 178–9, 221
  United Kingdom 59, 62, 66, 67–8,
    75–6, 79
  and women's labour force
    participation 17
Coluche 118
COMETT programme 194
Committee on Social Justice (UK) 64
competitiveness:
  and new risk policies 10
  and welfare policies 75

Conservative Party, policy discourse of
    62–4
convergence, and new social risk
    policies 231
corporatist welfare state 13
  and care spending 15
  and labour force participation 21
    women 17, 18
  and labour market activation
    spending 19
  and new social risks 23–4
    response to 221–5, 230–1
  and pensions 238
  see also France; Germany; Switzerland

decommodification, and welfare
    reform 14
demography, and ageing population 3, 6,
    88–9
Denmark, and European Union 194
Duisenberg, W. 13

economic growth:
  and development of welfare state 1
  Germany 223–4
  Switzerland 163
  trends in 6
  uncertainty of 2
economic policy:
  and development of welfare state 1
  and European Union 21–2
  and Keynesian paradigm 12
  and monetarist paradigm 12–13, 232
  Spain 138
education:
  and employment 4
  Finland 101
  Spain 141
  Sweden 101
  and unemployment 4, 36, 60
  vocational training 46, 47
elderly care:
  Finland 89, 90, 93–6
  France 120–1, 127–9, 131, 222
  Germany 42, 42–4, 51, 222
  neglect of 235–6
  and Nordic welfare states 88
  Spain 155–6

elderly care (*cont.*):
  Sweden 89, 90, 93–6
  Switzerland 166
  United Kingdom 59, 61–2, 66, 67, 68, 76
employment:
  atypical:
    Finland 100–1
    France 119
    Germany 35–6
    Spain 147
    Sweden 100–1
  and care responsibilities 3
  and education 4
  and labour force participation rates 3
  low-skilled 21, 36–7, 46–8, 103, 152
  see also part-time work
Employment in Europe survey (1996) 4
equal opportunities:
  and European Union 189, 195–202, 206
  see also gender equality
ERASMUS programme 194
European Central Bank 209
European Commission:
  and employment policies 194
  and enforcement 209
  and European social policy 189
  and gender equality 195, 197
  and Open Method of Coordination 191
  and policy learning 190
  and social inclusion 202–3
  and Spanish economy 146
European Council:
  and employment policies 192, 194
  and gender equality 196
  and new social risks 210
  and Open Method of Coordination 191
  and social inclusion 202
  and social policy 189, 209, 210–11
European Court of Justice 196
European Employment Strategy 13, 19,
    191, 192–3, 194, 196, 205, 209
European Labour Force Survey, and family
    models 16–17
European Parliament:
  and gender equality 195–6
  and social inclusion 202
European Trade Union Congress 197
European Union:
  and accession countries 205
  and activation policies 19, 22, 206
  and ageing population 3, 6
  and child care 193, 196, 206–7
  Community Action Programme 203

  and decision-making 186–7, 189,
    190, 202
  economic policy co-ordination
    21–2
  Employment White Paper (1993) 21
  and equal opportunities 189,
    195–202, 206
  and European Social Model 191
  Growth and Stability Pact (1997) 6, 187,
    191, 209
  impact on national policy-making 58,
    80, 185, 189, 208–9
  labour market policies 189, 190, 192–5,
    205–6
  Medium Term Action Programmes
    193–4, 196, 203
  and National Action Plans 191, 203
  and new social risks 21–3, 192–206,
    210–11, 216–17
  response to 11, 186, 187–8, 229–30
  and Open Method of Coordination
    190–2, 193, 194, 196, 203, 209,
    211, 243
  and parental leave 196, 208
  part-time work 206
  and policy-making 186–7
  and poverty 202–4, 207–8
  Poverty Programme 189
  and private pensions 5
  and Single European Market 185, 188
  Social Action Programme 188–9, 190,
    196, 203, 204
  Social Charter 188, 209, 210
  Social Dimension 189
  and social exclusion 202–4, 207–8
  Social Fund 193, 203
  and social inclusion 22
  and social policy 22, 185, 186, 187,
    188–90, 210, 229
  Social Protocol 202
  Structural Funds 196
  and subsidiarity 190, 204, 229
  summits:
    Barcelona (2002) 196
    Essen (1994) 191, 192
    Laeken 203
    Lisbon (2000) 191, 196,
      203, 204
    Luxembourg (1997) 193
    Stockholm (2001) 196
    Strasbourg (1989) 188
  and unemployment 205
  and welfare state reform 190–2

European Women's Lobby 197
exchange rates, and currency
    speculation 6

family:
    and development of welfare state 1
    family policy:
        Finland 92
        France 130-1
        Switzerland 163, 164
    Germany, family structure 17, 32-4
    and new social risks 5, 8, 10
    and social care 2
    in Spain 137, 140, 141, 143-5, 146, 155
    and traditional welfare settlement 14
    see also work/family balance issues
family models:
    dual carer 16-17
    dual earner 16, 17, 90, 91, 141
    modified industrial 16, 17
    reverse industrial 16, 17
Family Policy Strategy (Finland) 92
Fehr, Jacqueline 178
fertility:
    and short-term contracts 92
    Spain 140, 141-2
Field, Frank 73
Filatov, T. 93
Financial Services Agency (UK) 73
Finland:
    activation policies 99, 217-18
    adjusted unemployment benefit 103-4
    and adult education 101
    and ageing population 88-9
    child care 90, 92-3
    and dual earner households 90, 91
    and elderly care 89, 90, 93-6
    and employment 88-9
        atypical 100-1
        low-waged 102-3
    Family Policy Strategy 92
    and immigrants 105, 106
    and income inequality 102, 103
    and labour force participation 20
    labour shortages 94
    and new social risks:
        emergence of 88-91, 96-7
        politics of 107-9
        response to 217-20, 241
    parental leave 91-2
    part-time work 92, 101
    pensions 101, 106, 107-8
    as service state 90

and unemployment 89, 97-9
    employer subsidies 99
    immigrant 105
    long-term 98, 99, 103
    low-skilled 103
    youth 98
and welfare state change 106-7
welfare state popularity 107
and women's labour force participation
    90, 91-2, 217
work/family balance issues 91-2
see also Nordic welfare state
Finnish Labour Force 2020 94
flexibility, and welfare reform 14
Flückiger, Yves 165-6
France:
    activation policies 124-7, 133, 222
    and atypical employment 119
    and benefit targeting 132-3
    and child care 15-16, 117, 129-30,
        131, 221
    elderly care 120-1, 127-9, 131, 222
    family policy, duality of 130-1
    and 'insertion' policies 122
    Job Substitution Allowance Scheme 127
    labour market 222
        changes in 119-20
        and early retirement 119-20, 126-7
        making work pay 124-6
        and older workers 126-7
        reform of 236
        women's participation 18, 121, 129,
            130, 131, 221
    lone parents, and poverty 122
    and minimum income 123-4
    and national solidarity 132
    and negative income tax 126
    and new poverty 116, 117, 118
    and new social risks:
        emergence of 116-22, 131-3
        policies for 122, 230-1
        policy impact 131-3
        politics of 132
        response to 221-5, 240
    part-time work 119
    paternity leave 130
    Pension Steering Committee 127
    pensions 4, 120, 127, 224-5, 238
    social exclusion 115, 116, 117-19, 131
    social insurance 116-17, 222-3
    Special National Employment Fund 127
    and trade unions 116, 125, 132
    and unemployment 117, 124

France (*cont.*):
    traps 119
    youth 21
    welfare state:
        dualisation of 116, 221
        impact of new risk policies 131–3
        reform obstacles 115–16
        structure of 115
    and women 15
    work/family balance issues 121–2,
        129–31
    and working poor 119
    see also corporatist welfare state
Franco, Francisco 137

gender:
    and division of labour 15
    role changes 32–4
    and traditional welfare settlement 14
    see also gender equality; women
gender equality:
    Germany 40–1
    Spain 144, 145, 157
    Switzerland 170
    see also equal opportunities
Germany:
    and abortion reform 40
    activation policies 48, 222
    Agenda 2010 48, 51
    and benefit cuts 48
    and care insurance 42–4, 49, 50–1
    and child care 33, 38–9, 40, 41–2,
        51, 221
    and economic growth 223–4
    and elderly care 42–4, 49, 51, 222
    and European Union 194
    and family structure 17, 32–4
    and gender equality 40–1
    gender role changes 32–4
    and labour market 222, 223–4
        atypical employment 35–6
        characteristics of 34–5
        de-standardisation of employment
            35–7, 44–6, 51
        dependent self-employment 36, 44
        and low-skilled unemployment 36–7,
            46–8
        and mini-jobs 35, 44, 45
        reform of 236–7
        vocational training 46, 47
        and wage subsidy 47–8, 51
        women's participation 15, 18, 33, 38
    lone parents 32, 34

    and new social risks:
        emergence of 32–7, 50–1
        politics of 51, 233–4
        response to 221–5, 231, 240
    and parental leave reform 39, 40, 221
    part-time work 35, 39, 40, 44
    and pensions 4, 37, 45–6, 49–50, 51,
        224–5, 238
    and personal social services 37
    policy debates and developments 38,
        50–1
        de-standardisation of employment
            44–6, 51
        and frail elderly 42–4
        low-skilled unemployment 46–8
        and welfare markets 37, 49–50, 51
        and work/family balance
            38–42, 50
    and poverty 33–4
    and privatisation of welfare 37
    and subsidiarity 34, 40, 46
    and unemployment 36–7, 46–8, 224
        youth 21
    weak service infrastructure 34, 50
    and welfare state change 31, 37
    see also corporatist welfare state
globalisation, impact of 2
government, and new social risks 8–11
Greece, and dual earner households 17
Green Party (Germany), and women's
        labour force participation 38
Growth and Stability Pact (1997) 6, 187,
        191, 209

Hartz Commission 240
Health and Social Care Act
        (UK, 1990) 62
Hombach, Bodo 47

immigrants:
    Finland 105, 106
    Sweden 104, 105–6
Ireland:
    and dual earner households 17
    and low pay 21
Italy:
    and dual earner households 17
    and women 15

Job Seeker's Allowance (UK) 63
Jobcentre Plus (UK) 72
Jospin, Lionel 124, 130
Juppé, A. 128

Kohl, Helmut 32, 39
Kuhn, T. 11

laborem exercens 38–9
labour market:
  changes in 4
  European Union policies 189, 190,
    192–5, 205–6
  France 222
    changes in 119–20
    and early retirement 119–20, 126–7
    making work pay 124–6
    and older workers 126–7
    reform of 236
    women's participation 18, 121, 129,
      130, 131, 221
  Germany 222, 223–4
    atypical employment 35–6
    characteristics of 34–5
    de-standardisation of employment
      35–7, 44–6, 51
    dependent self-employment 36, 44
    and low-skilled unemployment 36–7,
      46–8
    and mini-jobs 35, 44, 45
    part-time work 35, 39, 40, 44
    reform of 236–7
    vocational training 46, 47
    and wage subsidy 47–8, 51
    women's participation 15, 18, 33, 38
  and new social risks 4, 5, 8, 10, 19–21
  politics of reform 236–7
  Spain:
    atypical employment 147
    and 'dead-end' jobs 152
    dual 152
    features of 146
    and flexibility 151–2, 157
    reform of 237
    women's participation 139–40,
      141–3
  Switzerland:
    participation in 19–20
    shortages 178
    women's participation 161
  United Kingdom:
    access to employment 60–1
    activation policies 19, 69–72, 75–6
    mobilisation 65, 68
    policy 63
    reform of 237
    women's participation 15, 18, 59,
      66–7, 79

see also activation policies; part-time
    work
legitimation:
  and Keynesian paradigm 12
  and monetarist paradigm 12–13
Lenoir, R. 117–18
Lewis, J., and gender division 15
liberal welfare state 13
  and care spending 15
  and labour force participation 21
    women 17, 18
  and labour market activation
    spending 19
  and low pay 21
  and new social risks 23, 24, 107
    response to 225–7, 231
  see also United Kingdom
lifelong learning 101
LINQUA programme 194
lone parents:
  Germany 32
  and poverty:
    France 122
    Germany 34
    United Kingdom 59–60
  United Kingdom:
    and child care 66
    and employment 59, 69, 71, 76, 79
low pay 21
  Finland 102–3
  Germany 47–8, 51
  United Kingdom 71
Luxembourg Income Study 3

Maastricht Treaty (1994) 6, 189,
    194, 210
maternity insurance, Switzerland
    175–8
maternity leave, Switzerland 164–5
maternity pay, United Kingdom 68
Maxwell, Robert 64
Mediterranean welfare state 13
  and care spending 15
  characteristics of 216
  and labour force participation 21
    women 17, 18
  and new social risks 23, 24
    response to 227–9, 231
  and role of family 140
  see also Spain
minimum incomes:
  France 123–4
  Spain 152–4, 155

minimum wage:
  Spain 153
  United Kingdom 71, 76
minorities, and new social risks 8, 10, 24
Mitterand, F. 123
mobilisation:
  and New Labour policies 65, 68
  and new risk policies 10, 14, 242, 243
motherhood, and labour force
    participation 17, 66-7

National Carers Strategy (UK) 67-8
Netherlands:
  and labour force participation 20
  and modified industrial family
    model 17
  and private pensions 4
New Deal (UK) 70-1, 76
New Labour:
  policy discourse of 58, 64-6, 79
  realignment of 240
new social risks:
  and ageing population 3
  citizen's perspective 7-8
    management of 8
    and minorities 8
    and state intervention 8
    and younger people 8
  definition 2-3
  differences from old risks 9-11
  emergence of 23, 216-17
  and European Union 21-3, 192-206,
    210-11, 216-17
  and European welfare states 215
  and expansion of private services 4-5
  and family 5, 8
  government perspective 8-11
  and labour force participation 3
  and labour market 4, 5, 8, 19-21
  and minorities 8, 10, 24
  and mobilisation of labour 14
  particularity of 8, 10
  and policy paradigm 23, 232
  politics of 11, 216
    institutional context 232-4
    and labour market reform 236-7
    and policy communities 241, 242
    and power resources 241-2
    and welfare state reform 237-9
    women and paid work 234-6
  response to 23-4, 216-17, 230-1, 242-3
    and convergence 231
    corporatist countries 221-5

European Union 229-30
liberal countries 225-7
Mediterranean countries 227-9
Nordic countries 217-20
and path dependency 231
and policy communities 241, 242
and power resources 241-2
and realignment of policy actors
  240-1
and welfare regimes 13-21, 216-17, 230
and welfare state change 5
and women 14
and work/family balance 15-19
see also individual countries
Nice, Treaty of (2000) 190, 210
Nordic welfare state 13
  and care spending 15
  and elderly care 88
  features of 88
  and labour force participation
    19, 21
    women 17-18
  and labour market activation
    spending 19
  and new social risks 23, 87-8, 96-7
    impact of 109-10
    politics of 107-9, 233
    response to 217-20, 230, 241
  and privatisation 97
  welfare spending 88
  see also Finland; Sweden

old social risks:
  characteristics of 8
  differences from new risks 9-11
  politics of 11
Organisation for Economic Cooperation
  and Development (OECD) 4-5

Palme, Olaf 234
parental leave:
  and European Union 196, 208
  Finland 91-2
  Germany 39, 40, 221
  Spain 144
  Sweden 91
part-time work:
  and European Union 206
  Finland 92, 101
  France 119
  Germany 35, 39, 40, 44
  Spain 147, 151-2
  Sweden 92, 101

Switzerland 164, 172
United Kingdom 59, 66
paternity leave:
    France 130
    United Kingdom 68
path dependency, and new social risk
        policies 231
Paugam, S. 118
pensions 237–8
    and corporatist welfare state 238
    erosion of commitments 9
    and European Union 5
    expansion of private 4–5
    Finland 101, 106, 107–8
    France 4, 120, 127, 224–5, 238
    Germany 4, 37, 45–6, 49–50, 51,
        224–5, 238
    politics of reform 237–9
    Spain 148–50, 238
    Sweden 4, 101, 106–7, 107–8, 238
    Switzerland 4, 165–6, 170–3, 238
    United Kingdom 4, 5, 61, 63–4, 72–5,
        79, 227, 238–9
PETRA programme 194
Pickering review 74
Pierre, Abbé 118
Pierson, P., and permanent austerity 7,
        24–5
Pisani-Ferry report 126
policy communities, and welfare
        reform 241
policy paradigm:
    Keynesian 12
    monetarist 12–13, 232
    and new social risks 23, 232
    notion of 11
political systems, and development of
        welfare state 1–2
politics, and new social risks:
    institutional context 232–4
    and labour market reform 236–7
    and policy communities 241, 242
    and power resources 241–2
    and welfare state reform 237–9
    women and paid work 234–6
Portugal, and labour force
        participation 20
post-industrial society:
    and new social risks 3–5, 215
    and welfare state change 7
poverty:
    and dual employment 3
    and education 4

and European Union 189, 202–4, 207–8
    France 116, 117, 118
    Germany 33–4
    and lone parents 34, 59–60, 122
    and Nordic countries 219
    and retired people 61, 78–9
    United Kingdom 59–60, 61, 76–9
power resources, and welfare reform 241
private sector, expansion of services 4–5
privatisation 4
    Germany 37
    and Nordic welfare states 97
    United Kingdom 62
productivity, long-term decline 6
public-private division, and new social
        risks 8

Raffarin, Jean-Pierre 126, 129
recommodification, and welfare
        reform 14
Rome, Treaty of (1957) 21, 194, 195, 202

Sailas, Raimo 92
Sandler review 74
Scharpf, Fritz 47
Schopflin, Pierre 128
Schröder, Gerhard 32, 48
self-employment, Germany 36, 44
Single European Act (1986) 6, 194, 195
social care:
    and ageing population 3
    and the family 2
    spending on 15–16
    and women 3
social exclusion:
    and education 4
    and European Union 202–4, 207
    France 115, 116, 117–19, 131
    Spain 152, 157
social groups, and resource allocation 14
social inclusion, and European Union 22,
        202–3
SOCRATES programme 194
solidarity, and welfare state 9–10
Spain:
    activation policies 146–7, 152–4
    decentralisation 138, 150–1
        and policy innovation 154–6, 158,
            241
        and welfare development 157–8
    economic policy 138
    education 141
    and elderly care 155–6

Spain (*cont.*):
  and family:
    and de-familisation 144
    dual earner model 141
    importance of 137, 140, 155
    shock-absorber role 140
    strategies of 143–5
    transformations of 137
    and youth unemployment 146
  and fertility rates 140, 141–2
  and gender equality 144, 145, 157
  labour market:
    atypical employment 147
    and 'dead-end' jobs 152
    dual 152
    features of 146
    and flexibility 151–2, 157
    reform of 237
    women's participation 139–40, 141–3
  low-income benefits 152–4
  minimum incomes 152–4, 155
  minimum wage 153
  and new social risks:
    emergence of 139
    and policy development 147–8
    politics of 234
    response to 227–9, 240–1
  parental leave 144
  part-time work 147, 151–2
  and pensions 148–50, 238
  and political consensus 138–9,
      148, 157
  and service provision 139
  social exclusion 152, 157
  social spending in 138
  social transformation of 137–8
  Toledo Pact 148, 150, 234, 238
  and trade unions 153–4, 155
  and 'underground' economy 146
  and unemployment 140, 157
  and welfare financing 140, 150–1
  and welfare state reform 148
    youth 145–6
  and women:
    caring/domestic work 139–40, 142–3,
        144, 156–7
    education 141
    political activity 157
    positive discrimination 145
  work/family balance issues 145
    and emergence of new social risks
        139–41
  see also Mediterranean welfare state

Storélu To, L. 117
stratification, and welfare reform 14
Streeck, Wolfgang 47
subsidiarity:
  and European Union 190, 204, 229
  Germany 34, 40, 46
  Switzerland 164
Sueur, Jean-Pierre 128
Sure Start programme (UK) 67, 68, 75
Sweden:
  activation policies 100, 217–18
  adjusted unemployment benefit 103–4
  and adult education 101
  and ageing population 88–9
  and atypical employment 100–1
  child care 90, 92–3
  and dual earner households 90, 91
  and elderly care 89, 90, 93–6
  and employment 88–9
  and immigrants 104, 105–6
  and income inequality 102
  labour shortages 94
  and new social risks:
    emergence of 88–91, 96–7
    politics of 107–9, 233
    response to 217–20, 241
  parental leave 91
  part-time work 92, 101
  and pensions 4, 101, 106–7, 107–8, 238
  as service state 90
  and unemployment 89, 97
    immigrant 104
    long-term 98, 100
  and welfare state change 106–7
  and women's labour force participation
      15, 90, 91–2, 217
  work/family balance issues 91–2
  see also Nordic welfare state
Switzerland:
  activation policies 162, 173–5
  and ageing population 163
  child care 164, 165, 178–9, 221
  and economic growth 163
  and elderly care 166
  and family policy 163
  and family, role of 164
  and gender equality 170
  and labour market:
    participation in 19–20
    shortages 178
    women's participation 161
  and maternity insurance 175–8
  and maternity leave 164–5

and new social risks 169
    adaptation to 182–3
    as contested issues 180
    parliament and policy-making
        179–80
    politics of policy-making 180–3
    response to 221–5, 240
part-time work 164, 172
and pensions 4, 165–6, 238
    and new career profiles 170
    occupational pension reform 172–3
    and women's career profiles 170–1
political system 233
    and coalition government 168–9
    and federalism 167–8
    and interest groups 169
    and policy-making process 167–9
    referendums 168, 171, 177
    and reform difficulties 161, 164
    and separation of powers 167
and retirement age 171
social expenditure 162
and subsidiarity 164
and unemployment 163, 173, 224
and unemployment insurance
    173–4, 224
welfare state:
    adaptation to new social risks 182–3
    old risk orientation 162, 163
    social expenditure 163
    structure of 161
women, role of 163–4
work/family balance issues 164–5
and working poor 165, 169
see also corporatist welfare state

Thatcher, Margaret 189
Thatcherism 57
Third Way, and New Labour 65
trade 155
Triponez, Pierre 177
Turner, Adair 74

unemployment:
    demand-side approaches to 6
    and education 4, 36, 60
    and European Union 192–5, 205
    Finland 89, 97–9
        immigrant 105
        long-term 98, 99, 103
        low-skilled 103
    France 117, 119, 124
    Germany 36–7, 46–8, 51, 224

and poverty 60–1
    Spain 140, 157
    Sweden 89, 97
        immigrant 104
        long-term 98, 100
    Switzerland 163, 173, 224
    youth 19
        Finland 98
        France 21
        Germany 21
        Spain 145–6
        United Kingdom 60, 63, 76
Union of Service Sector Employees
    (Finland) 92
United Kingdom:
    benefits 63, 71
    Changing Welfare State 65
    child care 59, 62, 66, 67–8, 75–6, 79
    and civil society 66
    and elderly care 59, 61–2, 66, 67, 68, 76
    and European Union policymaking 58,
        80, 189
    income levels 60–1, 78
    Jobcentre Plus 72
    labour market:
        access to employment 60–1
        activation policies 19, 69–72, 75–6
        mobilisation 65, 68
        policy 63
        reform of 237
        women's participation 15, 18, 59,
            66–7, 79
    lone parents 59–60, 66, 69, 71, 76, 79
    and low pay 21
    manufacturing industry 58–9
    maternity pay 68
    means testing and universalism 69
    and minimum wage 71, 76
    and modified industrial family
        model 17
    National Carers Strategy 67–8
    and the New Deal 70–1, 76
    and new social risks:
        emergence of 58–62
        and realignment of Labour 240
        response to 66–75, 225–7, 240
    part-time work 59, 66
    paternity leave 68
    and pensions 4, 5, 61, 63–4, 227, 238–9
        reform of 72–5, 79
    policy discourses:
        Conservative 57–8, 62–4
        New Labour 58, 64–6, 79

United Kingdom (*cont.*):
    political characteristics 57, 79, 233
    poverty:
        assessment of policies 76–9
        child 78
        and lone parents 59–60
        and retired people 61, 78–9
    and privatisation 62
    Sure Start programme 67, 68, 75
    Tax Credits 78
    and unemployment:
        education 60
        youth 60, 63, 76
    and welfare reform 61–2
    work/family balance issues 59–60, 66–9
    Working Family Tax Credit 71
    Working Tax Credit 72
    and worklessness 70, 76, 79
    see also liberal welfare state

welfare markets, Germany 37, 49–50, 51
welfare, new politics of 216
welfare reform:
    and policy communities 241
    and power resources 241
welfare state:
    and ageing population 3, 6
    challenges facing 1–2
        government capacity 6–7
        restricted resources 6
        rising demand 6
    and change 5, 7
        resistance to 10
    erosion of legitimacy of 7
    favourable development conditions 1–2
    functions of 2
    and gender divisions 15
    Keynes-Beveridge model 2
    Keynes-Bismarck model 2
    and Keynesian paradigm 12
    and monetarist paradigm 12–13, 232
    and new social risks:
        and welfare reform 237–9
        and welfare regimes 13–21

and permanent austerity 7, 24–5
policy making in 9
regime categorisation 13–14, 216–17
see also corporatist welfare state; liberal
welfare state; Mediterranean welfare state;
    Nordic welfare state
women:
    advancement of 2
    assumptions about activities 15
    and care responsibilities 3
    and labour force participation 3, 15,
        17–18
        corporatist welfare state 17, 18
        European Union 206
        Finland 90, 91–2, 217
        France 18, 121, 129, 130, 131, 221
        Germany 15, 18, 33, 38
        liberal welfare state 17, 18
        Mediterranean welfare state 17, 18
        Nordic welfare state 17–18
        politics of 234–6
        Spain 139–40, 141–3
        Sweden 15, 90, 91–2, 217
        Switzerland 161
        United Kingdom 15, 18, 59, 66–7, 79
    and new social risks 14, 234–6
    political weakness 233
    in Spain 139–45, 156–7
    Switzerland:
        and pensions 170–1
        role of 163–4
    see also gender equality
work/family balance issues:
    Finland 91–2
    France 121–2, 129–31
    Germany 38–42, 50
    and new social risks 15–19
    and Nordic welfare states 88
    Spain 139–41, 145
    Sweden 91–2
    Switzerland 164–5
    United Kingdom 59–60, 66–9
working class 7
Wresinsky, Père 118